"But I Digress…"

"But I Digress..."

A selection of his best columns

DARREL BRISTOW-BOVEY

ZEBRA

Published by Zebra Press
an imprint of Struik Publishers
(a division of New Holland Publishing (South Africa) (Pty) Ltd)
PO Box 1144, Cape Town, 8000
New Holland Publishing is a member of Johnnic Publishing Ltd

First published 2003

1 3 5 7 9 10 8 6 4 2

Publication © Zebra Press 2003
Text © Darrel Bristow-Bovey 2003

Cover photograph © *Style*

PUBLISHING MANAGER: Marlene Fryer
MANAGING EDITOR: Robert Plummer
PROOFREADER: Ronel Richter-Herbert
COVER AND TEXT DESIGNER: Natascha Adendorff
TYPESETTER: Natascha Adendorff

Set in 11.5 on 15.5 Adobe Garamond

Reproduction by Hirt & Carter (Cape) (Pty) Ltd
Printed and bound by Paarl Print, Oosterland Street, Paarl, South Africa

ISBN 1 86872 669 X

www.zebrapress.co.za

Log on to our photographic website www.imagesofafrica.co.za for an African experience

To those editors who made it easier to write:

*Tony Proudlock, John Battersby, Andrew Walker, Jovial Rantao,
Jeremy Gordin, Maureen Isaacson, Alf Hayter, Gus Silber, Jeremy Maggs,
Chris Nicklin, Chris Roper, Kate Wilson, Louise Steyn, Mike Moon,
Cara Bouwer, Peter Bruce, Clare O'Donoghue, Andy Davis,
Brendon Cooper, Steve Pike, Fiona Zerbst, Katherine Butt, Collin Howell,
Leverne Gething and of course the incomparable, inestimable
and suavely cosmopolitan Robert Plummer.*

But mostly to Robert Greig, arts-and-culture editor of The Sunday
Independent, *who for no good reason gave me my first
writing job and my first column, and without whom
I scarcely know where I would be now,*

and

*Marlene Fryer, who asked me to write my first book, thought up
the subject for the first book and made sure that I wrote my first book.
And the books since.*

Contents

Preface

I HAVE ALWAYS WANTED to write the preface to a book of collected columns. *My* columns, preferably. When I was younger, long before I started writing for a living, I could imagine no exercise of writing more glamorous. I would read Clive James' prefaces to his volumes of television columns and feel a pang of envy far sharper even than any I experienced while reading the columns themselves.

Clive James brought to his columns a weight and seriousness that anchored them not merely to the page – an extraordinary achievement in itself – but to a deeper and wider and solemnly impressive tradition of writing. Weight and seriousness are always attractive to a young man with aspirations, but sometimes in James' columns I found I could do without them. Too often they seemed to come too obdurately in the way of the words. Whatever else a column should be, however serious it is, I have always held it should be light – not necessarily light in the sense of having skimpy or non-existent subject matter, although those are some of my favourite columns, but in the sense of being light on its feet, or the way the sun catches the water and dances in those hours when it is not too overbearingly overhead. "I would not believe in a god who does not know how to dance," wrote Nietzsche, and I think the same is true of columns. (That was a favourite trick of James' – quoting dead German philosophers. Often in the original.)

Clive James is one of the funniest and most luminously gifted columnists in print, but every so often I would find myself wishing his words were more like pebbles worn smooth by the sea, less like perfectly formed miniatures chiselled of the seamless rock quarried from Mount Parnassus. Ah, but a preface is not a column, so when he took the opportunity, in each of his three collections, to wax serious and weighty about his own writing, I lapped it up. What could be more satisfying, I wondered, than to be called upon to dedicate a few thousand thoughtful words to your own words? The columns themselves are just stepping stones to that dizzy moment of carefully modest self-indulgence. A preface! *The* preface! *Your* preface! Oh, let the trumpets sound.

Which may be why I find it easy to write the columns, and almost impossible to write this preface. I have learnt, over the past six years, that I do not do serious and weighty very well. The only columns I have ever scrapped and re-written are those of which I went to sleep thinking: "Now *that* was a fine piece of writing. Now *that* will show the world that I am a serious writer." Thinking, as Ed Wood famously thought about *Plan 9 From Outer Space*, "That's the one they'll remember me for."

On each occasion I have arisen the next morning, re-read the polished masterpiece and expunged it on the spot, blushing furiously. When I try to write with weight and seriousness, I invariably produce the kind of turgid, belly-stroking mush that deserves to be roughed up by the cool kids and stuffed into a gym locker after school. There is nothing weighty I can say that I cannot more effectively say lightly.

So alas, having waited six years for the chance to loom serious in this preface, I shall have to let the moment slip. I know nothing useful about writing, anyway. Writing for me is a breathless mixture of desperation, blind fear, animal instinct and the dumb luck to stumble across the right word every so often, the way a hungry child lost at night in a dark forest might accidentally stumble across a piece of gingerbread that doesn't have a witch attached. The columns which I look back on now with the greatest degree of approval are those I wrote in my regular panic of self-doubt, which I submitted in defeat, fully expecting a curt reply from the editor saying, "Well, we gave it a try. Perhaps there is some other field of endeavour to which you might find yourself better suited. Professional kick-boxing, say. Or singing." I still expect that reply. I am expecting it now.

Since my first-ever television column in August 1997 (the first column collected in this book), and not counting feature articles, reviews, books, travel writing and occasional work for television and radio, I have written on average more than 100 000 words in columns every year. It was difficult to turn down new columns, because I could never find in myself the confidence that the columns I already had would not next week be cancelled due to lack of interest. The drawbacks to that turn of mind are over-work and a constant throbbing, free-floating anxiety; the benefits remain the desire to make each column count, to be able to think, *Well, they won't fire me for this one.* "We that live to please," wrote Samuel Johnson, "must please to live", and I know what he meant.

One lesson I have learnt is that in order to keep writing well, you must believe not only in what you write, but where you are writing. Only once has that belief failed me: I found myself contributing regularly to a publication I had come to actively dislike, in which I had – vain beast! – grown embarrassed to appear. As my respect for the page upon which I wrote diminished, my respect dwindled for the writing itself. When that happens, you are better off becoming a professional kick-boxer, or auditioning for *Idols 3*.

It was difficult making a selection from nearly a thousand columns. I solved the problem by not making any decisions at all, and handing over three lever-arch files of clippings to my editors and publishers at Zebra Press. Being an editor and a publisher in South Africa is thankless and shamefully under-rewarded, but it is heroic work. I am very fortunate to have found the editors and publishers with whom I work. If there are any obvious omissions here, it is not their fault. It is probably because I forgot to make a clipping that week.

I am sometimes asked whether I enjoy watching as much television as I do for my *Sunday Independent* column, or whether I am really as enthusiastic about sport as I pretend in *Business Day*. Would I not rather, people ask, be writing about more serious matters? Matters of weight, say, and seriousness? To which I reply: no. Or rather, I don't understand the question. Television and sport are two of my most deep-seated and abiding pleasures, nay, joys. They have given me comfort and solace – and the sorrow, fury, heartache and delight so necessary for any healthy relationship – longer than any human being besides my mother, and I rather fancy they will still be around when I am an old man solitary upon my sofa.

Besides, if you cannot find weight and seriousness in television and sport, where do you hope to find it? All the world is in there, all the dreams, folly, futility and splendour of which we are made, and I hope I have, in some varying degrees, made clear in the course of these columns why I think so. A cricket series, say, is – like a Shakespearean tragedy – more a mirror than a window. We look into it to see elements of ourselves writ large or small or refracted through a prism. If we bring nothing to it, we can hardly hope to carry anything away. I take great joy from these things, and writing about them is a fiery distillation of that joy. At all times except the last few hours before deadline, I can hardly believe my luck.

The same is true of the other ephemera of modern life. The annoyances and regrets and secret yearnings that animate the lifestyle columns – the problems of sex and dating and drugs and neighbours and babies and male bonding and flying economy class and whatever else it is that attracts the attention long enough to be written – these are the thousand tiny brushstrokes that combine to make the picture of being youngish and single and me in the modern world. If the picture is less likely to be found hanging on the walls of the Hermitage or the Louvre than it is to be prestiked to the wall of a kindergarten classroom with the crayon lines slightly smudged, the fault lies more with the footling obsessions of the painter than with the wider world he lives in.

Finally, I am asked with some frequency about the Chalk 'n Cue. Does it exist? Is there a Porky Withers? What is Hairy Mike's dark secret? Who is Sad Henry? The answer is yes, these people exist, and one day, more formally, their stories will be told. Yes, there is a Chalk 'n Cue. And if you have bought a copy of this book, you are just the sort of person who would be welcome there. So this is my invitation to you: come around any time. Show Karl the barman a copy of this book, and tell him I sent you. The first drink's on the house.

DARREL BRISTOW-BOVEY
JOHANNESBURG
AUGUST 2003

1
Television

Miss South Africa

SUNDAY INDEPENDENT, 10 AUGUST 1997

I T HAS BEEN a long time since SABC TV has been able to turn the heads of the viewing public, so the staff and presenters were justifiably excited about the fact that the 1997 Miss South Africa pageant was once again "on public television, where it belongs".

Precisely where it belongs is a moot point, although the trash can of history might be a good place to start looking. On the evidence of last Saturday night's pageant, the programmers for M-Net must be congratulating themselves on a job well done.

Showing a laudable instinct for economy, the SABC decided to scale down the extravaganza side of things this year. This was just a plain old vaganza, which is not necessarily a bad thing. The trick, though, is knowing exactly where to cut corners. On the plus side, no American so-called television stars presented the show; on the downside, three local so-called personalities did.

I could have forgiven much about the vaganza – the unsynchronised dancing, the insistent pink and red colour scheme, the sets that seemed to tremble and sway with each high-heeled step and twirl – if I hadn't had to listen to the light and witty banter between Ursula Stapelfeldt, Tsepo Mabona and someone introduced as "the multi-talented Simon Jones".

To be fair, the embarrassment factor is a staple at events of this type worldwide. Watch any show from the Oscars to the Artes, and prepare to cringe. Scriptwriters who can put together perfectly good stage directions can't write dialogue worth a tinker's cuss. It almost seems to be a condition of employment. Come now – did I *really* hear Ursula tell us that with their makeovers and new hairdos the contestants had been transformed into "orbs of magic"?

At least she didn't have Tsepo's job of complimenting each contestant as they appeared in their slinky silver swimwear. "She's a real rainbow child!" announced Tsepo about Swimwear #1.

"Have a great one, Yolanda," he urged Swimwear #2.

"Keep on smiling!" he begged Swimwear #3. I could barely keep my eyes on the shimmering orbs of magic.

Besides not buying decent dialogue, the producers also bungled by cutting back on the lighting budget. Perhaps as a sop to Islamic fundamentalists, or in an attempt to defuse the radical feminist critique, the lighting technicians swathed the contestants in a shadowy cloak from the calves up. I fiddled with the brightness button, I shone a torch at the screen, I took pills to dilate my pupils – nothing worked.

Alas, nothing could conceal the horror of the evening gowns. "Look out!" I screamed when the first contestants appeared swaddled in one of Derek of Di Patri's nightmarish visions. "There are triffids growing out of your chest!" And there were! From their upper parts burst a bloom, a bower, an effulgence of foliage. Each poor girl cowered behind a corsage from the Black Lagoon, a corsage fed upon amphetamines and steroids and nuclear waste, monsters of chlorophyll that looked set to turn upon their hosts. It was a like a vegetarian version of *Alien*.

Still, I suppose there is something in all of us that responds to the tack and cheese of even the most downmarket vaganza. Who could fail to be thrilled by the musical number featuring the dancing security policemen and their borzoi dogs? Who could stop themselves cheering whenever the camera-on-a-crane panned over the conductor's bald spot as he exhorted the National Symphony Orchestra to ever greater heights of musical excellence? (Seventeen times, if my figures are correct.) Ah, the footlights, the greasepaint, the tears and the tiaras ... there is not much that even the most subversive TV producer could do to take the shine from the sequins of a Miss South Africa contest.

Glued to our sets for Diana's match and dispatch

SUNDAY INDEPENDENT, 7 SEPTEMBER 1997

T HE LAST THING the world needs right now is more column centimetres about Diana. The international media have this past week worked themselves into a frenzy over her death, like piranha trying to cram in a final mouthful of flesh from one of the 20th century's great cash cows. Still, this is a television column, and this week television was all about Diana.

As far as I can work out, Diana's achievement is unique. She is responsible for not one, but two of the West's great "what-were-you-doing-when?" moments. Strangely, I was watching television on both occasions.

When I was 10, my Standard 3 teacher brought her Sony Trinitron television set to the classroom and we all gathered round to watch the royal wedding. Though a welcome break from long division and the reproductive cycle of the frog, it was a dull affair, made still more so when the visuals froze so Equity could block out Dame Kiri te Kanawa's singing. The ceremony had little to offer besides a germ of sexual hope in the breast of every little boy with knobbly knees and sticky-outy ears – a flicker of faith that the future might yet provide us with our very own princess. It was all a bit of a fairytale, really, but on that day, Charles was truly our king.

So as entertainment it was a bit of a dud, but we stuck with it to the bitter end. There were two reasons for such tenacity: firstly, a romantic determination to see the whole *schpiel* consummated with a kiss; secondly, the overwhelming sense of global connectedness.

The kiss, frankly, was a disappointment. It was dutiful and passionless and applied like local anaesthetic, and many a keenly watching 10-year-old might have had the first inkling of the depressing gap between fairytale and real life. But the power of sharing a moment with an audience of millions remains undiluted.

That is one of the uncomfortable seductions of Diana's death: watching CNN or *BBC News* on Sunday morning, each of us could join in a worldwide experience that briefly erased our individual and our national specificity. That illusion of connectedness is fleeting and invariably deceitful, but it is one of the truly modern thrills and often guilty pleasures of our age.

When it came to the actual coverage, there wasn't much to choose between CNN and the BBC. Both were thorough and professional, and both were quick to put together packages of highlights of the princess's life, which they recycled over and over throughout the day.

As befits responsible media organs, both took care to frown upon the paparazzi for their thoughtlessness and insensitivity. It also took them both more than 24 hours before they thought to mention the names of the driver who was killed and the bodyguard who was injured in the crash. It's a small thing, I know, but it might have meant something to the friends and families of the two men. It might have added a touch of humanity to all the newsworthiness.

Something else that's newsworthy is our very own truth commission. Not only does it command regular media coverage, but it also appears to be stimulating a peculiar form of tourism. *Focus Features* (SABC3, Monday, 10pm) was devoted to the visit of Ariel Dorfman, the Chilean playwright and poet. I had known Dorfman only through his ponderous and somewhat turgid play, *Death and the Maiden*. After Monday night, I now also know him through his ponderous and extremely turgid poetry.

The documentary opened with the bizarre sight of Dorfman creeping through the veld after a giraffe, singing what appeared to be an atonal Chilean drinking song. Soon he left the giraffe behind and turned his attention to the city. Even sooner, I started missing the giraffe. Dorfman, we discovered, was in South Africa largely to lurk around the truth commission hearings and to share his feelings on the matter with the people of South Africa. He wasn't shy to do so.

I am always reluctant to blame individuals for the impression they convey in carefully edited documentaries, but if Dorfman isn't a pompous, self-important bore in real life, then the makers of *Focus Features* were extremely cunning in making him appear so. It's bad enough that we were forced to welcome into our homes verse that included lines like: "If you could take one word with you to the future/What is it to be?" But, under the banner of intellectual cross-pollination, we were further treated to the sight of Dorfman in a humorously pink shirt, wandering from place to place explaining to locals exactly what was going on in their country. I found myself in the weird position of wishing he would read more poetry.

The lowest point of the show was Dorfman in the District Six museum, explaining to us – us! – at great length what District Six was and why it was bulldozed. I could perhaps have overcome my irritation if the man had shown any signs of clear historical thinking, rather than lapsing into statements like: "The tragedy of District Six was that 20 years later, there was a place called Sarajevo, and something very similar happened."

Sarajevo and District Six? Similar? I have heard Martin Locke make more sense than that. Not satisfied, Dorfman popped up again on Robben Island, pronouncing that: "Robben Island is a distillation, a concentration, an essence of what South Africa was."

Oh really, Ariel? What makes you say that? The penguins? The lime quarries? The communal backgammon board? Gah.

But such quibbles were beside the point. The poet was speaking (in an American accent) and we were expected to listen. I don't mean to sound parochial here, but if we really needed some ill-informed, self-impressed versifier to talk a bushel of patronising nonsense to the camera in exchange for a free holiday, we didn't need to bring one all the way from Chile. Surely we have enough muttonheads of our own.

• Hot Medium's Chilean Poet Award for the worst piece of television goes to the new advert for Always sanitary pads. It features a personal testimony from a satisfied customer, concluding with the words: "I tried it, I like it, now I'm sticking to it." Which surely begs the question: Then aren't you wearing it the wrong way round?

Mother Teresa should have been blonde

SUNDAY INDEPENDENT, 14 SEPTEMBER 1997

G OD BLESS MARTIN LOCKE. I can always rely on him to restore my perspective and preserve my sanity.

In this past week leading to the announcement of the Olympic bid result, I must confess I temporarily lost my head. Won over perhaps by the patriotic charm of a thousand Pick 'n Pay and Nedbank adverts, I allowed my previously unshakeable indifference to the fate of the games to be, well, shaken. Like a mugging victim who has fallen into the Randburg Waterfront and imagines he is being swept down-river toward the sea, I allowed myself to be caught up in the momentum and rainbow-coloured razzmatazz of the big day.

So it was that I settled down to watch the big occasion with growing nervous anticipation. I had all the usual Big Match symptoms: racing heart, dry mouth, a craving for harmful substances. I cared. I cared immensely. Then on came Martin Locke.

Martin is my perpetual reality check. Always obey Hot Medium's basic rule of thumb: if Martin Locke is excited about something, it is not very important in the greater scheme of things. As soon as I remembered that, and as soon as Martin uttered the words, "Welcome to this glorious city of Cape Town. The heat is on, as the famous song says!", I knew I was going to be all right.

Martin Locke is one of nature's great survivors. Reincarnated countless times as a DJ, a magazine show host, a wannabe jockey and now, most amusingly of all, a sports presenter, Martin has outlasted his way into our hearts. His boyish enthusiasm is more vigorous by the day, his verbal buffoonery grows ever more endearing. No one can inject gravitas into his voice after a South African defeat like Martin can. David Dimbleby last week describing the procession of Princess Diana's funeral cortège came across like Jerry Seinfeld by comparison.

This is Martin's great gift. He makes us laugh, he makes us cry, he makes us resolve to wear skin protection when going out in the sun. More humble than Trevor Quirk, smoother shaven than Max du Preez, taller than Baby Jake Matlala, Martin is a TV man for all seasons. Love him, hate him, it's no fun ignoring him.

Sadly, however, I couldn't enjoy Martin as much as usual last weekend. Small, wizened, deeply tanned and difficult to understand, Martin has always somehow reminded me of Mother Teresa of Calcutta.

Mother Teresa's sad death offers an object lesson in the politics of popular culture. Television viewers would have searched the channels in vain for the same elaborate memorials and life assessments that marked Diana's passing. People can obviously mourn whomever they choose, but it gave pause to notice how Diana's death was trumpeted as the passing of a great humanitarian, whereas Mother Teresa instantly became not much more than a historical footnote.

I was never necessarily the Mother's greatest fan: I found her views on condoms and birth control somewhat perplexing given the sprawling mass of suppurating overpopulation in which she lived and worked. Still, if anyone deserves to be deeply mourned as a self-sacrificing force for good in the world, it is surely her.

The problem, of course, is that she wasn't young, blonde and sexually active. What emotional problems she may have had, she kept to herself. I doubt she had a bulimic moment in her life. Mother Teresa did not live a soap opera, and the television cameras didn't encourage an artificial intimacy with her. She didn't have the same problems as us, so how could we hope to identify with her? Why should we even try?

How about this for the perverse power of the popular media: the vast majority of common people around the Western world imagine they had more in common with the noble-born Princess of Wales than Mother Teresa, the champion of the poor. I call it the soapiefication of society.

Noot vir Noot – game show of the Galapagos

SUNDAY INDEPENDENT, 23 NOVEMBER 1997

PERHAPS THIS IS a classic case of cultural bias, but I find *Noot vir Noot* (SABC2, Saturday, 6pm) inexplicable.

Being a responsible TV critic, I feel it is my duty to make sense of what is, to me, a truly baffling cultural phenomenon, but time and again I am defeated. It nags at me, that show, it torments me with my own inadequacies. I can never rest for knowing that another episode is out there, oblivious to me, smug and self-sufficient in its indecipherability. It will not yield. I am an urban Ahab, and Johan Stemmet is my Moby Dick.

The biggest problem is knowing which analytical tools to bring to bear on the beast. Sociological? Anthropological? Psychological? Each week I tune in, notebook in hand, volumes of Freud and Lévi-Strauss opened to relevant pages, trying to draw a bead on my target. Each week it snorts and shimmies out of range with the glimmer of a sequinned waistcoat and the reverb of an electronic synthesiser.

The more I think about it, the more convinced I become that Darwin would have the answer. Watching an episode of *Noot vir Noot* is like watching footage of a *National Geographic* expedition to the Galapagos Islands. It's a strange and fascinating world, populated by bizarre creatures with weird skills and survival techniques.

The Galapagos archipelago was so valuable to Darwin because, pristine in its isolation, it offered him an opportunity to study the effects of natural selection and environmental adaptation in a more or less closed system, undisturbed by outside influences or competition. Of course the Galapagos spawned some odd critters, but few more foreign than those I see every Saturday night.

For those without scientific curiosity, who haven't experienced the fearful fascination of *Noot vir Noot* at first hand, it is a game show of sorts, in which a variety of guests identify snatches of tunes presented by Johan Stemmet and his in-house band, the Musiek Fabriek. Ah, but so bland a description can't begin to convey the sense of dislocation that accompanies watching the show. The (English-speaking) viewer becomes a stranger in a strange land, bereft of recognisable cultural cues or points of familiarity.

Consider the Musiek Fabriek, in their variegated plumage of pink, purple and sunset-orange, and wonder at the environment that would have encouraged such perverse evolutionary adaptation. But more than this, more than the hairstyles and white canvas belts and unearthly moustaches, consider their principal means of communication. Consider the music.

Who makes that music? Where does it come from? Why does every episode of *Noot vir Noot* remind me of Valentine's Day in some infernal, interminable Kardies of the mind? Is it just me, or is that music the aural equivalent of a bunch of carnations, a red inflatable heart at the end of a stick, one of those small fluffy teddy bears holding a sign saying, "I love you beary much"? Most astonishingly, what extrasensory affinity do the contestants have with this music?

Because each of these individuals possesses an arcane knowledge so esoteric, so abstruse, that it leaves me dumbstruck, humbled by the rich diversity of nature. They listen to a note (no kidding – *one* note) banged out on the synthesiser, and are able to identify "Ek verlang na jou" by Gé Korsten, or "My liefde is soos a warm hasie" by Carike Keuzenkamp. These are preternatural skills. Like the greater blue-gilled Galapagan iguana, these people make use of instincts and abilities that are no longer available to their distant, mainland relatives. This is a case of evolution taking the road less travelled.

Noot vir Noot is a time capsule of a particular cultural strand or species of Afrikanerdom. It is endlessly intriguing, inexplicably entertaining, and to an outsider, hopelessly impenetrable. Like the Galapagos, it should be preserved intact, not only for the contribution it makes to our cultural biodiversity, but as rich research material for the naturalists and cultural anthropologists of the future.

That's no duck, that's Ally McVeal

SUNDAY INDEPENDENT, 28 JUNE 1998

S HOULD THE SPOOKY day come that I accidentally receive a transfusion of blood from Felicia, and find myself suddenly taking seriously Oprah's suggestion that we all keep Gratitude Diaries, my first entry will be: I am very grateful that I don't know anyone who even vaguely resembles Ally McBeal.

Ally McBeal (SABC3, Mondays, 9.30pm) is rapidly gathering something approaching popularity among 20- and 30-something white South Africans. Set in what I gather is a Canadian law firm, it is billed as a sophisticated sitcom. By "sophisticated" I presume they mean it doesn't have a laugh track. As for the sitcom, I see plenty of sitting but precious little comedy.

The show is a kind of three-step guide to first-year philosophy, a fabric-softened, tumble-dried wrangle with ethics, existentialism and Humean uncertainty. Like the academic career of many a feeble BA student, it takes its entire dramatic impetus from Ally's utter inability to make up her mind. Should I laugh? Should I cry? Should I pout more? Could I pout more? The next time I speak, should I finish one sentence before starting another? These are not, sadly, questions that ever receive the correct answer.

"Hi, I just wanted to … if you're sure you're not busy … because if you are I can come back some other … no really, it's no problem … oh, if you're really sure … if you're sure you're sure … ha ha … just wanted to say, you know, good morning."

Ally is played with diffident blankness by one Calista Flockhart, a name to give anyone an existential crisis. I don't like saying her name out loud – it sounds like a remedy for the kind of intimate female condition I'm not at all comfortable talking about.

She has two methods of dramatising her various crises of confidence. In the first, popular in some households, she blinks while pouting into the middle distance. In the other, a favourite in my neighbourhood, she blinks while pouting at the floor. You can almost hear the self-help mantra in her head: *I blink, therefore I am.*

Perhaps the greatest entertainment the show offers is the intellectual and aesthetic challenge of deciding precisely which barnyard animal it is that Ms Flockhart so closely resembles.

General consensus tips the poultry family, with the proud goose topping the polls, though the humble duck is rallying strongly, but I favour another of our farmhouse friends. Those languorously curling lashes, those curiously motile lips, that intolerable slowness of reaction – that's no duck, that's Ally McVeal.

It's astonishing, this ethic of agonising self-doubt with which the Americans infect our TV screens. Ally is just the latest in a noisome line of long-faced whiners who don't know how to be happy. From *thirtysomething* in the eighties to the latest baby-cursed series of *Mad About You,* we are subjected to an unending stream of self-consciousness, a narcissistic dissection of every impulse, obsession and pre-packaged emotion they can scrounge together.

Small wonder that women are reading books about running with wolves, and men have to take Viagra – there are no simple pleasures left in sitcom land. It's a fidgety, squirmy, over-refined world in which "because I enjoy it" isn't a good enough answer any more.

That's why *Seinfeld* (SABC3, Thursdays, 9.30pm) will be so sorely missed. It's not that prissy Jerry who makes the show, nor Elaine, nor even the all-powerful Kramer. No, it's George who gives us hope each Thursday – George Costanza, the most sneaky, selfish, amoral, un-self-doubting liar and cheat ever to grace the small screen with his sly, balding schemes. George is everyman – he is you, he is me, in our weak, beery, most conscience-free moments he is everything we want to be. He is the Wizard of Id.

Down the hatch with Keith Floyd

SUNDAY INDEPENDENT, 5 JULY 1998

I 'M NOT MUCH of a cook. Washing dishes, yes – it is soothing, sensual and one of the few activities besides shaving off your moustache that offers you both immediate solitude and the subsequent gratitude of others. In addition – shameful confession – there is something nostalgically comforting about the amniotic warmth of the suds.

But cooking, no. Brinjals and measuring jugs and sliced fingertips are not fit companions, even for a sensitive man of the nineties. Besides which, there is always someone at the dinner table who says: "Oh, it's so nice to eat some *plain* cooking for a change."

So much worse are cooking programmes on television – they're ordinarily all bright lighting and phoney sets and fussy little kitchen nerds like Graham Kerr with their smug tips about how to keep your mushrooms fresh. Which is why Keith Floyd is so surprisingly welcome a visitor in the Hot Medium household. Few are the middle-aged men who can beetle on to my screen and say, "Hello, we are making the most amazing fish soup," and expect to be around long enough to enjoy a pre-dinner cocktail.

Floyd's Fjord Fiesta (M-Net, Fridays, 7pm) – try saying that with a mouthful of martini olives – is Keith's culinary voyage through the frozen waters and endless afternoons of a Scandinavian summer. He was there to "interpret local cuisine", but judging by the volume of wine and aquavit he siphoned down, the chief attraction for Keith was that sundowners last all day and all night.

He was having a hard time impressing the locals. We joined him as he lovingly prepared a meal for the officers of his cruise ship, including a special beetroot cream he had invented for the occasion. The first mate scowled at her plate. "This is not in the Norwegian way of preparing beetroot," she intoned accusingly. The captain just frowned and scraped his teeth with his fork.

Small wonder Keith kept reaching for the brown paper bag, muttering, "It's time for my mid-morning slurp." His next stop was an outdoor cooking session at the site of the 1st International Herring Festival. Sadly for the organisers of the fest, it was deserted, save for the intrepid Keith and his assistants (whom, to his credit, he never once called his herring aids).

Spurning the regional delicacy of fermented herring – a dish available from local restaurants only as takeaways – Keith whipped up a kind of fins-and-all stir-fry, using whole, gutted herrings. I wish he hadn't. It was a cruel picture – their horrible wide eyes staring up helplessly from the pan as Keith prodded at them like some infernal Marquis de Sardine.

But enough of the frying puns. Keith was getting desperate. His next cooking location was down the pit in what he gamely admired as "the world's biggest iron-ore mine". If the scenery was about as gripping as an Ingmar Bergman movie, Keith himself rose to new heights of alcoholic entertainment. Oh happy moment of television magic when he accidentally reached for a beaker of neat brandy instead of his usual crisp chardonnay.

"Oh my god," he spluttered, "have you ever done that? Picked up a stranger's drink and nearly thrown up over the bar?" Worse things will happen if you pick up a stranger's drink down at the Chalk 'n Cue, Keith.

You can't help liking Keith Floyd, prickly old cuss though he may be. He marches across the screen extracting such generous yet unabashedly selfish pleasure from the simple indulgences of life that I'm almost tempted to try one of his recipes. Any man who can stand in the midst of the world's most dour and fleece-lined beach party, surrounded by po-faced herring enthusiasts, sample a raw sea-urchin and say, "Mmmm, good for the sex life" … well, I'll wash the dishes for him any time.

I wouldn't even open a packet of paper plates for the makers of *The Avenues* (SABC3, Mondays, 9pm). A new local drama series, it's not so much an avenue as a suburban cul-de-sac, littered with bad ideas and crumpled scraps of dialogue that were rejected by SABC1 continuity announcers for being too facile.

The only reasonable explanation for the unutterable direness of the writing is that it is scripted and directed by someone born entirely without ears. No one who has ever heard people speak could possibly force an actor to say those lines. It would be too wantonly cruel. A man scolds his children in an annoyed tone of voice – is this enough to let us know that they have annoyed him? Oh no. We have to hear the echoing voice-over. "These children will drive me to distraction."

The man and his wife are arguing at breakfast. He criticises her family. "My family are good, solid people," she replies, with all the verve and authenticity of a papier-mâché grapefruit, "and good, solid people are what you need for a dynamic society."

A good, solid colonic irrigation is what you need after digesting this script. Mind you, the direction did provide one viewing highlight. Whenever two people are talking, the camera swings laboriously from one to the other and back again, as though the filmmaker were a handicam-toting Japanese tourist taking in the sights at Sun City. On one occasion – ever to be treasured – the camera swung from man to woman and back again, but found only a blank expanse of wallpaper where the man had been. The actor, caught up in the drama of the moment, had taken an unscripted step backwards.

Why are local English productions so accursedly poor? They descend on us like one of the plagues of Moses, like the sufferings visited upon Job, like the wrath of Olympian gods for the hubris of the early Greeks. What have we done to deserve such stern treatment? It makes me long for a Nordic beach party and a glass of chilled aquavit with a frozen herring for a swizzle stick.

The humiliations of charity

SUNDAY INDEPENDENT, 20 DECEMBER 1998

To THE LEFT, bounce, jiggle … to the right, lunge, wheeze … ooh, you'll have to excuse me if the column is a little breathless this week. It's hard to type while bouncing and jiggling, and when you throw lunging and wheezing into the equation, well, I just hope I don't come out sounding like Barry Ronge, that's all.

I am trying to get in shape, you see, to avoid a repetition of the kind of humiliation that was my lot earlier this week. While others were putting their Day of Reconciliation to its more traditional use — road accidents and public drunkenness — I was sacrificing my hamstrings and dignity in the name of charity.

"It's an aerobics workout for the benefit of children with multiple sclerosis," the organiser had lilted cheerily. I couldn't think of anything that children with multiple sclerosis had done for me lately, but I didn't want to appear petty.

Pettiness would have been the sensible option. I am not, it is safe to say, inclined to athleticism. There are whelks and barnacles clinging to rocks in the Western Cape with more get-up-and-go. There are oysters being served on a bed of ice with Tabasco and lemon juice with a healthier cardiovascular system. The last time I broke a sweat — besides the occasion when I accidentally tuned in to Michelle Garforth's travel show without wearing my hessian hood and beeswax earplugs — was Black Thursday 1993, when I misplaced my TV remote control and had to change channels manually until Mr Delivery arrived.

In preparation for the workout, I settled down to watch a morning of fitness-product infomercials, but soon I had to stop, owing to a low tolerance for the word "buns". A blonde was wearing a leotard so tight I wasn't sure which part of her body she was waggling at the camera. "Do you dream of firm, tight buns?" she purred. "Try the Bunblaster." The hell I will.

So it was unfirm of thigh and with buns unblasted that I took to the aerobics floor with the few other media types who hadn't fled to Cape Town to escape all the jouncing and biggling. For decorum's sake, I shall draw a veil over the proceedings. Suffice to say that you haven't tasted shame until you've been publicly caught cheating at a charity event in benefit of the handicapped. "That man with the red face isn't sitting all the way up in his sit-ups!" I heard the piping voice of a small child. The crowd hissed its agreement. Someone threw a paper cup at me in disgust.

After that I tried my best, but in the field of physical activity my best isn't significantly different from my worst. One of the organisers circulated through the crowd, pointing at my star-jumps and murmuring, "That's what you look like when you have multiple sclerosis."

"Shame!" gasped the crowd, emptying their pockets into the collection box.

It is, of course, an untrue accusation. I am insufficiently co-ordinated to have multiple sclerosis – one sclerosis at a time is about all I could handle without dropping something.

Even worse, as I lay gasping for air like a coelacanth on a Madagascan beach choking on a carelessly discarded leg-warmer, was seeing the ageless Gordon Mulholland dashing through his routine like a young gazelle.

"Bunblaster?" I gasped from the floor.

He smirked mysteriously. "So they call me," he rumbled.

Packed in ice and taking intravenous doses of Deep Heat, I was fundamentally out of sympathy with the idea of charitable causes by the time I watched *Christopher Reeve – A Celebration of Hope* (M-Net, Sunday, 7pm), a fundraiser for a foundation that Reeve established to find a cure for spinal injuries. It confirmed my suspicion that selfishness and apathy, while socially unproductive, are far more aesthetically pleasing human traits than public displays of compassion and empathy.

Reeve himself, strapped in the chair, was elevated in the audience so that everyone could see him. There is an extraordinary power of presence to be derived from sitting immobile in a Hollywood gathering of luvvies and hand-wringers. In tragedy, Reeves has achieved a stature and dignity elusive in the days when he was known only for being a 1970s Superman and appearing in a string of rotten movies.

If only those around him would have picked up some tips in underplaying a scene. "Hope lights a candle instead of cursing the darkness," sighed Winona Ryder moistly. A gentleman in the front row hobbled from the auditorium when a cliché accidentally rolled from the stage and crushed his foot.

Amy Grant sang a song, the first line of which began: "Sometimes it's hard to remember to keep your feet on the ground." Reeves blinked in surprise, or perhaps indignation.

Willy Nelson arrived to strum a, er, foot-tapping tune, which must have made Chris wish he'd lost sensation in his ears too. Jane Seymour flowed on stage, serene as a bottle of hair conditioner, seemingly thinking everyone was there to see her. She started talking about "a movie I acted in with Chris, called *Somewhere in Time*".

Everyone clapped, as they did every time Reeve's name was mentioned. "Oh, thank you," said Jane coyly. Everyone frowned. "I know it's a great favourite of many people," she gushed, perhaps thinking of the same people who consider *Chains of Gold* to be John Travolta's best movie.

It's an unworthy thought, but I can never escape the feeling that charity events are more for the benefit of the charitable donors than for the recipients. It was a thought that stayed with me at the climax of the show, when Reeve was wheeled on stage. The audience rose to give him a standing ovation. A particularly thoughtless tribute, I would have said.

• Hot Medium's I'm-Doing-Anything-To-Avoid-Writing-About-Christmas Award for the most careless television commentary goes to Mungo Poore, reporting on the Sterkfontein fossils on the 8pm News (SABC3): "When the hominid fell into these caves," opined Mungo thoughtfully, "he probably had no idea of the fuss he would cause three-and-a-half-million years later." Mungo, that's probably true.

Darker side of Christmas lurks in every living room

SUNDAY INDEPENDENT, 27 DECEMBER 1998

CHRISTMAS IS THE great leveller. Perhaps if I had risen from a Muslim tradition I would be writing: "Eid is the great leveller"; but such are the vagaries of birth and life.

It is easy to be flippant about Christmas, to make sly references to Boney M and that new terror from the north, Helmut Lotti, to dwell on the Coca-Cola origins of Santa Claus and his red-and-white suit, but ultimately Christmas, with its memories and hopes and its excessive consumption of cheap sparkling wine from glasses bought at Clicks, comes down to one thing: fear. Christmas is the great celebration of deep, unshakeable, inescapably personalised fear.

Whether it be fear of the past or fear of not being able to recreate the past, our frenzies of eating, buying, drinking, remembering, forgetting are driven by the ghastly apprehension that we are alone, that childhood has gone, that that fugitive sip of champagne at the lunch table between the first cracker and the first roast potato will never again taste as good as when we were not allowed to take it.

I have in my possession a small plastic compass that came tumbling from a Christmas cracker when I was a chubby lad of nine, testing my strength against my sad-eyed Aunty Lynn, who wore too much make-up, even for the 1970s, and always smelt inexplicably of Old Spice. The needle of the compass was wobbly, but always pointed north, no matter which way I twisted it. Even at the bottom of the next-door neighbours' swimming pool, with a large magnet and, for some reason, a brick, that needle never moved away from the big N.

"At least you'll never be lost," lied Aunty Lynn. " And you'll always be able to find your way home."

It was an obvious lie – a lie that became increasingly more obvious as I grew older – but at least it was a comforting one. I will take one comforting untruth over a thousand desolate honesties. That is what I appreciated about Aunty Lynn – for all her unsettling personal characteristics and easily imagined personal unhappiness, she was a comforting figure. Isabel Jones is like that too.

Aunty Isabel is a true South African hero – the local equivalent of the men of 911, or a similar service in a fantasy world where free, speedy, efficient assistance is but a phone call away. Whenever I shut my eyes and think about the nativity – an increasingly less frequent occurrence – the three wise men always have the faces of Desmond Tutu, Willem Heath and Isabel Jones.

Isabel was doing her bit for the festive season this week on *Fair Deal* (SABC3, Mondays, 6.15pm). Her target, for a change, wasn't a swindler, charlatan or mail-order shyster but mince pies, traditionally a subject of some indifference in the Hot Medium household.

Mince pies, I have always felt, are the unwelcome relatives at the Christmas table. While not exactly prone to getting drunk, feeling up the host's wife and telling loud stories about the good old days in Rhodesia, they still don't really fit in, do they? Offering neither the comfort of a solid meat-'n-potatoes scoff, nor the hot, silently screaming fuzziness of a healthy tot of Yuletide spirit, they seem to lurk without fixed intent, undesired, a strange remnant of someone else's idea of Christmas.

"Ooh, I couldn't possibly, I've had so much already" – those are the words most familiar to the veteran mince pie who's seen a Christmas or two in its time.

Undaunted, Isabel rounded up a trio of what she called "celebrities" to blind-taste a selection of retail pies. Mark Gillman was one, and a pair of actors from *Isidingo* (SABC3, weekdays, 6.30pm) were the others. That should tell you something about how many celebrities hang around in Johannesburg over the Christmas season.

They boldly tucked into their samples. "The pastry's crumbly," complained the first *Isidingo* gourmet.

"The pastry's supposed to be crumbly," murmured Isabel diplomatically.

"I've never tasted a mince pie before," mentioned the second connoisseur. Isabel smiled bravely.

Gillman, meanwhile, was fumbling for some wackiness. His entire radio career is built upon the twin pillars of being wacky and shouting into the microphone. On television you are not allowed to shout into the micro-phone. "This mince pie tastes like … tastes like … this!" he mugged, grabbing something from the table in front of him. Unfortunately the camera failed to follow his hand, so we will never know what he grabbed. I suspect, however, it was another mince pie. How Isabel must have wished she was still dealing with swindlers, charlatans and mail-order shysters.

On Christmas Eve I shunned SABC's various treasure troves of festive tunes (if it's not sung by Sacha Distel, I just ain't interested), and turned instead to the baubly wonders of satellite. Sadly, there was no Christmas Channel – which makes me wonder exactly how the Osmonds make a living these days – but I happily settled down to *The Wizard of Oz* (TNT Classic Movies, 11pm).

I have always considered *The Wizard* to be a far more appropriate Christmas film than those other staples, *The Sound of Music* (in which Julie Andrews tries to sing the Nazis into submission) and *It's A Wonderful Life* (in which Jimmy Stewart demonstrates the socially productive aspects of attempted suicide).

It is an unsettling film. Things stir beneath the surface of the story – fearful things, only half-apprehended by children, and the more powerful for that. With its witches and flying monkeys and unreasonably cheerful midgets, there is a dark shadow rimming the candy colours and heel-kicking tunes of Oz. It is, I think, the shadow of adulthood, of the farm back in Kansas with its mortgage and its freak tornadoes and failed crops.

Watching the young Judy Garland, pumped to the pigtails with diet pills and amphetamines, turning her face to the skies and to the future, yearning to be somewhere over the rainbow, I couldn't stop myself whispering: "Stay right where you are, babe."

A night with Monica Lewinsky

SUNDAY INDEPENDENT, 14 MARCH 1999

WHEN I WAS 11, as cute as a grazed elbow in short pants and haversack, dreaming of growing up to be an ichthyologist or Joe Hardy or, in my more solitary moments, that woman from the Morkels advert, I conceived a fascination for a girl in my class. In fact, we all did, after it became known that Shirley Whiteside had gone all the way with Craig Barnsley, an oafish youth in Standard 5 who, with an unrelated passion, used to waylay me on the way home and make me eat grasshoppers.

I had only a fuzzy grasp of what going all the way might entail. Surely Shirley didn't actually swallow the grasshoppers? (I used to stow their chewed-up corpses under my tongue, grinning and mumbling with a studious nonchalance, then covertly spit them out once Barnsley had released the downward pressure on the back of my head. It is a technique that even today serves me well in editorial conferences.)

Still, Shirley was pretty hot stuff among the boys of Mrs Kincaid's form class – we speculated endlessly about the events of that hot Durban afternoon beneath the frangipani tree while Mr and Mrs Whiteside were at work. Steven Kenton thought it had happened in the shady ditch behind the woodwork room, but no one ever listened to Steven Kenton.

Shirley was the focus of a small-boy curiosity of almost unbearable intensity. I would lie awake at night in a restless fever – in the morning the sweat stains on the pillow (if you tilted your head and squinched up your eyes) described the silhouette of Shirley Whiteside. When she played those mysterious games on the playground with the other girls, involving a length of elastic and plenty of squeals, her calves flexed unfathomably and her ponytail shimmied and trembled with the impenetrable secrets of adulthood.

Happily, I never learnt what went on at the bottom of the Whitesides' garden. As a result, my imagination prospered, and the sticky, tawdry disappointments of grown-ups had to wait until I was, well, grown up. And a good thing too – adolescence would have been positively unbearable without the comforting throb of itchy-fingered anticipation.

All of which may do little to explain why I felt so unshakeably empty and depressed while watching Jon Snow interview Monica Lewinsky last Sunday (*Carte Blanche*, M-Net, 7pm). "You have the right to see it all" is *Carte Blanche*'s oft-repeated motto, a sentiment with which I am in hearty disagreement.

Frankly, the world would be a great deal more attractive with a few more veils and secrets and frilly petticoats, several degrees more appealing if it maintained hidden areas of tangled undergrowth and deep shade, dark places where daylight never reaches.

The Lewinsky affair, of course, was never the stuff that dreams or fantasies are made of. It was a tatty little episode, as dull and workaday as a suburban husband flirting with his neighbour's wife over the Sunday afternoon braai, as routinely tiresome as an attractive woman being interviewed by Tony Sanderson. It would be dreary enough to watch it unfold in real life; to watch it on television was to feel one's own life shrink to the stature of a dripping garden tap.

There was a listless diversion in spotting how many sexual double entendres Snow could weasel into the interview ("What did you hope would flow from the relationship?"), but the pleasure soon congealed.

There was a brief interest in determining which of the two better carried their weight. Monica, though looking as slinky as a bag of charcoal briquettes tied in the middle, edged a narrow victory by virtue of her tactically sound legs-crossed position, which broke up her outline; Snowie just slouched in his chair with his belly thundering upwards like the dome on Capitol Hill.

There was even the perverse entertainment of watching Derek Watts acting like some husky-voiced shill for a Mills and Boon serial at each ad break: "He needed lovin', she was ready to oblige," Derek twinkled throatily. "After the break we pick up the story!"

But these were temporary pleasures. Ultimately nothing could disguise the fact that we were watching a perfectly ordinary young woman describing a depressingly ordinary encounter with her boss. "Did you feel a sexual connection?" demanded Snow delicately.

"Yes," she said patiently.

"Did it make you tingle?" said Snow, drawing on a lifetime's experience of cheap soap operas.

"Tee-hee," said Monica Lewinsky.

Snow's high-school debating-club gravitas rapidly became comical. "The sex was very one-way, if I may put it in a male sense," he murmured, smoothing his tie. Monica frowned, as though displeased at the thought of him putting it at all.

"He was a quarter of a century older than you," persisted Snowie gravely, for all the world as though discussing a matter of international importance.

"Oh, but age is just a number representing how long you have been on the planet," said Monica confidently. There was no arguing with that.

She was likeable enough, was Monica, and bright in a general sort of way. She was the girl you see in orientation week at university – keen, well groomed, eager to be liked, drinking too much peach schnapps and giggling while she puts her hands in some postgraduate's trouser pockets. Her ordinariness was too stark; it made our voyeurism too suburban. If we're going to feel cheap, let us at least be entertained. Let's have some sensation in our sensationalism.

Everybody loves Oscar

SUNDAY INDEPENDENT, 28 MARCH 1999

I F AN OSCAR ceremony was held in a forest, and there was no one around to see it, would Tom Hanks' wife really exist? There are many arguments for holding Oscar ceremonies in forests – it would teach those wattle-and-daub Knysna hippies a damn good lesson, for one thing – but the prospect of Tom's foolery evaporating in a puff and a sniffle is perhaps the most appealing.

Hanks himself hogged a good deal of camera time during *Oscars 99* (M-Net, Monday, 8pm). There he lurked like a sinister scoutmaster in the second row, dewy-eyed and dimpling and practising the secret cub-scout handshake on himself. In a misguided effort to butch up, he has grown a scrappy new beard, which doesn't so much create the effect of a rugged leading man as much as it does a hairy eraser at the end of a pencil.

The Oscars play an important role in our collective sense of well-being. Far more revealing than *paparazzi* snapshots of Kate Winslet without her make-up or John Travolta without his cigarette, they offer a fleeting glimpse of what stars are like when they write their own scripts. Always remember Hot Medium's first law of social success: under no circumstances appear in public without a script. Spontaneity requires practice, and original thought is like original sin – it only ever happened once, a long time ago, to someone who wasn't you.

Whoopi Goldberg, sad to say, did have a script, yet still contrived to throw me into the torments of embarrassment with which I suffer through bad speakers. For some reason she chose to punctuate every sentence with the word "honey!" ("Wooo, honey, this is going to be a long night!"), as though she were a bad drag act opening for Billy Ray Cyrus in a honky-tonk bar.

Besides impersonal terms of endearment, there are two crimes unforgivable in a public speaker – one is repeatedly laughing at your own smutty jokes, and the other is noticing that no one else is laughing and demanding, like Whoopi: "Are you having a good time? Are you? Yeah!" All right!"

Much like those other dreaded interrogations, "Do you remember what you did at the party last night?" and "Are you sure you love me?", "Are you having a good time?" is a question only ever asked when the answer is bound to be roundly in the negative.

Blessed relief from Whoopi-Cushion Goldberg was the delightful dance number, which demonstrated that choreographer Debbie Allen has lost none of the talent or taste that made *Fame* such a must-see programme in at least four households around the world in the mid-1980s. Let those who mock the artistic value of the Oscars watch a long-haired, bare-chested Spaniard tap-dance the theme song to *Saving Private Ryan*, and blush. When the dancer flexed his pectoral muscles in a moving tribute to the fallen soldiers, I could scarcely contain my bravos.

But the magic of the Oscars lies in the winners' speeches. My immediate delight that Tom Yanks didn't win the best actor award was tempered by the realisation that Roberto Benigni had. Some may consider the chair-climbing antics of the excitable little continental chap charming, but I felt they lowered the class and tone that Debbie Allen's dancers had tried so hard to establish. "I am surging with the love," gurgled the little loon, once he'd made it up to the stage. "I am wanting to hug and kiss you all and put my tongue in your ears." Perhaps Hanks had slipped something into his *chianti*.

Steven Spielberg gave me pause for thought with his acceptance speech for best director. "I want to thank all the families who lost sons in the Second World War," he declared. I wonder: what would be the correct response if you were one of the families being thus thanked? "It's a pleasure" seems insincere. "Not at all, any time" likewise. Perhaps "Don't mention it" might be closest to the mark.

Anyway, it all paled next to Gwyneth Poltroon's speech. Even Whoopi paled next to that speech. As poised and gracious as a block of processed cheese, as concise and pleasing as a song by Celine Dion, it had me regretting that Benigni couldn't have won best actress too. It was fun counting how many different people in her speech she loved "more than anything in the world", but it did become a little morbid when she thanked her cousin Keith, who'd been dead these past years. "I miss you, Keith," she declared into the cameras, which raised the inevitable questions about whether the dearly departed watch the Oscars, and if so, whether M-Net or SABC3's coverage is favoured in the afterlife. I am inclined towards M-Net – it may be more long-winded than the SABC's edited highlights, but you've got to pass the time in eternity somehow.

Starship Election: Space 1999

SUNDAY INDEPENDENT, 6 JUNE 1999

T HE DEVIL HAS all the best tunes, M-Net has all the best sport, but the SABC – bless 'em – had the 1999 elections. I woke at 7.45 on Tuesday morning and turned on the telly, just in time to hear Vuyo Mbuli say: "The time is now 6.45."

Vuyo, looking neat and shiny as a newly peeled egg, was the left prong of the Election '99 broadcasting trident; Nadia Levin, looking confidently bouffant, was the right: but the real star of the show was the IEC centre, lurking in the background with screens flickering and counters turning, like the bridge of the Starship Enterprise. It has been a long time since an SABC production had such a lavish set, and Vuyo and Nadia weren't about to let the moment pass unnoticed.

"Here we are in the very hub of the elections," said Vuyo, for the first of many times.

"Yes, Vuyo, this is indeed the very hub," agreed Nadia.

"Everyone here has a chair," marvelled Vuyo, as the camera panned over rows of empty seating.

It was true: even Graeme Hart, the weather guy, had his own chair. Unfortunately, he didn't have his own microphone. His voice was like the faraway grumble of an approaching drought. When they did manage to mike him up, his voice was sombre in its appreciation of the magnitude of his meteorological contribution to democracy. Bereft of visuals, he was forced to make the climate come alive with facial expressions.

Fortunately for Graeme and viewer alike, the weather was fine. He hunched unhappily in his chair, blazer ruffling about his neck. There is nothing more poignant than a weather guy without his synoptic chart.

Nor was Vuyo inclined to let the humiliation end there. "I've been watching Graeme for years," he announced jovially, "and he always does it standing up. Maybe Nadia can discuss with him what it's like to do it sitting down."

If she had, I would have lodged an official complaint with the IEC. Wisely, the broken Hart made subsequent appearances squarely on two feet.

The SABC's was an ambitious operation, with outside units, roving reporters, even the odd bar graph. Yet more impressively, the presenters have picked up an international tip or two: they shrewdly adopted the CNN strategy of spending far more time telling us what in-depth coverage we're getting, than actually providing coverage itself.

Mind you, there wasn't much coverage to give. To the great satisfaction of everyone who isn't a journalist, the elections were as marrow-achingly boring as elections should be. Still, Vuyo soldiered forth undaunted.

"We've had some exciting moments already," he enthused. "Just now we saw Bantu Holomisa cast his vote!" As a highlight, it was meagre pickings, but we watched it over and again throughout the next hour, in glorious slow motion. Oh, wait a minute, that's not slow motion, that's the normal speed at which people vote. I can think of very few people who could make the act of dropping a slip of paper into a cardboard box look interesting. Grethe Fox, maybe, and Walter Matthau. John Cleese, if he did that funny walk. Marthinus van Schalkwyk and Bantu Holomisa? No.

For variety, the studio kept optimistically crossing to Jessica Pitchford in a helicopter. "What does election day look like from the air?" Nadia asked from the very hub of the elections. Jessica chattered away, but she must have been borrowing Graeme Hart's microphone. We sat staring at the skyline of Pretoria, hearing only the mocking whirr of rotor blades. From that vantage point, election day looked much like any other. A cloud drifted by, but I was inclined to ignore it.

Eventually Jessica's voice crackled into life: "We're flying over the IEC, the very hub of the elections ..." Down in the very nerve centre, Vuyo and Nadia had developed the unpleasant habit of crossing for regional updates.

That left those of us in Gauteng in the company of what appeared to be a pair of dressmaker's dummies in air-stewardess's uniforms. They were identified as Paula Slier and Noxolo Grootboom. Noxolo was the one whose lips had to be manually operated by the sound engineer; Paula was the one with the pop-eyed manner of a trout who'd been stunned by a blow from a grizzly bear. They eyed the camera in rubbery silence, as though afraid it might make an improper advance.

Embarrassingly, due to a technical glitch, the viewers could hear all the instructions the producer was murmuring into Paula and Noxolo's earpieces. Political analyst Sheila Meintjies stopped speaking. Paula goggled at her piscatorially.

"Thank you, Sheila," crackled the producer's voice.

"Thank you, Sheila," wobbled Paula.

"Now you, Noxolo."

"Thank you, Sheila."

Finally they could take it no more. "Let's cross to Jessica Pitchford, our eye in the sky."

There followed the familiar sound of rotor blades, then: "Yes, hi, we're flying over the IEC, the very hub of the elections."

Every so often, a music video was played. It was always a song called "The Rainbow Nation", rendered by two Spur waiters in black pullovers. Their accompaniment was a reedy tune picked out on an E-Zee-Play Organola. Their names, if you can believe it, were Bobo and Kellam. "The world is awakening," they crooned, as though masked intruders were tampering with their ingrown toenails, "to a global fee-ee-dom!" By all that's holy, who could like that song?

Back to the studio. "I really like that song," said Nadia.

Oh, there were wondrous times in the very hub of the elections, but by the time Vuyo and Nadia moved over to make space for Alyce Chavunduka, the fun was draining away. Without Vuyo's shiny dome to light the way, it all became a little dreary. There was simply no news worth reporting. By Friday, the circus had left town. "Welcome again from the IEC," said Vuyo, "a very hive of activity." I could take a hint.

When a hub is no longer a hub, it's time to leave.

I am Wat Siam –
TV in Thailand

SUNDAY INDEPENDENT, 9 JANUARY 2000

ON THE NIGHT before Christmas I hired a high-prowed wooden fishing boat and put out through the breakers, skimming fast across the surface of the Andaman Sea, as warm and dark as a glass of mulled red wine. The wake swirled and gleamed with faint phosphorescence, like the distant glimmer of the lights from a department-store Christmas tree that had slipped overboard and lay unravelled across the sea-bed. The moonlight danced on the sea like tinsel. After an hour I arrived at Buddha Island, a tiny, unlit dot off the west coast of Thailand. I made my gift of bottled water and loaves of rye bread and a small tub of Philadelphia cream cheese to the head monk. He spoke no English, and my Thai should be punished with a coconut-husk flail and sharpened length of bamboo, so the boatman translated as we stood under the rushing, swaying hurricane palms in the uncanny glow of a tropical full moon.

It is a tradition in these parts to bring gifts to the monastery, and to ask the head monk, who has a reputation for knowledge beyond ordinary ken, questions of the future. My principal curiosity concerned the cricket score, but while the Buddha was undoubtedly wise and good and even fun-loving, there was no suggestion He was a cricket fan.

"What can I expect from the new year?" I asked instead. The head monk looked at me narrowly, and pulled his saffron robes close about him. "Is it new year already?" he said. He was perhaps 60, but his muscles were taut and alive, like a school of fast-swimming ocean fish in a surgical glove. He was a persuasive advertisement for the clean life, or at least the life lived far from other people. He placed a hand on my upper arm and frowned. "Beware," he said, "of lawsuits."

It was an alarming thing to hear, so far from Jani Allan and the SABC, but southeast Asia is a place of surprises. It is also a good place for Yule-phobes such as myself to spend the season. The only sign of Christmas against which I stubbed my toe was a tinny album of carols playing in a department store in Kuala Lumpur.

The album was recorded by a Thai pub band specialising in Western music, which perhaps explained why it sounded as though a plantation of annoyed dwarfs were yelling "Sirent night! Hory night!" I bought my souvenir gift hamper of Malaysian rubber and fled. Behind me the dwarfs were building to a frenzy: "I'll pray my dlum for him, pa-lum-pa-pum-pum!"

It has been quite some journey to the east, but by the time you read this I shall be home. As I write, a water buffalo grazes in a rice paddy outside my window, and if I look to the left I can see a clipper in white sail following the current down to the Straits of Malacca and into the China Seas. I came in search of television, but I found the footprints of authors.

In the Bangkok Oriental hotel I took tea in the suite in which Somerset Maugham nearly died of malaria, and stood on the spot where Joseph Conrad slumped to the ground after too many rum toddies. In Singapore's Raffles I drank a gin sling on the porch where Noel Coward sat shuddering with dengue fever. I rode the same rails as Graham Greene up the Malaysian peninsula, and slept in the same compartment of the Orient Express that Wilbur Smith once infested. I tried to change compartments, but nothing doing.

Which is not to say that I entirely neglected my television duties. TV, unlike the portions served in local restaurants, is big in the Orient. On the River Kwai, barely 500m downstream from the infamous and strangely unimpressive bridge, a nearby settlement is visible only by the tangled thicket of television aerials rising above the bamboo and banana fronds. In the villages and farmsteads lining the railway through the Malaysian jungle, every small stilted shack housing rubber tappers and dirt-scrabble palm growers has a rickety aerial receiving all that local television has to offer.

In Thailand, that consists principally of the same overpitched game show that followed me about like a hungry mutt. Wherever there was television, there was that green and purple stage design, those seven Thais in animated conversation, that cheering, whistling audience. I spent many hours trying to puzzle it out, but I still haven't any idea how the game is played. All I could gather, by the succession of groans and crumpled facial expressions, was that no one had yet triumphed. Finally, after 10 days of such torture, the grand prize was won. I wasn't watching when it happened, I'm happy to say, but Dam, my driver, told me it had been a motorbike.

Dam was a font of invaluable information. When buying cobra's blood from a street vendor, he cautioned, always make sure it's fresh. "Watch the snake be kill," said Dam earnestly, "with own eyes." Apparently unscrupulous cobra-blood merchants will substitute the pre-packaged blood of the more common tree snake. Dam tutted at the depths of man's depravity.

Two days later I stood in a narrow Chinatown alley, carefully watching as my cobra was sliced open. The blood was decanted into a small plastic packet, such as you would use to wrap your child's sandwiches for school. I looked around eagerly, savouring the exoticness of the moment, but the vendors weren't watching me. They were peering through a half-open door at a flickering TV screen. I looked over their shoulders. A Barbara Cartland movie was showing.

Hugh Grant stood proud in Regency wig and ruffles. He appeared to be defending, or perhaps defiling, the honour of a simple country lass in blonde curls. He said something in Thai, and the snake vendors hissed approvingly. I sighed and sipped my blood. Everyone wants to be a critic.

White male TV columnists overthrow the world

SUNDAY INDEPENDENT, 6 FEBRUARY 2000

T HERE ARE MANY ways of insulting someone. One way that is surprisingly common is to give them a bunch of carnations on Valentine's Day. (Don't ask why, buddy, just don't do it.)

Another popular means of insult is to call someone nasty names. "Shane" is a nasty name, and so is "Gary", and I'm not crazy about "Dwayne" either.

The important thing about insulting someone, if you want the insult to sting, is to ensure that it is accurate and to the point. "You blocks, you stones, you worse than senseless things" has pleasing iambic pentameter, but it is not going to cause a roomful of *Simunye* presenters to burst into tears.

Similarly, when Steven Kenton the class bully took to calling Lance Denman "Four-Eyes" when we were all cruel youths, it caused more puzzlement than pain, since Lance Denman never wore glasses. Steven Kenton tried to explain that he was referring to Lance Denman's stammer, but once you have to explain an insult, you are lost.

"I-I-I-I don't know what you mean," Lance Denman would simply say smugly, and Steven Kenton would be nonplussed, if nonplussed is the word I'm looking for.

An ill-directed insult causes more mirth than soul-searching. Just the other day, for instance, someone hissed, not without venom, that I belong to something called "the white male media conspiracy".

Unless you're white, male and working in the media, it is hard to understand just how funny this is. Take a good look at the next white male media worker you bump into while returning your empties down at the bottle store – he can scarcely co-ordinate his own clothing, far less a sinister counter-revolutionary movement. We can't even put together a Sunday league cricket team, let alone conspire to overthrow the world with our white, male TV columns.

On the whole, conspiracies require a great deal more application, intelligence and energy than most human beings (white, male or otherwise) can bring to the job. If we have learnt anything from the past century, it should be that history unfolds not through planning and co-ordination, but through the unravelling of chance and circumstance, and the relentless dialectic of opportunity and opportunism.

The Nazis: A Warning from History (SABC3, Sunday, 9pm) should be compulsory viewing for everyone who complains there is nothing decent on television, and everyone who likes to abnegate his own responsibilities by pointing an indignant finger outwards. The idea of ordinary people being helpless before the hidden face of implacable power is perversely comforting, but it is a myth.

The West has long been made uncomfortable by the very fact of Hitler and his Nazis. How could such a man, and such a machine, exist in a civilised world? The easiest answer is to accept, at least partially, Hitler's own publicity: the Nazis must have been supermen, or supermonsters, cold-blooded and calculating, working tirelessly to achieve their diabolical masterplan.

The truth, as *A Warning from History* so strikingly demonstrates, is less dramatic and far more frightening. With extraordinary research and dazzling footage, the show brought Hitler snuffling and harrumphing to life. He emerged not as the dynamic Führer of legend – sleepless, burning with the inner flame of an infernal mission – but a lazy, rather stupid opportunist, who slept late, liked a pint, and even during the height of the war was most enthusiastically exercised by the prospect of a good meal and a movie.

Hang about, I realised with a lurch, watching footage of Hitler dozing on his couch while outside all the world was ablaze. *Take away the comical moustache, the jodhpurs and Nazi convictions, and that could be me.*

The machinery of Nazi government, which in retrospect looks such a model of fascist order and discipline, was revealed to be a bumbling and uncoordinated hive of jealousy and insecurity. Hitler was portrayed as a vague dreamer of bad dreams, an inspirational leader with scant grasp of the pragmatics or technicalities of dictatorship, who would speak aloud his visions for his squabbling acolytes and toadies to seize on random thoughts and half-ideas, and bring them to terrible fruition.

Worse, the documentary revealed the German people not as a brutalised, brainwashed people in the grip of jackbooted power, still less a community of Aryan devils with murder in their hearts, but as that sight so familiar to local eyes – a nation of ordinary people whose darker urges were encouraged by authority.

In a powerful piece of television, one Rezi Kraus, now a sweet-looking old lady of gentle habits and tender disposition, was confronted with a letter she had written to the Gestapo 50 years earlier, which had helped send a neighbour to the camps. She recognised her signature on the statement, but she could remember nothing of the letter itself.

She brooded awhile then burst out: "You know, I didn't kill anyone! I didn't even join the BDM, the girls' Hitler Youth!"

"Oh?" said the interviewer, expecting some burst of ideology, some impassioned self-defence.

"No," said Rezi Kraus, "there was no way my father would let his daughters travel all the way into town after dark to go to the meetings."

This is how the history of the world and of individuals lurches forward through a mixture of the political and the recognisably human, the horrific and the domestic. It is not the paranoiac world of conspirators and powerful cabals that we need fear in our dim apprehensions of power, but the libidinal world of power allowed to flow free, following the fault lines, seeking the low ground like water rushing toward the sea, our baser nature given space to flex and exercise and find its own path. In the history of the modern world, more harm has been done by weakness than by strength.

Fridges and fantasies

SUNDAY INDEPENDENT, 22 OCTOBER 2000

HAVE YOU EVER bought a fridge? Well, of course you have. If the readership profile of the quality Sunday newspaper is to be believed, you are probably an educated, employed professional with a respectable income. Congratulations. Such pillars of society as your good self generally do buy refrigerators. Indeed, I shouldn't be surprised to learn that you have bought more than one refrigerator in your time. Perhaps even several, which seems a little profligate, but no doubt you had your reasons.

I raise the subject because, like a saint going marching in, I have recently joined your number. Not so much the "employed professional" part; more the fact that I have myself recently bought a fridge. No big deal for you perhaps, but a harrowing experience for a man who has never given much more thought to the refrigerator than to wonder how to move it closer to the couch without damaging the carpet.

Refrigerators are substantial items. They represent many things. Food, mainly, and ice for the bourbon, but also a home. More than that: a home you are making for yourself. My previous fridges have been other people's fridges. They have just been there, white and humming and uncertain of origin, like an ageing folk musician. This one is all mine.

There is so much to consider when buying a refrigerator. Top freezer or bottom? Sticky-out handle, or handle recessed into the door? What is a crisper? And most agonising of all: should the egg caddy be built-in or detachable? The egg caddy conundrum haunted me through umpteen department stores and too many late-night conversations, even after I had recovered from the discovery that egg holders are officially called caddies.

I don't eat eggs, but a fridge is for life, or if not for life at least for the length of an average marriage, and no man wants to lie awake for the next seven years wondering if he was too hasty in the egg department.

I have plenty to say about my fridge, and indeed my new home, but I shall confine myself to this announcement: I welcome all house-warming gifts, with the firm exception of those rotten magnet-poetry sets, in which small magnetised words are scattered about with the implied invitation to visitors to arrange them in bursts of lyric poetry. No such set shall sully my fridge. No limply suggestive soft-porn phrases shall insult my eye when seeking morning milk for my coffee; no grisly metaphors or vapid aphorisms shall arrest my appalled attention while dashing for another six-pack at half-time. There are few things more loathsome than other people's ideas of poetry. Fridges are for making beer run cold, not my blood.

That is quite enough about fridges. Forgive me, dear reader, but I have been lingering with good reason: firstly, because instead of watching television this week I spent my evening with hammer and ratchet and grease-stained overalls, trying to repair the little light inside the fridge. (It went off when the door was opened, and on when it closed again, and don't ask me how I know.)

Secondly, because buying a refrigerator, or perhaps reading about one, is precisely the kind of domestic drudgery that drives a certain kind of reader into the arms of fantasy fiction.

Gormenghast (M-Net, Tuesday, 8pm) is a remarkable series, but it is not my cup of mead. The kind of perfectly realised alternative world that underpins Mervyn Peake's trilogy, as with Tolkien and to a lesser extent CS Lewis, is immensely attractive to many people.

They find comfort in it, and freedom. A world limited only by your imagination (actually, someone else's imagination) is just what they're after. And I am not only talking about the losers at university who wore capes and organised role-play games and drank mulled wine at their parties. There are perfectly decent citizens who find pleasure in fantasy. Not me.

Well-wrought fantasy fiction arouses in me a sensation approaching terror, a feeling of being perched on a ledge at a sheer cliff face above an abyss in the howling darkness. The opening hour or so of *Gormenghast* captured the experience. Gormenghast is a kingdom somewhere, sometime. It is big enough to be everything, or so it feels when you're inside it. On screen it throbbed with the terrible quality of a dream – the colours too vibrant, the scale too impossibly huge. "Welcome to the vastness," murmurs the mad Earl of Groan to his new-born son Titus, and the words sent a dark echo through me.

I dislike dreams because I am always small in them. Not in the svelte sense (those are waking dreams), but in the sense of the world being too big, beyond my ability to understand or be understood. So it is with Gormenghast.

Early in the episode the hero-villain Steerpike escapes from the purgatory of the castle kitchens and scales the roof of the world, walking along a narrow rooftop with his head in the sky, seeing Gormenghast for the first time, aghast. It exhilarated Steerpike; it horrified me.

The sets and costumes are a clutter of styles and artefacts from all cultures and times, thrown together without outward order or logic, as in a dream: Siamese *wats* and Viennese frock coats, Ottoman drapery, moustaches from the Raj, Copernican beards and Dickensian libraries, a throne from the Versailles court of Louis XVI ... together they seem to make a sense that can't be apprehended: the most frightening sense of all. I am fearful of worlds I cannot understand.

Gormenghast has its conventional weak points. The acting at times is too broad – all shouting and facial expressions and accents so thick you could cut them with a bicycle, as though the Two Ronnies were performing *Alice in Wonderland*, or the cast of *Big Okes* had wandered onto the wrong set. But the vision is whole and complete. It is vast and strange.

It makes me want to curl up and read a crime novel by the soft light of my fridge.

Missouri's living dead elect one of their own

SUNDAY INDEPENDENT, 12 NOVEMBER 2000

I HAVE NEVER BEEN to Missouri, but it has always fascinated me. One of my heroes, Mark Twain, was born and raised there, and his finest novel, *The Adventures of Huckleberry Finn*, is largely set along the banks of the mighty Mississippi. In recent years, though, my interest in Missouri has become more appalled than admiring.

Missouri, like most states in the United States, has its own slogan. In the US a state is sneered at by its brothers if its essence can't be captured in two or three words and emblazoned on a motor car licence plate. Missouri is officially called "The Show-Me State". Why show me? It is from a speech made by one Willard Duncan Vandiver in 1899. "I come from a state that raises corn and cotton and cockleburs," said Vandiver proudly, "I am from Missouri. You have got to show me."

Which is to say: native Missourians are actually proud of having the regional characteristic that they will not or cannot understand something unless it is practically demonstrated. The Missourian takes as his defining feature that he is incapable of abstract thought.

It was Missouri that in the 1990s passed a law requiring that Biblical seven-day creationism be given equal teaching time with the new-fangled heresy of evolution. Schoolchildren in Missouri spend half an hour learning about fossils and the adaptation over millennia of hominids to their changing environment, and the next 30 minutes learning that men and women were made from a handful of dust and a spare rib.

Missouri once had a state law prohibiting women from driving a vehicle without displaying a sign warning other motorists. Ah yes, Missouri. As Bill Bryson once wrote: "It is worth remembering that Mark Twain got the hell out of Missouri as soon as he could, and was always disinclined to come back."

Why this disquisition on the Show-Me State? Because I am still marvelling at the fact that on Wednesday morning the good folk of Missouri elected to the US senate a man who had been dead for several months. Of course, in 1980, the American people elected as president a man who was dead from the neck up, and in this election have had to choose between two men dead from the eyebrows down, but still.

It was just one bright spot in a marathon session of viewing that is the highlight of my television year so far. *Election 2000* (CNN, all Tuesday night and Wednesday morning) was pure anarchic viewing pleasure.

Ross Perot set the tone in an interview with Larry King. "You know, Larry," Ross creaked reflectively, like Norman Bates's mother in a ruminative mood, "the Republicans and the Democrats are just like the Palestinians and, you know, them other group over there."

"The Israelis?" guessed Larry.

"Sure, the Israelis," agreed Perot. "Just like them, only, you know, not as violent."

With such an intro, it could hardly fail. Breathlessly I watched as events unfolded like a one-day cricket match. I cheered as the Democrats won Florida. I hissed as the Republicans won it back. I gave a happy hoorah as the recount was announced.

"We're going to be here a long time," said Bernard Shaw in the CNN studios. I poured bourbon on my cornflakes and leaned forward happily.

What made it the more enjoyable is that Bernard and his presenters were in for the long haul with me. Everyone in the studio had their own turf: Bernie and his team were on the Big Desk, Wolf Blitzer was looking lovably bristly over at the Balance of Power Desk, and one Hal Bruno was forced to stand beside what looked like a weatherman's synoptic chart.

"How you doing, Hal?" asked Bernie at around 10am our time.

"I've been standing for the last 10 hours, how do you think I feel? Back to you at the Big Desk, Bernie," said Hal through clenched teeth.

As the broadcast entered its 13th hour, Bernie and the gang veered between hysteria and downright prickliness. One Ed Kast – some manner of Florida state election official speaking to the team from ground zero – seemed personable enough, but as far as information went, he may as well have been a Missouri voter.

The Big Desk was not amused. "How long will it take to recount the votes, Ed Kast?" asked William Schneider.

"We'll start as soon as we can," Ed Kast assured him.

"Yes, Ed Kast, but how long will it take?" snarled Schneider.

"Well," said Ed Kast, "that will depend on how long it takes to recount the votes."

In between the election coverage, CNN provided all manner of interesting news from around the world. I learnt that Truck Expo 2000 is currently being broadcast live on Romanian television. A man wearing a paste-on Eastern European moustache appeared in front of a poster of a truck to tell us that it is a great day for Romanian television.

"It is not just trucks," he said, "but also truck parts and truck accessories." I was just raising a spoon of cornflakes to toast the fact that I am not a Romanian TV columnist when we were back in the studio. William Schneider was thumping his forehead on the Big Desk, softly keening: "When can we go home? When can we go home?"

"Breaking news!" announced Bernie gamely. "The election is not over. Let me repeat that: the election is not over!"

William Schneider looked up hopefully. "Are you wrapping up, Bernie?" he asked.

"No, no," said Bernie, "I just wanted to say that before I forgot it."

By that time I was beginning to flag. Twelve hours is a long time to watch someone else's election. Unlike Bernie, I was not being paid overtime. As I staggered to bed, I heard William Schneider's head hit the desk again.

"Wake up, Bill," begged Bernie, "we've got Ed Kast back on the line."

A Christmas story

SUNDAY INDEPENDENT, 24 DECEMBER 2000

THERE ARE FEW good Christmas stories. Christmas stories, by and large, are too caught up in their own Christmasness to be any good as stories. Indeed, Christmas stories are similar to Christmas cards – their purpose is not to be honest or to entertain, but to perform a dutiful and imprecise sort of gesture.

They always have a message. Messages do not make for good stories. Messages should either be sealed in a bottle and thrown into the sea, or written in lemon juice in the white space between the lines of the story. If the readers want the message badly enough, let them hold up the page to a naked flame.

(I have tried that, incidentally – faithfully following the good Ms Enid Blyton's instructions. But perhaps the lemons available to English children in the 1930s were of a more subtle sort than those available today. I never had the invisible writing resolve itself into brown lines before my eyes. All I had were scorched fingertips and on one occasion an invisible map of my back garden that went up in a frightening burst of yellow flame. It didn't matter, I suppose. I hadn't buried anything at the spot marked X more valuable than a silver napkin ring, and I had no one to whom to pass the secret map who would have had the slightest idea what to do with a loamy napkin ring.)

Worse than a message is the burden of a Christmas message. Christmas stories are supposed to embody in some way the true meaning of Christmas. The trouble is that no one really knows what the true meaning of Christmas might be, which leads to an awful lot of guff.

There are only so many times that a sensible person can stomach Jimmy Stewart discovering what a wonderful person he really is (*It's a Wonderful Life*) or those two chumps in O Henry's *Gift of the Magi* giving each other overpriced Christmas presents. Closest to the truth was Scrooge in *A Christmas Carol*, who discovered that you can buy the affection of the townsfolk by being free with your cash.

I am dwelling on the problem of the Christmas story, you may have guessed, because I don't feel like writing about television. I feel like telling a Christmas story. I couldn't invent one that I liked, so I turned to real life.

I considered telling the true tale of a girl with whom I went to school, whose name was Carol. We called her Christmas Carol, partially because she was head of the choir, but also because she had a bulbous, shiny nose. The last I heard of Christmas Carol, she had married a man from Qatar, converted to Islam and is now living somewhere in Yemen, where I can only hope she has found a veil large enough to conceal her nose. But the story of Christmas Carol lacked zip.

Let me tell you this story instead. It has no message, but that is as it is in real life. My grandfather was a prisoner in an Italian camp during the last world war. He had been a gunner with the Eighth Army in the deserts of North Africa, and had been captured and interned somewhere in Italy. He was hazy with the details: men of my grandfather's generation seldom spoke about the war. He did tell one tale. It involved Christmas Day, 1943: the day he called and made slam in no trumps while playing bridge in the shade of a pine tree beside the camp's exercise yard. Never before and never since would my grandfather call and make slam in no trumps.

His bridge partner on that occasion was an Italian guard, whose name I have forgotten. If I tell you it was Luigi, you will guess that I am guessing. Luigi was a young man, almost a boy, just like my grandfather. He was friendly and occasionally brought the prisoners chickens. My grandfather taught him English, but didn't bother to learn Italian in return.

They spoke about home, and played bridge and football together. Luigi didn't get along with the other Italian guards, for reasons that can only be guessed at, but thanks to Luigi, my grandfather always said, the day that he called and made slam in no trumps was the happiest Christmas of his life.

After the war my grandfather returned home and played out the remainder of an undistinguished bridge career, pausing only to set in motion the chain of events that led to, well, me. Luigi disappeared into the gloom of post-war Naples.

In 1993 I was living in Cape Town. A week before Christmas, I went to a local picture shop to frame a sepia photograph of my grandfather as a young man. I had recently discovered it in a dusty box in a garage; it would be a Christmas present for my mother.

The framer was an old man. He stared at the photograph a long time. I was anxious to be going, but he told me a story. It was a story about being a young man in the war, and working as a guard in a prisoner-of-war camp, and about a South African friend, a prisoner, who made the unhappy months bearable, and how later he had remembered the stories of Cape Town, and had moved south, and been happy since.

He spoke in perfect English, with an Italian accent. He had never seen his friend again, but hoped he would. Perhaps they would share Christmas lunch together again. Perhaps they would play some bridge.

And there the story ends. My grandfather had died a month before, and Luigi died a few months later. They had lived the past 40 years within five kilometres of each other, and had never stopped playing bridge.

It would have been nice if they could have met that Christmas, and called and made one final slam in no trumps. Sometimes it would be nice if life were like a Christmas story.

The more the marrier

SUNDAY INDEPENDENT, 22 APRIL 2001

I AM NOT IN the habit of judging other people's lifestyles. Well, actually I am, but I wasn't about to admit it in the very first sentence. I am informed that some people are in the habit of reading only the first sentence of each article in the newspaper, and I want to leave them with a good impression of me. Although, now that I come to think of it, I don't really give two hoots (which in owl currency is the equivalent of one human damn) for the opinion of the kind of individual who would only read the first sentence of this column. If I could take that sentence back I would, but what's done is done, I suppose.

So yes, actually, I *am* in the habit of judging other people's lifestyles, but of all the lifestyles I have had cause to tut over, it is Alex Joseph who gets the most unequivocal thumbs-down. Who is Alex Joseph? You may well ask. Alex Joseph was a featured guest on *The Jerry Springer Show* (DStv, Series Channel, daily, 10pm). Unusually, Jerry ventured out of the studio to visit Alex on his ranch. It was a dusty sort of a ranch, without much by way of grass or crops or even livestock, but Alex was happy. Alex purred and preened like a cat that has managed to get its paws on some other cat's saucer of milk. But there the comparison ended. Despite a small and scrubby beard, Alex is not as furry as a cat, and whereas a cat has nine lives, Alex Joseph has eight wives.

To have one wife, you might say, is good fortune. (You also might not say it, especially if you have one.) To have two wives is careless. To have six and seven and eight wives is to be interviewed by Jerry Springer, and when you're being interviewed by Jerry Springer, you must have some inkling that somewhere on life's bendy byways you've taken the wrong turn.

Mind you, the extended immediate family of Alex Joseph was a good deal more harmonious than most of Jerry's guests. They huddled together in the yard and beamed for a group photograph, like a box-framed collection of sun-faded Tretchikoffs.

Alex told us that he and his wives have produced 25 children and 733 grand-children. Well, he may not actually have said 733, but after a certain point what difference does it make? Alex's ranch is located outside Big Water, Utah, which would encourage a lesser and cheaper columnist to make a series of leering jokes involving, you know, bigness and water. But Big Water, Utah is beyond a joke. Big Water, Utah is one of the ugliest places I have ever seen. There is nothing there except wives. We took a tour of the compound. "All the wives have their own houses," said Sarah, the chief wife, "except for some wives, who share."

The houses were decorated with home-made cushions and bean bags and quilted things. On the wall of each house was an embroidered motto: "The more, the marrier". No, I just made that last bit up.

Why would Alex do such a thing?

"To take a wife is a responsibility," said Alex, squinting philosophically into the dust, "and the bigger the man, the more responsibility he bears."

Marrying eight women at the same time struck me as a foolhardy way of proving your manhood. On the whole, I think I prefer the Xhosa tradition, where all they do is cut off a piece of your penis.

Alex has started his own church, and in a sense his own congregation. It is called "The Church of Jesus Christ of the Solemn Assembly". It's almost as if he wants to be laughed at. We had dinner with the family. Now *that* was a solemn assembly. "The problem with the world today," said Alex as he buttered both sides of his bread, "is that women get married when they're 20 and change their minds when they're 30. They change men like diapers." Which made you fear a little for the personal hygiene of the little 'uns. They must be looking forward to turning 10, so they can change those diapers already.

Alex's plan to eliminate the problem of the changeability of women involved marrying his most recent wife when she was 15 and he was 53. She had been signed over as his bride when she was nine years old. The only thing Alex's wives change like diapers is their diapers.

And yet they all seemed content enough. Whatever the disadvantages of plural marriages – I can imagine, for instance, that one would be reluctant to take the family on a cruise ship with a "women and children first" policy – Alex wasn't complaining and the ladies weren't contemplating a change. And who am I to criticise? I can scarcely get a date on a Saturday night, and this nutter in Utah lands eight uncomplaining wives. He should be a hero to us all. But he isn't.

TV in Yemen

SUNDAY INDEPENDENT, 13 MAY 2001

SALAAM ALEIKUM, my friends. You will notice that I begin this column with a common Arabic expression. That is because I have just returned from Yemen (or, as some would have it, *the* Yemen), where common Arabic expressions are even more common than they are elsewhere.

That particular expression either means "Peace be upon you", or is a way of ordering extra salami and cucumber on your pizza. I am rather inclined to the first interpretation, because I frequently said *salaam aleikum* in my travels through the wadis and highlands of southern Arabia, and not once did anyone point me in the direction of the nearest Italian trattoria.

Of course, when you are in the Yemen, the nearest Italian trattoria is a continent away. There is a Pizza Hut in Aden, mind you, but no one really knows what its purpose might be. Locals stand outside and giggle at its architecture. The only customers are CIA investigators probing the sinking of *USS Cole* last year.

You can tell the CIA investigators a mile away. They have tattoos of mountain lions and biceps the size of a Yemeni waist and are always eating pizza out of cardboard Pizza Hut boxes. I shared a lift with one in an Aden hotel, and as the doors closed I asked how the investigation was going. He raised his head from the Pizza Hut box and adjusted his black plastic earpiece. "How do you know who I am?" he demanded. I smiled cryptically and tapped the side of my nose. He had to restrain himself visibly from throwing me in a headlock.

Western foods haven't made much impact in Yemen. I ate a camel-meat kebab somewhere in the Hadhramawt, the lush, palm-filled valley on the fringes of the endless sandy wastes of the desert the locals call *Rub al-Khali*, the Empty Quarter. It was tasty. It tasted like chicken. No, it didn't – it tasted like beef, but leaner. I suppose you might say it tasted like ostrich. Most of the time I ate chicken. That, I am pleased to say, *did* taste like chicken.

Yemen has shunned most of the eyesores of Western consumerism, but I have yet to visit the country that doesn't boast more satellite dishes than a man on horseback can count in a hundred days of galloping, as the old Yemeni saying goes. In Al-Hudaydah, on the Red Sea coast, I lay back under a spinning ceiling fan, draped myself in a swatch of muslin and settled in for an evening of television.

The greatest hazard to anyone thus approaching the intriguing and often opaque Arabian culture is the ubiquitous Arabic music video, in which, without exception, a portly fellow wearing loose shirts and immodestly snug-fitting trousers dances around a foxy lass with handmade eyebrows. He tries unsuccessfully to plight his troth for two minutes, 25 seconds of the song, while the foxy lass jangles her jewellery and looks unavailable.

How depressing, you might think, but fear not: you can tell by the waggle of the gentleman's eyebrows and the suave way he ruffles his moustache that he knows how the song ends. Finally, in the last five seconds, the foxy lass smiles and melts and accepts his troth and the pair scamper off screen, presumably en route to a good plighting.

Fortunately, the satellite service offered a full bouquet of channels from around the Arabic-speaking world. I tuned in to a Moroccan channel, or was it from Dubai? It was a live broadcast of a stage play. Two Moroccans in chinos and bowling shirts stood on stage, just outside the spotlights. Every time the spotlights tried to settle on them, they sidled away again. The spots danced around on stage trying to find them, a delicate pattern of loops and squiggles, as though the lighting guy were spelling out swear words in Arabic. In the foreground, a dwarf was speaking on a phone.

I couldn't follow what they were saying, of course, but apparently it was a comedy, because the two Moroccans kept slapping each other on the back and yelling their lines in unison, which is something they also do on e.tv sitcoms to signify a punchline. Ah, the universal language of comedy.

You could also tell it was funny because the 17 people in the audience kept chuckling. You could tell there were 17 people because a camera kept panning over them. Every time they noticed the camera, the audience members would wave and pull faces and try to pull their friends' jerseys up over their heads. It must have been a little puzzling for the performers. It was puzzling for me, but perhaps it was an innovative scheme for luring audiences back to live theatre: "Come to our play – you could be on television!"

I tried to tune in to the Saudi Arabian channel, but the service wasn't operational. What an opportunity lost. I lay there a long time, trying to imagine the wonders of Saudi television. A curtain draped over the screen, perhaps, with low voices in the background discussing the price of oil and laughing. ("Tell me, how much oil actually goes into a barrel, Sheik Ahmed?"

"Hmmm, not entirely sure, Ali. As much as we feel like, I suppose. Don't tell the Americans, heh heh heh."

"Heh heh heh.")

There are many reasons to visit Yemen, the land of Sheba and Sheherazade and the *Arabian Nights*, but television is not among them. I left the hotel and took a walk along the seafront, where groups of men sat and smoked and played dominos and drank strong, sweet coffee. Everyone invites a stranger to sit with them.

I chose a table that spoke English. "How you like Yemen?" someone asked.

"I like it better than Jerry Springer," I said, which is my way of giving a strong compliment.

"Who is Jerry Springer?" they said. Suddenly I realised all over again what a beautiful country I was visiting.

Father's Day

SUNDAY INDEPENDENT, 24 JUNE 2001

L AST SUNDAY WAS Father's Day, and I forgot all about it until *The Story of Fathers and Sons* (SABC3, Sunday, 5pm) reminded me.

It was a documentary celebrating what some goof wearing a back-to-front baseball cap was pleased to call "the mystical, spiritual bond between father and son". I have always wondered why people mistrust the emotional and the material so much that they feel obliged to reach into the ether to account for the strength of their feelings.

No matter. Much of what was most moving on the show was conveyed without words: the scene in which Dad hugs his son who has just struck out in Little League; Dad kneeling to hug the son who cannot walk; Dad and son standing together in the fine awkwardness of a pair who love each other, but aren't sure what to say to one another. As is usually the case, when words *were* used they tended to flatten the experience.

"Love is painful," said one dad, "because it hurts when the one you love is taken away." Well, yes.

"I think it's hard to plant a tree," said some bearded hippie dad, "and then watch it, uh, walk away from you."

I could forgive the show much. It is a subject that is especially close to me. I have wanted a son for precisely 22 years now, which is also the length of time that I have wanted a father.

When I was a small boy the wallpaper in my room was decorated, somewhat mysteriously, with recurring patterns of cowboys, locomotives and trout. The cowboys wore chaps and six-shooters, the locomotives billowed soot, the trout leapt high, eyes wide, fishing line trailing from their mouths towards an unseen rod. In order to calm myself after a particularly alarming episode of *Squad Cars* on the radio or *Bonanza* on television (the Ponderosa ranch had cowboys and locomotives aplenty, but I was always troubled by the conspicuous absence of trout), I would lie awake in the half-light, counting the figures on the wallpaper. On bad nights I would count a full wall-and-a-half before falling asleep.

One night, after the episode of *Bonanza* in which Little Joe fell into a fever and was captured by the Apaches, my father came in and sat on the edge of my bed and began talking. He spoke for a long time. His black silhouette blocked my view of the wallpaper.

Then he stood and said: "You may not understand all this now, but one day when you're grown up you'll remember these words." I remember that clearly. What I don't remember is anything he said before that.

Almost certainly it was some useful life lesson that would have spared me immense inconvenience and discomfort – how to avoid an over-friendly scoutmaster on a scout camp, perhaps, or the truth that only tennis players and newborn infants can wear white socks in public without social disgrace. Perhaps it was his recipe for making the perfect brandy-and-ginger ale, a drink for which he had an unreasonable enthusiasm.

In certain long dark nights of the soul I have come to the conclusion that if I could only remember those words, all the secrets of adulthood would be revealed to me. I have sat staring at the *Greater Oxford Dictionary*, bitterly musing on the fact that all his words are in there – I just have to arrange them in the correct order.

Some weeks after that particular episode of *Bonanza*, my father had a stroke, was hospitalised and died. His words, unless one day I suddenly grow up and remember them, are lost forever. Which is not to say that he didn't leave me illuminating tips to light my way through this long valley.

"Never mix your drinks, when you can get the barman to mix them for you," was an enduring favourite, sometime after the fourth little tin of ginger ale had been emptied.

On the subject of marriage, his advice was simple: "If you want a happy relationship," he said, "never, never, never do the washing up." At that time he was on his third marriage, so he must have known what he was talking about.

I don't know that his absence in my childhood affected me that much. It simply meant that my mother had to watch a lot more games of schoolboy rugby than she might otherwise have preferred, and that there was no one in the house big and strong enough to prevent me playing music as loud as I liked.

My mother being a good, sweet person with a strength of will incapable of matching my sulks and tantrums, it also meant that I had my own way through adolescence and consequently had nothing against which to rebel. An absence of discipline meant I had to invent my own – a masterstroke of parenting by implication.

People learn many useful things from their fathers. To this day I don't know how to change the oil in my car or repair a leaking water pipe. I had to teach myself to drop-kick a rugby ball and how to bowl an in-swinger, which is why every so often I still unintentionally produce the mystery delivery that neither swings not goes in.

Instead I contented myself with the stories and memories he shared of his own life as a bouncer and a romancer and a conman and a child of the Great Depression. You learn wisdom not from being told wise things, but from proximity to wisdom. And wisdom is simply another word for living well. I don't know what my father told me that night, which means I can never decide it was mistaken.

His more useful gift to me is the idea, however false, that there is a truth, and that if I live well enough I may one day find it. Perhaps one day I will even learn how to make the perfect brandy-and-ginger ale.

Forget phobias, find a fix for Felicia

SUNDAY INDEPENDENT, 1 JULY 2001

THERE ARE MANY things that frighten me. People driving white BMWs, for instance, and dinner parties where only couples are invited, and the Williams sisters, and anyone below the age of 25, and falling overboard in the middle of the night and bobbing in the wide and ink-black sea, yelling unheard as the yellow lights of the ship are slowly swallowed by the darkness. These are all scary things, and I haven't even mentioned colonic irrigations and conceptual artists and sausages.

But fearfulness, like happiness, is a shadowy trick of the mind.

Leave it to work away at the corner of your vision and it will grow obligingly, following its own laws and dusky twists of logic. But look at it closely and it simply melts away, like a journalist when it is his turn to buy the round.

Unless, that is, your fear is a phobia. A phobia is an irrational fear, felt with irrational force, so there is no remedy for treating it rationally.

There is, I can reveal, a clinic in the suburbs of Pretoria that takes what I can only describe as an overly aggressive approach in dealing with Felicia-phobes. Who among us does not tut and even cluck at reports of grown men and stripling children being strapped to their seats, their eyelids clamped open and tapes of Felicia on e.tv being endlessly replayed before their transfixed eyes?

Oh, the humanity. After such knowledge, what forgiveness?

At night in the dormitories, out-of-work SABC newsreaders are employed to sit on elevated chairs and read and reread a paperback copy of Felicia's autobiography to the sleeping unfortunate. The autobiography is called *Dare to Dream*. The sleeping unfortunate dare not.

Fears and especially phobias were Felicia's subjects on her show this week. Her first guest was a genial hypnotherapist called Terry Winchester.

"We have a phobia because we fear the unknown," announced Terry genially, or perhaps hypnotherapeutically.

Not me, mate. I know exactly what it is I fear about watching Felicia's show. I fear waking up one day in a bed in a dormitory in a clinic in the suburbs of Pretoria, with my head bandaged and a portion of my brain missing because the doctors had decided it was time for drastic measures.

Felicia had a variety of frightened people in the studio with her. Mainly, they were frightened by snakes and spiders. That suited Felicia just dandy, because she happened to have a variety of snakes and spiders ready to hand.

A doctor popped up to caution that treating phobias by trying to force the phobics to confront or touch the object of their fear is bad medicine and counterproductive.

It was an extraordinary thing to watch: Felicia appeared to be listening. She scrunched up her face and cocked her head on one side, as she does when she wants to appear to be listening.

She even nodded thoughtfully, as people do when listening. Then when the good doctor had finished, she scooped up the snakes and spiders and resumed chasing people around the studio, trying to force them to touch the objects of their fear. Felicia had not been listening.

We met Kylene, who is afraid of spiders. "I don't want to see a spider," said Kylene. "Shall I bring in a spider?" said Felicia. "No," said Kylene. "Let's bring in a spider!" yelled Felicia.

Along came one of Felicia's assistants, with a spider. "I want to see how close we can bring it to you," crooned Felicia in a tone of voice you wouldn't expect to hear outside of a dank dungeon in a medieval monastery.

We met a fellow in the audience who confessed, rather boldly, to a fear of buttons. "Oh," lamented Felicia, "I wish I had a big bucket of buttons with me, so I could see how scared you are of them."

Was the man afraid of swallowing a button, or being swallowed by a button? Did he snort contemptuously and with bitterness whenever someone used the expression "cute as a button" within earshot? How did he feel about people named Button? That saucy Jenni Buttton? Lauren Hutton? Hal Sutton? Pizza Hutton? Roast leg of mutton? We never found out.

I had other things on my mind. It is always fun to watch recent fads in American sitcoms come limping onto our TV screens, rag-tag and single-file and dragging their paltry ratings behind them in the muddied snow, like Napoleon's army entering Russia after an especially stern autumn.

Some of My Best Friends (M-Net, Fridays, open time) is the most recent attempt to tap into the American insight that friendships between homosexual men and heterosexual men are a rich mine of heartwarming, slide-slapping, life enriching humour.

I watched the first episode with interest. A gay man and a straight man share an apartment in New York. The gay man has a problem, because he doesn't have a female friend with whom to empathise and shop. The straight man has a problem, because he has a girlfriend who expects him to talk. But ho! There is a solution. They gay man and the straight man share the girlfriend! Everybody's happy!

I telephoned my friend Daniel, who happens to live in New York. "Daniel," I said, "you're gay." "That's true," he replied. "So how come," I demanded, "we so seldom enjoy heartwarming, side-slapping, life-enriching humour?"

"What?" said Daniel. "What I'm getting at," I persisted, "is why haven't we ever shared a girlfriend?"

There was a long, transatlantic silence.

Daniel is an old and dear friend. He knows me well. "Darrel," he said at length, "are you struggling to finish a column again?"

The highs and lows of weather

SUNDAY INDEPENDENT, 26 AUGUST 2001

I SHALL NEVER LOOK at weather the same way again. As of now, my pleasure in isobars has flown and the delights of frontal lows have evaporated like morning mist in the rising sun. I am unmoved by partly cloudy conditions. Synoptic charts delight not me; no, nor isobars neither. I wouldn't go so far as to say that this most excellent canopy, the air, appears to me nothing but a foul and pestilent congregation of vapours, but the thought is not far from my mind. It was not ever thus.

I was never really a fan of weather, precisely. I liked it well enough, but only when it was good weather. When it was bad weather I was less enthusiastic. I wasn't one of those fanatics who liked the weather for its own sake, who keep barometers mounted on their walls and nod and tut knowledgeably when the mercury drops a notch.

Far less was I one of those suburban meteorologists who have installed an inverted plastic cone in their gardens and at the end of each month record the rainfall figures in a special logbook they keep in the top drawer of the sideboard, beside the telephone directory. (I once met a man in Durban who could tell you the rainfall in millimetres of any month of any year, stretching back to February of 1964. I am led to believe that he would offer to do so as a party trick. I remember his wife having an extremely haunted look and a tendency to bury her head in her hands.)

So I was never one of the true weather nuts. My principal interest in the weather was what it could do for me. But the weather did offer me this special pleasure: it brought Graeme Hart into my life.

Graeme Hart was not, on the face of it, the kind of public figure you would expect to make an enormous impact on anyone's inner sense of being. Faintly beige in colour, mournful of mien and bearing altogether too close a resemblance to a better-fed version of Mr Burns in *The Simpsons*, Graeme Hart was no one's pin-up. His principal recommendation was that he was unflappable, personally inscrutable and knew how to impart the weather with the proper gravitas.

Not for him the cheery smile, the playful waggle of the eyebrows, the humorously patterned necktie. Graeme always delivered the weather as though just off screen balaclava-clad terrorists were holding an Uzi to the heads of his loved ones and snarling in Eastern European accents: "Right, read the weather, Mr Hart, and I suggest you make it good – or else." I sometimes think Graeme Hart became a weatherman just to give me the opportunity to use the word "lugubrious" in public without fear of ridicule.

But Graeme gave me peace and continuity. He has been around forever, cool, unmoved by the ructions and fluctuations of the world outside the weather. Did Graeme blink when Kuwait was invaded or when the space shuttle exploded? Does Graeme have an opinion about Robert Mugabe or the plight of the East Timorese? No, sir. Graeme Hart was a pool of unchanging calm, an unwinking pole star in a swirling, spinning, ever-expanding universe of quarks and black holes and supernovas.

Graeme Hart was history, damn it. He is a veteran of the Mafeking wars of the late 1970s. Who else but Graeme and I will remember the astonishingly passionate battles that raged in the letters pages of the nation's newspapers, regarding the correct spelling of Mafeking on the weather map? Should it be Mafekeng? Mafeking? Mafikeng? If Graeme Hart knew, he wasn't telling. He was not trafficking in Mafeking. We need Graeme Hart. We need him, I tell you.

Who else in the entire world knows how to find Gordonia on a map? Including the Gordonians?

And now he is gone, and what will we do without him? We will have to content ourselves with Simon Gear, that's what. I don't mean to be unkind to Simon "Reverse" Gear, but he is stepping into an awfully large pair of Hush Puppies, and I don't feel he is going about it the right way. Besides bearing a superficial resemblance to how you would imagine the young Graeme Hart to have looked (if Graeme Hart was ever young), Simon Gear has not learnt much from the master.

Besides the uncanny knack of positioning himself directly between the camera and whichever region he is currently describing on the map, the Gearster lacks Graeme's steady constancy of delivery. His weather reports have three distinct phases.

The first is characterised by a kind of breezy optimism. He greets you with a jaunty air and a roguish twinkle in his eye. If he had a cap, it would be at a rakish angle. This time, he seems to be thinking, everything will go much better. This time, I'm the man. Then he runs into difficulties. In the second phase he resembles a car trying to drive off with the handbrake up. He starts the sentence, and you can tell the sentence wants to go, but it just can't seem to get moving. "And, uh, uh, there's … uh … there's a cold front over … over … um …"

The third phase comes when he has realised that he has spent 40 per cent of his time transmitting 10 per cent of his script. Then he breaks out into a horse-racing commentator's urgent patter. Where will the high-pressure system end? "It's Port St Johns on the outside, Tzaneen on the rail but closing fast is Pretoria Kimberley East London Beaufort West and that's all from me, goodnight."

Never mind. There is a long road ahead. Weathermen are not made, or replaced, overnight. Perhaps one day I will be dandling my grandchildren on my knee and saying: "That's Simon Gear, the weather guy. I remember the first time he wore that suit."

Oh brother, Big Brother

SUNDAY INDEPENDENT, 2 SEPTEMBER 2001

S O GEORGE ORWELL had it backwards all along: the biggest fear for the future is not that Big Brother will be watching us; it is that we will all be watching *Big Brother*.

Big Brother (DStv, 24 hours) came seeping onto our screens this week and it would have taken more moral conviction and strength of will than a mountaintop full of Tibetan monks to have kept it out. Among the many things that I am not – blond, for instance, and good-natured, and a patient driver, and to be trusted not to read through your e-mails if I am bored and you are out of the room – a Tibetan monk is pretty well near the top of the list.

Along with the rest of South Africa's chumps and suckers, I was so far bowed under by the sheer weight of media hype and hullabaloo that last Sunday night saw me hunched before my television screen waiting for ... for ... come to think of it, I didn't really know what I was waiting for; and now I know even less.

Good thing for me Gerry Rantseli was there.

"There are still some people who are wondering what the fuss is all about," burbled Gerry in the pre-launch show, looking something like a glove puppet who has escaped from its hand and is joyously planning to flee across the countryside. "Well, now, believe it or not, I'm going to explain it to you."

Oh, I believed her, all right. Why wouldn't I? It's her job.

I had more difficulty believing her co-host, someone calling himself Mark Pilgrim. When first I glimpsed him, he was towelling himself off after a dip in the jacuzzi, presumably as a cunning measure to demonstrate the range and picture quality of the hidden cameras.

"I'm trying so hard not to let you see my Charlie," said Pilgrim proudly. I could only encourage him in his endeavours.

"We can see you, Mark," whooped Gerry. "We can see you. You can hide but you ... we can still see you."

It was sorry viewing.

The show had such a long and laborious build-up, you would think Gerry and Pilgrim might have spent some of that time thinking about what they were going to say on the big night. Apparently not. Gerry, given the brief to be excited, hit upon the dramatic stratagem of telling us she was excited. She hopped from one foot to the other in front of a skimpy crowd of M-Net employees holding helium balloons. You wouldn't call it a throng, exactly. It was more of a thong than a throng. "It's so happening out here. I'm so excited I don't know what to do with myself," she gurgled.

Behind her the crowd started chanting: "Run, little glove puppet, run." No, they didn't, but I would have if I'd been there.

It was all a little embarrassing. It was like being at a bad party where everyone is standing around looking at each other but one person is drunk and running around shouting: "What a great party!"

As bad as Gerry and Pilgrim were, however, I would rather spend a year locked in the boot of a car with them than three months in a house with that shower of twisters who somehow managed to bob to the top of the contestants' barrel. Looking at them, you could only blanch and tremble and hang a piece of garlic around your neck to imagine the black-hearted villains who didn't make it through the selection process.

There is not a one among the 12 that I would allow into my home – not even if they were delivering furniture – and yet for the past week those blighters have been, well, blighting my living room with their infernal babble and chatter. I switch them off, of course – I have not yet fallen entirely under the evil eye – but I find myself at peculiar moments thinking, "Hmm, I wonder what those halfwits in Randburg are up to now." And then I switch on and sit a spell and see if anything interesting is happening.

And sure enough I receive my rightful punishment. I have watched them mow the grass and make fires and smoke cigarettes, none of which is a gripping spectator sport. I can watch *myself* doing those things, damn it. In fact, if I scootch down in my chair right now and catch a glimpse of myself reflected in the computer screen … nope, it's no more exciting when I do it. And yet can I stop switching over to the 24-hour channel? I cannot.

Fortunately I have not yet reached that sunken state where I can identify all the swines by name, although their faces are already beginning to hoot and screech at me in my feverish waking dreams. I am becoming concerned for my mental health. It isn't right that I should know that the yodelling girl who wears a cowboy hat has a dog named Savannah. It is generally my policy not to have any truck with individuals who name their pets, or indeed their children, after brands of apple cider, yet there she is in a corner of my lounge each day.

Just this morning I found myself wondering about Bradford's stated goal of winning the million rand and "travelling around South Africa fighting crime". Will he make himself a cape and mask? Will he build himself a Bradfordmobile? Will he wrestle Ferdinand to the ground and shave the hairy crime that is his shoulders? I am dismantling my satellite dish today. This must stop while it can still be stopped.

September 11

SUNDAY INDEPENDENT, 16 SEPTEMBER 2001

I WAS WATCHING THE cricket test match on Tuesday afternoon when a friend called and told me to turn on my television. "My television is already on. My television is always on," I replied sternly. It doesn't do to have people questioning your work ethic.

"Turn to CNN," said my friend, and there was something in her voice that caught my attention.

Soon I had forgotten the cricket. I watched, like the rest of the world, in whirling disbelief as scenes from Hollywood played out on my screen. It was all purest cinema, as though it were the alternate ending of a lost Bond movie in which 007 had somehow failed to foil the improbable and frankly impractical plot of the evil super-villain, who plans to paralyse the United States and panic the free world for inscrutable reasons of his own.

Perhaps the most astonishing thing about the footage was just how astonishing it was. It has long been the argument of old-fashioned stick-in-the-mud media critics, such as myself, that today's hyper-realistic special effects, in which anything that can be imagined can be made real, has the effect of gradually and progressively numbing the viewer to the experience of life outside the cinema. After you have seen a famous icon or national monument being destroyed on the big screen, as in movies such as *Deep Impact* and *Independence Day*, I would have assumed that the emotional force of watching the same thing in real life would somehow have been diminished.

Nothing of the sort, as it turns out. In a peculiar way, it made the experience of seeing the towers of the World Trade Center disappear in a cloud of dust and rubble seem even more surreal, yet more difficult to comprehend. Your first reaction is to blink it away as a scene from a film, but when you rationally return to the fact that this scene, which can only have been from a film, is *not* in fact from a film, the disjuncture is even more baffling and boggling.

It is always instructive to watch the same news event unfolding on rival channels. Sky News (DStv) seemed to have the edge in efficiency, not only breaking information first (they had news of the Pittsburgh crash at least 30 minutes before CNN), but offering a wider range of snap opinions and specialist interviews. Those interviews also tended to be more helpful, while the CNN team seemed to be under instruction to ask each guest the question that should live in infamy: "As a New Yorker/American/member of the fire-fighting fraternity, how do the day's events make you feel?" Not surprisingly, the answer to that question remained fairly constant. No one was much pleased by the day's events.

CNN did have the edge, however, in the all-important story-headline department. While Sky opted to label its coverage: "Terror in America", which was accurate enough though a little uninspired, CNN boldly declared: "America Under Attack", which is altogether more snappy.

It was interesting to watch the coping strategies coming into play. At first the Americans hid behind a numbing wall of circumlocution. "If you listen carefully, in the background you can hear the sirens from the mobile anti-fire apparatuses," intoned one reporter in Manhattan as a cavalcade of fire engines swept past.

"Here in the casualty ward there are many people dealing with issues relating to or stemming directly or indirectly from involuntary smoke inhalation," declared a field reporter from St Vincent's hospital.

Soon, however, they were moved to displace their shock with anger, and the anger didn't take long to find its obvious target. Within hours we were being told that US intelligence sources were fingering "the Islamic extremist Osama bin Laden" as the culprit, a comforting source of speculation, given that US intelligence sources hadn't been able to give even the slightest prior warning that four hijacked passenger flights would shortly be used as weapons of terror.

Shortly thereafter, the channel managed to scrounge up footage of five or six happy Libyans dancing a jig, apparently celebrating the news of the attack on America. Even if one overlooks the questionable news value of watching a handful of foreign civilians in a hostile nation reacting for a TV camera, there didn't seem to be much in the handbook of responsible journalism to encourage cutting the footage with images of weeping New Yorkers and showing the montage on a repeating cycle all through the next day.

Far from America – though arguably not far enough – there was a peculiar and almost perverse pleasure in the communality of Tuesday evening. Wherever you went, groups of people were clustered around television sets in restaurants and bars, supermarkets and shop windows. Strangers at check-out tills started conversations about the fifth missing airliner; newspaper vendors at traffic lights asked me if I had heard any fresh news on my car radio. For an afternoon at least, people were drawn together by the sense of shared occasion, as we had been during the Gulf War, during the 1994 elections, during the 1995 Rugby World Cup. It was an event we could all share, and something deep inside us thrilled to that.

"At least it gives us something to watch other than *Big Brother*," said my friend on the phone, later that night, as we sat in different cities, unable to stop ourselves watching the same video footage being replayed for the umpteenth time. It was kind of funny, but neither of us felt like laughing. There are times, as TS Eliot nearly said, when humankind cannot bear very much reality television.

Not even St Helena offers safe haven

SUNDAY INDEPENDENT, 14 OCTOBER 2001

Ahoy, me hearties. Avast and belay and thar, unless my eyes deceive me, she blows. Oops, you'll have to excuse me today. I am fresh back from the sea, the call of the running tide still ringing in my ears, the fine salt spray still blurring my eyes, a faint odour of harbours and seagulls still clinging to my clothing. I have been on the distant island of St Helena, as you would have noticed had you also been on St Helena.

St Helena is, I am told, as far away as you can get from any continental mainland without needing an oxygen pack and retrorockets. It is a remote place of rainforests and volcanic ridges, of shipwrecks and Georgian houses and a tree on which, if family legend be true, my grandfather once carved the initials of the woman who would become my grandmother, when he passed that way between the wars.

My grandfather was a little vague as to the precise whereabouts of that tree. He would puff contentedly on a pipe and say, "It was on a hill." Perhaps that was his little joke. The whole of St Helena is a series of hills. It only stops being a hill when it briefly becomes a series of steep-sided valleys. I had promised – rashly, it now seems – to bring back a photograph of the initials. Could I find the tree? I could not.

Eventually I resorted to etching in the initials with a rusty nail. I cunningly carved them high on the trunk to take growth into account, but then I couldn't remember whether a tree trunk grows from the top or the bottom. I decided to carve another set of initials, and take another photograph, just to be safe, but as I was doing so a weather-worn local wearing a floppy hat and Wellington boots came tramping round the bend.

"Eee," he said, or words to that effect. "You can't go carving on our trees."

I blushed. "No, no, they're my grandmother's initials," I reassured him. He looked at me with eyes that wished St Helena were a little further away from the mainland, and hurried away, no doubt to make sure his children were safely indoors.

The only way to reach St Helena is a five-day voyage on the RMS *St Helena*. I had gone to sea to take a break from television, but by the time I reached the island my eyes had been sufficiently soothed by the blues and whites of the wide-stretching ocean that I was ready for a little cathode action. They do have television on St Helena, and have had for a couple of years now, but when I arrived I soon realised that TV was a controversial subject.

"It will be the ruin of this island," one old gent told me, casting eyes to the heavens. "You can see it already. The language of the children. And the clothes they wear. And how they cheek their parents."

An elderly lady confirmed his forebodings. "Moral decay," she told me. "Children see those gangsters on television, running around with guns. One of these days someone is going to bring a gun to the island, mark my words." She leant closer and lowered her voice. "I shouldn't tell you this, as you write for newspapers, but last month my son left his wallet on the front seat of his car, and when he returned," she paused for dramatic effect, "it had been stolen."

I tried to work up some appropriate sympathy. "Window broken, eh?" I said, clucking.

She looked puzzled. "No, no," she said, "they opened the door."

I was curious to see what foul electronic outpourings could corrupt a community so pure no one locks their cars. What evil was being injected from across the waters? Porn channels? Snuff movies? I turned on the telly. It was M-Net.

It is disconcerting to venture more than a thousand nautical miles into the pitching blue, only to be confronted by a Currie Cup rugby match when you get to the other side. I watched the Currie Cup rugby match, of course – it is something like a conditioned reflex – but afterwards I felt ashamed.

That afternoon I walked up into the mountains and down into Daffodil Valley to find Napoleon's tomb – bare and slightly forlorn in the shade of the towering Norfolk pines – and I tried to stand there and think about Ozymandias and the fate of all things human, and how dreams and vaulting ambition must in the end turn to grass and suchlike improving thoughts, but all the while I couldn't shake the feeling that Marius Roberts or Gerry Rantseli was peering over my shoulder.

And then a terrible thought occurred to me. For the next four days as I made my way around the island, visiting the Boer War cemetery, swimming in the wild southern Atlantic, chasing tortoises around the gardens of the governor's mansion, I tried to ignore that thought. I tried to push it aside and to the back of my mind, but like a medieval witch or an unhappy childhood it kept resurfacing. The thought was simple, yet terrible: I wonder what is happening on *Big Brother*?

I resisted as long as I could, but like a souse returning to the bottle, one night I switched on. As I sat there in a funk of self-loathing, my neighbour popped round to borrow a cup of sugar. She glanced at the screen. "Oh that," she said, wrinkling her nose. "Can you imagine that anyone would watch it? Eee, we all listen to the radio when that comes on."

She left, and suddenly I felt bathed in the warm light of St Helena. Outside, folk were chatting over garden fences or washing their cars. No one was watching *Big Brother*. Oh blessed isle. Suddenly I understood why French emperors would come here to retire.

It takes a lot of money to look this cheap

SUNDAY INDEPENDENT, 18 NOVEMBER 2001

'I THINK THE EYES are the windows of the soul," said Tammy Faye, "so whenever one of my special friends dies I always ask if I can have their glasses." It was one more reason not to be a special friend of Tammy Faye Bakker. The thought of her perched at the foot of my deathbed like a shoulder-padded homunculus, just waiting to put the pennies over my eyes and make off with my spectacles, is not one that encourages me to make a happy noise unto the Lord.

The Eyes of Tammy Faye (M-Net, Monday, 10.15pm) was filled with noises unto the Lord. Some happy, others more like a strangled cry. Tammy Faye Bakker was the wife of Jim Bakker, the chipmunk-cheeked televangelist who first popularised religious television programming of the sort that revolves around saying "Hosanna" and asking the viewing public for cash donations.

Big Jim used many of those donations to build Heritage USA, the religious theme park that at one time was the third most popular tourist attraction in America. He also had a one-night stand with a Playboy bunny and was eventually jailed for misuse of subscriber funds.

Jim himself was interviewed, fresh from the penitentiary, posing with his new wife, wearing a Melton blazer and wire-rimmed spectacles and a swish new haircut. Prison does strange things to a man – in Jim Bakker's case, it made him resemble Glen Hicks. All the same, you can't hide those cheeks; he still looks as though he is concealing wads of hundred-dollar bills in his mouth.

The real focus was Tammy Faye, a Southern Baptist Zsa Zsa Gabor with facial make-up as thick as she is tall. "Tammy Faye was always religious," said her brother. I think his name was Tommy Faye. "When she was little she had a wart on her finger and God told her to dip it in the Communion cup on Sunday. It worked."

One more reason not to invite Tammy Faye around for drinks. I wouldn't care to lay on a punchbowl only for Tammy Faye to discover she has a carbuncle on her toe.

Jim and Tammy Faye's television empire had humble origins. We watched lurid 1970s footage of Tammy Faye operating a finger-puppet. As the Bakkers' Praise The Lord network expanded, she added another finger-puppet.

While Tammy Faye's fingers did the talking, Jim's principal task was to ask for money. I still can't get over his trademark sign-off. Just before the closing credits, he would look out at the audience and say, quivering with the effort of holding back a guffaw: "Jesus loves you, heh heh heh, he really does."

Today, watching it, you think: "How did he get away with that?" True, audiences are no less gullible nowadays, but televangelists are thoughtful enough to wait until they are off-camera before they openly laugh at the rubes.

Whatever their other crimes, for me the Bakkers' greatest sin was the part they played in kick-starting the modern trend for turning private moments into public performance. No less than Oprah, Tammy Faye was one of the great TV weepers. She wept with sorrow, she wept with joy, she wept with her mind on something else and her eyes restlessly roaming round the studio.

When she became addicted to prescription drugs, she lived the recovery in the open, for the gratification of her electronic parishioners. When the financial brouhaha broke, Jim and Tammy Faye filmed their last show sitting on the porch of their mansion. "And now," said Jim, "before we leave our home, Tammy Faye will sing 'The Sun Will Shine Again'." And she did. She did a lot of singing. Next to the finger-puppet, song was Tammy Faye's medium.

The show became a kind of winking, nudging celebration of Tammy Faye's post-Jim life. A walking trademark by virtue of her Crayola-box make-up and mascara that make her eyes look like two fields of sooty asparagus spears, she rose to cult status when she remarried, then waved her second husband goodbye as he in turn was jailed for embezzlement.

To lose one husband to the fraudsters' penitentiary is bad luck; to lose two is to become the butt of a nation's jokes. To become the butt of a nation's jokes is ultimately to find your way into their heart.

The documentary might have been a serious look at the American cash-for-redemption industry, or it might have been a serious examination of one woman's relationship with sudden wealth and a weird kind of showbiz, but in the end it was neither of these things. The show was narrated by RuPaul, a famous drag queen famous mainly for being famous. RuPaul was a dead giveaway – the show was not about a ruined televangelist's wife, it was about a Camp icon. We watched Tammy Faye at 60, having glamour portraits made and trying to pitch a puppet show to ponytailed young network executives. She was the very embodiment of the Camp female.

Exaggerated to the point of sexlessness, the Camp female is celebrated for being unaware precisely how she comes across to the world. Tammy Faye is so fabulously like a Bible-waving Dolly Parton drag act that you imagine she can't possibly not be doing that on purpose. But she isn't. Like Judy Garland or Marilyn Monroe, she talks ironically about herself but can't actually see the irony. She is her eyelashes. The celebration of her Camp is the celebration of her inability to grasp precisely why it is that life is always slightly beyond her control.

The problem with Camp is that, by definition, it illuminates nothing beyond itself. Showbiz glamour is skin-deep, but Camp doesn't even get as deep as the skin. It is as deep as the last layer of cosmetics. The documentary was contemporary irony at its most empty. It posed knowingly, but it had nothing to say. Tammy Faye wasn't a woman, she was just a cultural reference. Not even a televangelist's wife deserves that.

Survivor: Africa

SUNDAY INDEPENDENT, 9 DECEMBER 2001

A FRICA IS A big place. How big is Africa? Oh, it's very big. It is bigger than, say, Milwaukee. It is bigger than disco ever was. It is bigger than you and it is bigger than me. It is bigger than both of us put together. People who say foolish things like "It's a small world" need only spend a day with a WeedEater, trying to mow Africa, to realise precisely how foolish a thing that is to say.

I think we can agree that Africa is a big place. Still, as big as it is, 10 minutes of watching *Survivor: Africa* (SABC3, Tuesdays, 7pm) is enough to suggest that it is not big enough.

Survivor: Africa does what the combined tourist authorities of the African continent cannot do at the moment: it brings a group of Americans to a place in Africa that is not Cape Town. Specifically, it brings them to an especially arid stretch of savannah in a Kenyan game park.

You know it's Kenya because there is footage of Masai warriors leaping in the air in the traditional dance of welcome. You know it's the savannah because one of the Americans mentioned being in the jungle, and whenever Americans talk about the jungle, they always mean the savannah.

Americans, when they are away from home, can make the world seem like an awfully small place. Not all Americans, admittedly, are like the American with whom I once shared a luncheon table on a cruise boat on the upper Nile. (The Nile, incidentally, is also in Africa, although I had to spend several increasingly surreal hours trying to convince the American of that fact.)

This American lady at lunch stared dolefully out of the wide picture window, just as the grand ruins of the temple of Edfu came floating into view, slow and shimmering like a mirage left over from a thousand years ago.

"Don't you just get sick of these old rocks?" said the American lady, without the hint of a smile.

It is the kind of story that people usually make up about Americans, but it really happened. Not all Americans are like that lunching lady, but when they are, there are few cultural experiences more primally gratifying than banding together to laugh at them. Ordinarily when we laugh at them, Americans don't say much in reply: they just hold up a dollar bill, and we blush and fall silent and shuffle away to watch some rugby. Which is why *Survivor: Africa* is such a boon and a godsend: not only have we American tourists to laugh at, but we have American tourists in a position where their money cannot help them.

From the moment in the first episode when a contestant scanned the savannah like Alan Quartermain in sunscreen and neatly pressed khakis from JC Penney and said, "This is Africa, man, this is the jungle. There are lions and tigers and bears out there," I knew we were in for a treat.

This week the poor saps had to drink beakers of warm cow's blood, fresh tapped from the vein by willing Masai. It is one of East Africa's most stirring traditions that the Masai herdsmen shun their greens and steaks, living on a steady diet of blood and milk. Personally I have never quite recovered from the occasion on the plains of Tanzania when I wandered past a thorn tree and came across a couple of amiable Masai munching on a peanut butter sandwich, but I am all for a stirring tradition.

The Yanks actually did quite well when it came to drinking the blood. Better than, say, I would have done. It was a little disappointing.

We were on firmer ground watching them throw away their vats of drinking water because they were too heavy to carry on a forced march.

"Ho ho," we said, down at the Chalk 'n Cue. And also: "Stupid Americans." We even slapped each other on the back. And how we hooted as we watched them try to make fire by rubbing twigs or clacking rocks together.

"These Americans know nothing!" gurgled Porky Withers happily.

"Ho ho," we agreed.

Ordinarily someone would have produced two twigs or a pair of rocks and invited Porky Withers to demonstrate precisely how fire should be made, but we were having too much fun laughing at the rich folks. No one wanted to spoil the mood.

Our deepest, darkest motivation in watching, of course, was the unspoken hope that someone would be eaten by a wild beast. Isn't that a terrible confession? But it's true. Deep down inside there is a wicked voice that wants to say to some glubbering Yank nursing a bite wound: "So, how cute do you find *The Lion King* now?"

We want to lay claim to the authentic experience of wild Africa, even if the closest some of us get to wild Africa is a Nando's chicken with extra peri-peri. The fact is that we are protective of Africa, precisely because being African is the last thing we have left to boast about.

Living in a game park doesn't have much to do with living in Africa – and it is not something that many of us would be in a position to do any more successfully than the average American – but it represents an idea that we defend with jealousy. We laugh at the Americans because it is a way of asserting that we live in Africa, that we live *here*, even if the *here* in which we live is more like America than it is like the wild savannah. We laugh at the Americans because it makes us feel good about being us.

But also, of course, we laugh at the Americans because, well, because it's fun to laugh at Americans.

What is Mark's shuttle worth?

SUNDAY INDEPENDENT, 28 APRIL 2002

WERE YOU EXCITED about Mark Shuttleworth going to space? Were you? Really? Good for you. Hold on to that inner child. Dandle it on your knee. Kiss it better when it cries. As for me, I did not much care that Mark Shuttleworth went to space. I kind of lost interest in him when he moved to London.

For all the genuine enthusiasm I could work up on Thursday morning, he was just some rich guy buying a ticket on a really expensive flight. The biggest novelty about it was that the flight lasted longer than most, and the rich guy didn't fly first class. He didn't even fly economy class. He was packed away into an overhead baggage compartment; the kind of overhead baggage compartment where the air hostesses don't even come around and sell you a packet of peanuts. Mark Shuttleworth has just become the world's most uncomfortable paying passenger – except for people flying Kulula.com, of course. But it was preferable to flying Kulula.com. Whatever other drawbacks the Soyuz TM-34 might have, at least it left on time.

My attitude towards the project was sceptical from the beginning. Frankly, I just didn't think it was a good deal. *You* would have to pay *me* $20 million to get me to squeeze into some clanking 1960s Russian tin-can along with two odd-smelling continentals and trust myself to the technology of a nation that can't even get its women to match their shoes to their hairnets while they queue to buy half a loaf of bread; all in order to spend several days urinating into a length of second-hand rubber tubing and saying things like: "Gee, look at that view" and "Say, Yuri, wasn't that my toothbrush you just used?"

But I wanted to be excited, I really did. I had watched *Buck Rogers* and *Battlestar Galactica* when I was young, and I was a dedicated fan of the first three *Star Wars* movies (it was a defining moment in the life of any young man of my generation when he had to sit down and decide who he would grow up to be: Luke Skywalker or Han Solo. Or Princess Leia, I suppose).

Plus, the newspapers were getting so worked up about the launch I figured it had to be special. I haven't seen the daily press this serious about a news story since the first series of *Big Brother*.

In the days before the launch, I tuned in to the *First African in Space* channel (DStv, channel 38). I would not say it drove the adrenalin levels up. It seemed to consist principally of replays of Derek Watts' *Carte Blanche* interview, followed by links with NASA TV. NASA TV is a thrill-a-minute educational service offering ways to make science fun. On the night before take-off (or T-1, as they say at NASA) the insomniac space enthusiast could tune in to a youth programme titled *Data Analysis and Measurement – Having a Solar Blast!*

I hoped that Mark had something more entertaining to watch on his last night on Earth. A history of light industry in the Ukraine, perhaps, or a Russian cooking programme. ("You in ze decadent vest haff ze Naked Chef. Ve haff ze Chef Who Couldn't Afford a Furry Hat and New Pair of Mittens.")

There was a moment, the day before, when I began to be stirred by the whole enterprise. The heart could not fail to respond to the footage of the rocket being brought from its hangar to the launch pad. It was slow and solemn, heavy with the weight of a great undertaking. Soyuz was sleek and strong and sexual, an enormous penis with nowhere to go but up. We watched the vast fuel tanks propping up the payload. "There is always the danger of premature ignition," cautioned the commentator. How true that is.

I began to warm to the occasion. It seemed noble and brave, and Mark Shuttleworth even managed to look a little dashing in his baggy blue cosmonaut overalls. Then again, anything that would get him out of those awful shorts and sandals is heartily to be applauded. The rocket itself was strangely moving. The craft and its supportive housing seemed almost nostalgic – all grey metal and mechanical locks and hand-stencilled flags over rivets and joins. It looked archaic, poignantly low-tech in a digital age. This was the same launch pad from which Yuri Gagarin rode a Vostok rocket into space half a century ago, and you would expect to find his car still parked out back.

But by Thursday morning my enthusiasm had waned. That's what bad TV coverage will do for you. The viewing audience was treated to an interminable static view from the cosmodrome. The rocket huddled in the lower left-hand corner of the screen while behind it, dwarfing it, the steppes of Kazakhstan stretched far away. Derek Watts described Kazakhstan as looking something like the Karoo, but from the empty grey awfulness of the view it more closely resembled the gigantic tongue of a man who drank too much vodka and smoked too many Pravda Filters last night.

The rocket was tiny against the numb blankness of the land. It looked small and not terribly grand; like something that would have difficulty reaching Vladivostok, let alone outer space and back. There was no countdown when it went. There was a wisp of smoke, a surge of flame, the rocket lifted and hovered a moment, as though the hand pulling the strings was not quite strong enough, then suddenly it vanished upward like a slim arrow aimed at the sky. Minutes later the fire of its afterburners looked from below like a winter sun glimpsed through high mist.

And then it was over.

I am glad Mark Shuttleworth is safe, and I hope he returns that way, but there my involvement ends. Those Russkis just don't know how to put on a show. Perhaps that's why they lost.

God is in the donations,
not the details

SUNDAY INDEPENDENT, 12 MAY 2002

I T CAN'T BE EASY, being God. It's not all fun and games and burnt offerings when you are the Light of the World. It's a full-time job, being the Lord of All.

Being omnipotent will certainly help you rattle through your chores of a morning, but what with all the delivering from evil and smiting of unbelievers and deciding who prayed hardest to win an Oscar or the Currie Cup this year, I would be surprised if you had a spare minute for yourself at the end of the working day.

I don't know where He found the time to dream up the duck-billed platypus, say, or earlobes, or fingerprints. In retrospect, I suppose it's not surprising that He never did get around to sending me the digital watch with the calculator and miniature space invaders game for which I begged each evening on my hands and knees when I was eight.

As if all that weren't enough, God also has to keep in touch with changing times. The march of technology waits for no one. When you wanted to get your message out to the world, it used to be sufficient to whip up a burning bush or a column of smoke or a talking donkey, but no more. Today God needs a satellite, and god knows satellites aren't cheap. This was the thrust of Benny Hinn's sermon on the *Satellite Night Praise-a-thon* (DStv, Events channel).

The praise-a-thon was part of a drive to raise money to buy a satellite for TBN, an American evangelist TV channel.

A silver-tongued shmooze artist named Benny Hinn stood at the podium in a small television studio that had been decorated to resemble a large modern church. A little balsawood here, some shiny gold fabric there, a painting on plaster or a stained glass window in the background, and the joint looked downright hallowed.

"That's right, saints," Benny Hinn was saying as I tuned in, "the Galaxy 5 is the most powerful satellite over North America! And we want it! The word of the Lord deserves only the best! But it's not cheap!"

I was flattered that Benny Hinn should refer to me as a saint. I have never really thought of myself as saintly. Certainly, watching Benny Hinn, I was beginning to have extremely unsaintly thoughts.

Evidently it costs some infinitely large and infinitely loving amount of dollars each month to keep Galaxy 5 in the air and broadcasting TBN to a grateful world. Whence do you think such riches shall flow? "Saints, you don't have to wait, you can call right now and pledge!" said Benny Hinn generously.

He held aloft a plywood model of Galaxy 5. "See! Doesn't it look just like a little angel?" he cooed. "Your dollars can put one more angel into the air, hallelujah!" I peered at the screen. I had never seen an angel before, but if Benny Hinn is to be believed, and I can't see any reason for him to lie, I can report that angels look very similar to wooden tomato crates with square wings made from tinfoil and bits of wire.

Benny Hinn seemed to feel that sending cash donations to the TBN network would secure peace in the Middle East and protect America from terrorist attacks.

"That is not a war between Jews and Arabs," he reminded us, "it is a war between God and the devil." It was unclear which side he aligned with God. Quite possibly neither.

"Let us pray for the safety of any Christians in the Middle East," said Benny Hinn pointedly. The rest of the Middle East's residents, he seemed to suggest, could look out for themselves.

"Now saints, remember September 11." Benny Hinn surged forward. "Prayer can keep the enemy away! But how can we speed our prayers? By satellite, that's how! Somebody say hallelujah!"

"Hallelujah!" said the accountants and bookkeepers of the TBN network.

Behind Benny Hinn on the stage, enthroned on gilt chairs with red velvet upholstery, sat Paul and Jane Crouch. Paul and Jane own the TBN network. Paul was resplendent in white suit and waistcoat and small white beard, looking like a pious Colonel Sanders. Jane was in the uniform of the televangelist's wife: she wore a voluminous pink skirt, and had pink hair roughly the size and shape of Ayers Rock. Her eyelashes were as long and dark as a formation of sooty asparagus spears.

Paul and Jane beamed and nodded and occasionally raised their hands in the air as Benny Hinn spoke. Whenever Benny Hinn mentioned money, they shut their eyes and swayed in a kind of rapture.

Benny Hinn suddenly broke off what he was saying. "You know what?" he said. "The Lord has just spoken to me. Right here in my ear. He has told me what to do. I'm going to pledge $10 000 myself."

Paul Crouch leapt from his throne in protest. "No, Benny, I can't let you do that!" he declared staunchly.

"Don't say no, Paul," said Benny. "I must do it. God is speaking to me. Saints, can you hear God speaking to you? He is, you know. And you can call and pledge right this very minute."

The call for cash rose in pitch and swelled like a Gregorian chant.

"Now don't get me wrong, saints. You cannot buy the blessings of God. But any farmer will tell you that you can't reap without sowing. Think of each dollar of your donation as a seed of faith."

It was hard to believe that it was all real and not some elaborate satire. "Every time you give a gift of money, you are raising a weapon against the devil!" purred Benny Hinn, brushing lint from his Armani suit. "God wants you to call now! I know God well. I spend a lot of time with him and I know He wants you to call."

It can't be easy, being God. You work hard all day, and then just look at who you have to hang out with.

An ordinary man who
had done extraordinary things

SUNDAY INDEPENDENT, 26 MAY 2002

I T IS EASY to be dismissive of television. In fact it is so easy that generally it is the people who watch it least who feel most qualified to dismiss it. "Oh, I never turn on the TV," they will say, with a tone of voice and cast of head and gleam of eye that suggests a certain pride in accomplishment, as though not watching television made them somehow smarter and more interesting than the rest of us who do. It is as though they feel that not watching television makes them better conversationalists, witty and thoughtful and more knowledgeable about Abstract Expressionism, say, or the causes of the failure of the Weimar republic.

I am not sure why they think this. It is not as if they use their non-television-watching time to read an improving book or learn a new language or solve Fermat's last theorem. If not watching television were a marker of great cultural or intellectual attainment, we might expect more Nobel prizes or contract bridge champions to emerge from the painted tribes of the Brazilian rainforests. Tibetan yakherds would be more in demand as guests at cocktail parties around the world. People who do not watch television are like people who live in Cape Town: they are irrationally proud of something which involves not doing anything in particular. The rest of us, poor slobs, have to try to be proud of the things we actually do.

It annoys me, frankly. People who can extract no value from a medium reveal more about themselves than about the medium. There are joys that television has brought into my life that I could have experienced nowhere else. An example was the chance encounter I had on Discovery Channel last week.

Aimlessly flipping through the channels, as I do of an evening while waiting for the drink to take effect, I landed midway through a show called *War Heroes*. The series is dedicated to remembering, and if possible interviewing, the men and women who in times of conflict have distinguished themselves by the kind of unthinking, reflexive selflessness that makes for heroism. It is the kind of selflessness – otherwise called bravery – that we all hope we have, but can never know until the moment comes when it is called upon.

I missed the name of the man being interviewed, which was somehow appropriate. He was known during the war as the Wheelbarrow VC. He was awarded the Victoria Cross for, among other things, running through the crossfire of no-man's-land to collect a wounded comrade, then braving the shells and shrapnel of an enemy mortar barrage to bring him back in, of all things, a captured German wheelbarrow. He is very old now, a slim man with fragile hands and Brylcreem in his immaculate hair, but his features are recognisably those of the impossibly handsome young man in the fading photographs. He sat beside his wife on a chintz sofa in the Essex countryside, frowning uncomfortably at his fingernails.

The Wheelbarrow VC refused to talk about his heroism. He refused to discuss or even describe what happened. After more than 50 years of living quietly in his country cottage, married to the woman who was his wartime sweetheart, he was embarrassed that someone should be making a fuss all over again.

In a private interview, his wife confided: "He doesn't like to be thought of as a hero. He always says that he did what he did because it had to be done, not because it was a heroic thing to do. That's why he won't speak about it."

I caught my breath. In the age of Oprah, that makes him a hero all over again.

In the sight of the man, sitting gently in an old darned cardigan, occasionally turning to gaze fondly through the window at a garden lovingly tended, a vegetable patch neat with marrows and watercress and beans, a small corner of a world he helped keep safe for a little while longer, there was something that moved me unutterably. He was a quiet, ordinary man, living a quiet, ordinary life, desiring nothing more than to continue in quietness and ordinariness and privacy, who had once done extraordinary things.

There was nothing staged in his reticence. In his awkward, fidgeting, dignified silence there was a glimpse of all that I find wonderful in human beings. I felt honoured to have seen it. And only television – of all the media that have ever existed – could have offered me precisely that glimpse.

The Wheelbarrow VC refused to contribute, so the show was pieced together with newsreels and clippings and the memories of the surviving members of his unit. One of his former comrades remembered how, every day for two weeks, the Wheelbarrow VC would leopard crawl across no-man's-land with a pocket of hand grenades to eliminate the Germans manning a forward machine-gun post. He was wounded in the shoulder by a German sniper, but he returned, again and again. The interviewer raised this with the Wheelbarrow VC. For the first time the Wheelbarrow VC ceased to look uncomfortable. He looked up, and in his faded blue eyes there was the fierce light of sudden emotion, and an expression of something like wonder.

"Every day they were killed," he said, "and every day there were new soldiers there. They knew they would die, but they kept manning the post."

He shook his head, and his eyes became moist and something caught at his voice. Unobtrusively, his wife lowered her eyes and pressed her knee against his. In the silence a clock ticked.

"The Germans," he said at last, still shaking his head in wonder and sorrow and something deeper that we who have not been to war can never understand, "those Germans were so brave."

Heinz Meanz Has-Beenz

CAPE TIMES, 5 JULY 2002

I DON'T LIKE HEINZ WINKLER. I'm sorry, but I don't. There is something about that smirking face and smug hairdo that makes me want to seize him by the lapels of his pizza-delivery-boy-moonlighting-as-a-male-stripper outfit and strike him firmly with both sides of my hand. In fact, the more I think about Heinz Winkler, the less I like him. He is young, allegedly attractive to women and on the brink of making more money than me. What's to like? He is the Jamie Oliver of South African pop music.

There are many things I dislike about Heinz Winkler, not least his name. What kind of a name is Heinz Winkler for a pop idol? Not since Engelbert Humperdinck has there been a name so unlikely to have me heaving my boxer shorts on stage. I don't know precisely what a heinz is, but I don't think I'd care to see one winkled in my presence. (Although, to be fair, he does have this over Engelbert Humperdinck: Heinz Winkler is in fact his real name. Unbelievably, Engelbert Humperdinck is a stage name. What could Engelbert's real name have been to have driven him to such a sobriquet? Jim Scrotum? Ben Dover? Adolph Hitler?)

Do you join me in spurning Heinz Winkler? Probably not. Chances are you are one of the squillions of local viewers spending your evenings and your monthly salary calling the Heinz Winkler vote line at cellphone rates. Gee, you must really like him. I have close friends and family members for whom I wouldn't pay cellphone rates.

At any rate, there is no real doubt that Heinz Winkler will win *Idols*. My man at M-Net first tipped me off three weeks ago that the sheer volume of calls suggests that the Winklemeister has a fan-base roughly the size of North Korea. Is there space in Stellenbosch to hide the population of North Korea? my man at M-Net asked me. Because all the calls seem to come from Stellenbosch.

This is causing some discontent in Johannesburg. Northerners take their Reality TV shows very seriously. These are the people, remember, who staked out the *Big Brother* house and threw messages over the wall hidden inside potatoes. That would not have happened in Cape Town, and not just because Capetonians do not go out of their way to greet new neighbours. People in Gauteng invest themselves deeply in the contestants, and they are beginning to suspect a conspiracy.

There was disapproval at that chucklehead Ferdinand winning the first *Big Brother*, but nothing was said because there was no one else that anyone especially liked. *Idols* is different. Not only have there been candidates clearly stronger and less annoying than the Winkster, but for the next few months we are not going to be able to switch on the radio without hearing the winner's rendition of "Islands in the Stream" or "Nelly the Elephant" or whatever fresh horror lies in store for us.

There is much at stake here. Johannesburgers are becoming suspicious of the rural areas of the Cape. "What goes on down there?" they say, narrowing their eyes. "Are there betting syndicates in Stellenbosch with automatic dialling machines? Are there units of Cape patriots with telephones funded by Jürgen Harksen and a brief to win at all costs?" Then they say: "If this goes on much longer, we'll just stop making Reality TV shows. Then what will they do?"

Good citizens of Cape Town, I know these people. They are not joking. It is too late for *Idols*, but *Big Brother 2* starts soon. Take my advice: let the northerner win.

I can't bare the Naked Chef

SUNDAY INDEPENDENT, 28 JULY 2002

I F YOU ARE a regular reader of this organ, you will know that I am no fan of the Naked Chef. It would be fair to say that between the Naked Chef and me, a great deal of love is not lost. We have never come to blows or anything, no matter what you may read in the tabloid pages of the yellow press, but relations between us are not cordial. Let's just say we do not speak to each other, and leave it at that.

There are many things I do not like about the Naked Chef. I do not, for one thing, like his lips. He has lips like the inside of a giant clam. I am afraid of standing too close to those lips in case they snap shut around my ankle and hold me immobile while the tide rises and slowly drowns me. Fortunately, I have devised a technique for neutralising the threat of those lips. Remember this simple manoeuvre if ever you find yourself in close proximity to Jamie Oliver and the rising waters of the seashore: place your right hand behind his head and press, with a firm and steady motion, his face against the nearest wall. A squelching sound will tell you when maximum suction has been attained between lips and wall. A few gentle backward tugs by the hair should ascertain firmness of bond. Congratulations! Jamie Oliver and his lips are now immobilised. You are safe! Plus, you won't have to hear a grown man use the words "Tucker" or "Yeh?" or say "Wicked" as an expression of approval.

It has been suggested that my principal complaint against Jamie Oliver is not his lips or his David-Beckham-meets-Keith-Floyd hairdo, or the fact that he has a vocabulary of fewer words than Marlee Matlin's mynah bird, or even that cutesy scooter that makes the ladies go "Awww". (Just wait until someone arrives to fetch you for a date on a scooter, girls. Then you'll really say "Awww".)

It has been suggested that my principal complaint has something to do with the fact that each year he sells more copies of his rotten cookbooks than you can shake a stick at. (And believe me, I have shaken many a stick at those books.) This allegation, while uncharitable, is regrettably true. Jamie Oliver is young, slim, attractive to the public and sells lots of books. His very existence is abhorrent to me.

But my better self sometimes asserts itself. "Perhaps he is not so bad when he is not mugging it up in the kitchen," says my better self. At which point I throw my better self in a headlock and shove my thumb into one of its eyes. So it was something of a relief to discover this week that the little swine is even more of a dunderhead when he's not mashing potatoes or jellying eels or whatever.

Jamie Oliver was a guest on *Parkinson* (BBC Prime, Monday, 10.30pm). He's a lovely old duffer, is Michael Parkinson. He brings to me the same comfort as Graeme Hart the weather guy, or a cricket test on a summery Saturday afternoon: it feels as though nothing can go too terribly wrong with the world as long as Parky is having a good old chuckle with his guests. "Ho, ho, ho, ho, hooo, dear me," says Parky during the course of a good old chuckle. When he is merely chuckling politely, he goes: "Ho, ho, ho. Yes." To a veteran Parky watcher, these variations are all important.

You could tell that Parkinson was slightly bemused at finding himself interviewing a chef in his early twenties with absolutely no life experience. "The secret of my success is that I am really passionate," said Jamie Oliver.

"Oh really?" said Parkinson, perking up at the scent of a conversation. "Passionate about what, exactly?"

This was a question Jamie Oliver had not asked his press manager. "Um, uh, well, everything, mate. Everything, yeh?"

Parky pondered. He didn't want to belabour the point, but there was really nothing else to talk about. "Presumably you're especially passionate about food?" he offered.

"Oh, mate," said Jamie Oliver, his eyes shining like a pair of faucets, "food is brilliant. Because you know, flavours are, well, they're a real experience, aren't they? Lovely. Wicked."

Soon Parky was stretching for something to ask. "Culinary fashions change so quickly," he ventured. "What do you think we will be eating in 20 years?"

Jamie Oliver's new vertical hairstyle quivered slightly in the gentle breeze of his deep thought.

"You know," he said at last, "the secret of my success is that I am very passionate …"

"Is it true that you have never read a book?" asked Parky.

"That's true, yep," said Jamie Oliver with a proud smile. At least, I think it was a smile – it is hard to tell with those lips. It was a shocking admission. Even the person I always believed to be the biggest cretin on television – Margaret from *Big Brother 1* – has read a book. If you will recall, she couldn't remember precisely the title of the book, "but I know it was by Danielle Steele". Think about that – Margaret with her suntan-lotion-stained paperback Danielle Steele is better read than one of the best-selling authors on the market today.

Thoughtfully, Parky had invited Elle McPherson on the show to make Jamie look better. "So, Elle," said Parky happily, "do you mind it when people call you The Body?"

Elle was ready for this question. "No, no," she said. "Bodies are good, because they have everything inside them, like, you know, a soul, and a spirit and … uh …" Polyps? Duodenal ulcers? Tapeworms? Sometimes, if you're lucky, selected bits of other people's bodies? We don't know. She never finished the thought.

"Anyway," said Elle, "it could have been worse. I could be called … uh … The Brain."

Parky chuckled. "Ho, ho, ho," he said. "Yes."

Bogie and Bacall look off-colour

SUNDAY INDEPENDENT, 11 AUGUST 2002

A ND SO THAT'S how *Ally McBeal* ended – not with a bang, but with a whimper. Come to think of it, that's also how *Ally McBeal* started – and carried on. Still, we have now seen the last episode, and a good thing too. No more pouting, no more hair-twiddling as a substitute for acting, no more of Vonda Shepard's theme song for the 1990s, "I've been searching my soul tonight".

Searching your soul is unseemly. You never find anything useful there – the car keys are generally between the couch cushions, and your parking ticket will not be found, no matter where you look. When you do put in a thorough search, standing at the parking payment machine with a small sea of plastic shopping bags around your feet, and you finally emerge with a parking ticket, like a happy gannet bobbing up with a pilchard in its beak, it is always the parking ticket you lost the last time you were at the mall. Where was it three days ago when you needed it? Where has it been in the interim? Ah, my friends, these are life's ineffable mysteries. You may as well ask why the caged bird sings, or how many roads a man must walk down before you can call him a cab.

Humphrey Bogart never searched his soul, or if he did, he had more class than to do it in public. That is one of the many reasons I am so fond of him. Bogart is a reminder of a better time; a cleaner, stronger, nobler time, when male movie stars were men, not pretty boys with expensive haircuts and bellies rippling like traffic calming zones. When life dealt Bogart the blows it deals us all – true loves arriving in our gin-joint with a new man on their arm; strange hoodlums socking us on the jaw when we least expect it – he responded as men should respond: with bourbon and a cigarette and a quiet determination not to let it happen again.

Bogart was not simple. He was not emotionless as Stallone or Steven Seagal or other modern so-called tough guys are emotionless. Sam Spade and

Philip Marlowe and Rick in *Casablanca* were troubled, sensitive beasts, prone to brooding and hurting and – in the scenes off-camera, solitary tears. The difference is that they didn't expect applause for being sensitive. They decided what had to be done, and they did it and bore the consequences like – if the Women's Day activists will forgive me – like men.

The Humphrey Bogart festival started on e.tv this week, and I settled in front of the *The Big Sleep* (e.tv, Monday, 10.15pm) as excited as a kitten. *The Big Sleep* was co-written by William Faulkner. The plot line is more prolix than Faulkner's novels, but fortunately the sentences are shorter. Bogart carried a gun, but his most effective weapon is the snub-nosed sentence, delivered like a poker dealer delivers a card: "Have you met Miss Sternwood?" asks the butler. Bogart's face is impassive.

"Yes," he says, "she tried to sit on my lap while I was standing up."

Later the supernaturally lovely Lauren Bacall loses her temper and flies at Bogart. He catches her wrist. "Careful," he says, without any inflection. "I don't slap around so good, this time of evening."

Bogart was so hard-boiled he hardly spoke the way other men speak. He seemed to hold his lower jaw immobile and move his upper jaw up and down. He specialised in playing lonely men toughing it out in a world of shadow and deceit, a world of pasteboard masks and moving scenery that conceal corruption and betrayal and death. And down these mean streets he stays true to his code of honour and tortured sense of duty. But scarcely had I started watching *The Big Sleep* when I realised that Bogart was up against a whole new threat.

The Big Sleep had been colourised. Some poor schlub in Ted Turner's diabolical workshop sat with digital paintbrush and pen and coloured in the black-and-white print, so that Bogart floated across the screen in lurid shades of newly peeled pink, like a hard-boiled lobster. It was awful. The point of film noir is that the hero wanders a world of black and white, in which nothing is black or white but washed with shades of moral ambiguity. The only thing ambiguous about the colourised print was the actual colour of Bogart's trench coat.

In the original it is an appropriate shade of slate; colourised, it suddenly took on precisely the mustard shade of Inspector Clouseau's coat. It was disconcerting to be half-expecting Philip Marlowe to ask people if they had a minkey. Fortunately, halfway through a scene the colourisers had a change of heart, or perhaps they ran out of mustard crayons, and the trench coat subtly metamorphosed to a queasy shade of green.

Precisely how aesthetically destitute would you have to be to prefer the colourised version? Ted Turner defended the process by claiming that the renovated prints would attract new generations to the films. This is something like painting bigger breasts on the Mona Lisa in order to bring her in line with contemporary tastes and draw a younger crowd to the Louvre.

I don't think I can bring myself to watch the other films in the Bogart festival. I love them too much to see them painted and peddled like tuppenny tarts. I will certainly not be watching a colourised *Casablanca*. There are few things that are sacred to me, but Ingrid Bergman's white dress is one of them. If I see her on that runway in shades of lilac or bottle green, I'll regret it. Maybe not today, maybe not tomorrow, but soon; and for the rest of my life. Here's not looking at you, kid.

It's a god's life

SUNDAY INDEPENDENT, 18 AUGUST 2002

I**T'S A DOG'S LIFE**, being God. Hang on, I've just realised that I'm not sure whether the expression "It's a dog's life" means it's a hard life or an easy life. Do dogs have a hard life? In Korea, yes, and it can't be much fun in Greenland with a sled tied to your back and a man in a furry parka yelling "Mush!" at you all day, but besides that dogs seem to have a soft enough time of it.

There must have been a couple of Buddhists over the generations who have been tempted to rack up a couple of bad-karma points so that they could come back as a dog and spend some good years being fussed over and scratched behind the ears and regularly fed a tasty dish of something nutritionally balanced and tail-thumpingly good. Of course, the risk is that you might collect too many bad-karma points and come back as a tapeworm, or a pimento, or something.

That's why I have never converted to Buddhism: too imprecise. There should be a schedule of benefits and punishments, as with frequent-flier miles: "Thirty acts of adultery earns 1700 bad-karma points, which equals reincarnation as a moose," for instance. Then you would be able to plan for the future.

But I digress. When I say: "It's a dog's life, being God," I mean that it can't be much fun. Oh, there must be plenty of fringe benefits. Good seats at all the big games, for instance, and you wouldn't have to worry about medical aid or retirement schemes. Plus, there are any number of tax-free corporate gifts, although after a while you might be looking for a little variety. "Enough with the burnt offerings already!" you might say. "What's with the thousands of years of burnt offerings? What's wrong with medium-rare every now and then? And would it kill you to throw in a nice blue-cheese sauce?"

Yes, there are some drawbacks to being God: You would know how all the movies end; it's hard to go for a quiet evening out without being recognised; people are forever doing awful things and saying it was your idea.

Mostly, though, I would get depressed by the kinds of people I would have to deal with every day. Heaven seemed like a good enough idea in the beginning

– you get to hang out with your buddies and no one ever has to get up early to go to work – but heaven must increasingly be resembling Cape Town: it's an attractive enough place, but all the interesting people are somewhere else.

Imagine, for instance, having to spend eternity in the company of Neleh and Vicepiah. Neleh and Vicepiah are not the names of twin towns on a Biblical plain earmarked for destruction, although they should be. Neleh and Vicepiah are the names of the last two contestants in *Survivor: Marquesas* (SABC3, Tuesdays), which ended this week. Throughout the series the two gals ran their respective campaigns on a two-pronged platform of evangelism and deceit. Neleh was a Mormon, and Vicepiah belonged to some other denomination that allows you to do whatever you want as long as you ask forgiveness afterwards.

"We pray to the same God," Neleh solemnly informed Vicepiah, in a moment of what passed for multiculturalism in America. It might have been a meaningful gesture if Neleh had been Palestinian and Vicepiah an Israeli soldier, but between two Christian denominations it was hardly an epiphanic moment.

They may pray to the same God, but they had different ideas about what God's best course of action should be. Neleh prayed that God would make Neleh win. Vicepiah prayed that God would make Vicepiah win. "I am proud of my spirituality," they both informed the camera. It was infuriating to watch two such smug individuals so utterly persuaded of their own virtue. Their faith had not made them behave any better than anyone else – it had just allowed them to feel good about it.

Perhaps I am just envious. It must be a pretty sweet deal to be able to act the way we are going to act anyway, and still have no doubt that it's all going to turn out well for us in the end. I have no beef with religion. I had a beef with Neleh and Vicepiah.

"I could never believe in a God that did not know how to dance," Nietzsche once said. I suppose I could never believe in a God that watched Reality TV.

The good news was that one of them was going to lose. The bad news was that one of them was going to win. Vicepiah won. She hooted. She hollered. "God is good!" she hooted and hollered. Neleh did not hoot and holler that God was good. Vicepiah thought God had made the right call. Neleh wasn't so sure. Neleh, you had the impression, was beginning to wonder if they really did pray to the same God. What if, she seemed to be thinking, my God was watching *Big Brother* instead?

The long reach of television

SUNDAY INDEPENDENT, 21 OCTOBER 2002

TELEVISION HAS A long reach, and it makes bonds where you would scarcely imagine bonds might be. I have just today returned from Namibia, and more precisely from the Skeleton Coast. The Skeleton Coast is the most extraordinary place I have visited. It is far, far from here, a place of dreams and fears, where the sky and the sea and the sand meet and make an agreement that does not take human beings into account. You cannot live on the Skeleton Coast of Namibia; you can only visit it, and each moment that you are there, you know you are there only on the sufferance of the sky and the sea and the sand.

On the Skeleton Coast the nearest telephone is 300 km away. The nearest television is further. It is a wild place. It is wilderness. On the shore I saw the bleached masts of 19th-century whaling ships, and jackals that roam the dunes and pick over the scrubbed bones of baleen whales. I saw hawks and gulls and lions that walk the sand, feeding on the slowest seals. There are elephants and dead men and a wind that never stops blowing from the sea. The foam mounts on the sand until the shore is like the trembling crest of some infernal beer.

The Skeleton Coast is a lonely place, but I was not lonely. I had good company. Among the company was a German man named Wolfgang. Wolfgang and I did not warm to each other. I am not proud of it, but I have an in-built prejudice against Germans. I don't seriously believe that the Maginot Line is in serious danger any more, but old habits die hard. (I mean my habit of mistrusting Germans, not necessarily the 20th-century German habit of wearing grey and invading their neighbours.)

Wolfgang was in his sixties, and although rationally I knew that means that he was too young ever to have piloted the Stuka that dive-bombed my grandfather's tank in 1944, still I looked at him askance. I began to feel like John Cleese. There were South African history buffs in the camp, and whenever anyone mentioned war, I found myself, as though possessed, turning to Wolfgang and saying, "They are talking about the Anglo-Boer War, you know. Oh, yes, the Anglo-Boer War. Gee, what a war, eh? Never mind, we're all friends now."

It was, you might imagine, awkward. My companion – an individual of immense diplomacy and good sense – took me aside and said, "Will you shut up about the war already? Who do you think you are, Winston Churchill?" But could I stop? I could not.

And then the peculiar thing happened. Around the campfire one night, someone mentioned Bing Crosby. I forget how Bing Crosby was mentioned in the distant sandy hollows of the world's most desolate coast, but he was, and what's more, he was not popular. Popular opinion on the Skeleton Coast, I am compelled to report, was not in favour of Bing Crosby. Good words were spoken of Jim Reeves, of all people, and Nat King Cole and Frank Sinatra, with which I can scarcely argue, but Bing Crosby received short shrift. For want of anything else to say, I offered: "Oh, Bing's not all bad. His daughter shot JR, for one thing."

That received the silence it deserved, but then Wolfgang turned to me. "You are right," he said. "Mary Crosby played Sue-Ellen's sister, Kristin Sheperd, and she shot JR."

I was astonished. "You know *Dallas*?" I said. Wolfgang leaned forward, and his khaki safari-vest rustled slightly under the intensity of his gaze. "I love *Dallas*," he said.

Wolfgang is a *Dallas*ophile. I too am a *Dallas*ophile. It is currently being repeated on the Series Channel (DStv), but my *Dallas* memories are vivid from the days I used to tiptoe out of bed at 9 pm on a Tuesday and peer around the corner of the living room to watch the doings of the Ewings over my parents' shoulders.

Occasionally I was caught and my mouth was washed out with soap (my father would have preferred to have washed out my eyes with soap, but my mother was a gentle soul), but still each Tuesday I returned. Sometimes I snuck outside and stood in the garden, watching *Dallas* reflected on an open window in the Durban summer night. I am still obscurely touched to think that my parents sought to shelter me from the horrors of the adult world by forbidding me to watch *Dallas*. If only they had just forbidden me to grow up, I am sure I would have been much happier.

I love remembering *Dallas*. It awakens in me the memory of the days when being an adult still seemed exciting. For the rest of the trip, Wolfgang and I tested each other on *Dallas* trivia. "Who was JR's lawyer?" Wolfgang asked. "Harv Smithfield," I replied with a smirk.

"What was the name of the corrupt *Dallas* sheriff?" I asked. "Fenton," said Wolfgang, shrugging.

On the whole, I blush to confess, Wolfgang had the edge with *Dallas* trivia. For one thing, he remembered the name of the nightclub where Audrey Landers as Afton Cooper sang when she was still Cliff Barnes' girlfriend. I had to concede.

From our *Dallas* connection, conversation grew. We spoke about being children and seeing things we were not allowed to see. We spoke about the small sorrows of growing older. We spoke about our fathers, and dying. We never mentioned the war.

Now Wolfgang is back in his small village outside Bremen, and I am on this page, fielding queries from friends about when I am going to update my photograph. It wasn't quite like the Christmas Day the soldiers called truce to play football in no-man's-land, but still it felt good. Now I have a place to stay, the next time I find myself in a small village outside Bremen. And we have *Dallas* to thank.

My kind of serial killer

SUNDAY INDEPENDENT, 3 NOVEMBER 2002

Now WHERE IS Hannibal Lecter when you really need him? I have of late been thinking about Hannibal Lecter. Hannibal Lecter, I am compelled to admit, is my kind of guy.

I have always liked Hannibal Lecter, I suppose, in a distant sort of way. He had a fine nose for perfume and a way with women that impressed me. Like John Malkovich chatting up Michelle Pheiffer in *Dangerous Liasons*, Hannibal Lecter in *Silence of the Lambs* touched a nerve deep in every young man's heart. "Say, I don't need a flashy car or an expensive haircut in order to interest the ladies," every young man realised, on some deep and perhaps inarticulate level. "All I need is to learn how to speak to them. Maybe not precisely like Hannibal Lecter speaks to Jodie Foster – in some circles that may be regarded as a little creepy, and not *all* women respond well to the rumbling threat of being eaten on the first date – but he does seem to know a thing or two about holding up his end of the conversation."

What was captivating about Hannibal Lecter in *Silence of the Lambs* was that he was himself captured. His power was the power of a low voice in the darkness, like a brooding fallen Lucifer plotting one day to get back up there where the air is rarefied. It was comforting to a young man. When you are a young man without money, a vehicle or much by way of desirable social resources, life can feel very similar to a solitary cell in a maximum-security prison: you can't go anywhere and you have to wear unattractive clothing and your only companions are other men in a similar social position with unattractive personal habits. Ah, but with a voice and a mind, Hannibal Lecter could transcend all that! And win an Oscar too! Hannibal Lecter was a quiet inspiration.

But last week, tucked up on the sofa with a barrel of fried chicken, a full heart and *Hannibal* (M-Net, Sunday, 8pm), it occurred to me that Hannibal Lecter on the loose is altogether a different proposition. I had not seen the sequel before, although I had nearly watched it one night in wintry Amsterdam when I was on my own and at a loose end. (Traditionally single men at night in Amsterdam find other entertainment than an Anthony Hopkins movie, but I was not much tempted by such ruddy delights. The human body is capable of many splendours and wonders, but I would like to keep some of them as a surprise for my middle age. Besides, even alone and in Amsterdam, there are some loose ends at which you do not want to be.)

I had chosen not to watch *Hannibal* that night, even though there was an English-language print showing in a theatre somewhere off the Kaizersgracht, because I was already lonely and cold and in a foreign city, with the canals stirring slow and dark and menacing. The last thing I needed was to feel lonely and cold in a foreign city with the pressing suspicion that I am being followed down the side alleys by a cannibal in a Panama hat. But last Sunday I was not lonely and I was not cold, and all of a sudden I found myself wishing that I had Hannibal Lecter on personal retainer.

In *Hannibal*, Hannibal Lecter is on the loose. Outside of prison, much of his personal power is dissipated. His voice and his personality are not as important – he can buy things and wear disguises and even become involved in tussles with the forces of evil. Well, the *other* forces of evil. It is, I suppose, a little like being a young man grown older. Life is a little easier and much more fun but not necessarily as dramatic. I identified far less with Hannibal Lecter in the second movie, but I approved of him even more.

Hannibal Lecter kills and eats people. Big deal, you might say. There are plenty of people who kill and eat people. But Hannibal Lecter's gimmick is that he prefers to kill and eat people who *deserve* it, not because they are immoral or unethical, but because they are without grace or taste. Oh, what a thought! The problem with serial killers is that they are so random. Worse: they are often fairly uncouth individuals themselves. What could be a more dismal fate than being randomly killed and eaten by some unshaven yob scratching his belly and listening to *The Best of Queen* in his pick-up truck? But if serial killers were calm and rational and dedicated to making the world a better place by removing, not the sinners and the harlots, but the bad mannered and the poorly dressed, I would be all in favour of them. Ah, would that there were a squadron of Hannibal Lecters.

Different serial killers resemble different understandings of God. I would love to believe in a God like Hannibal Lecter – an individual of taste and breeding, punishing those who jump queues or who have facial piercings or who bring babies to restaurants or who insist on telling you jokes. Sadly, in my limited experience, if God is a serial killer, he more closely resembles the Washington sniper. It is a random harvest.

Such at any rate were my thoughts, late of a Sunday evening, having watched Hannibal Lecter eat part of the living brain of Ray Liotta with a knife and fork. At such moments my mind turns frequently to improving the world. If only we could identify the part of the brain that enjoys *Big Brother*, and that makes people stand reading their transaction slip at the ATM instead of stepping aside already, and that invented the mullet hairstyle. If only we could, I might just turn Hannibal myself. Pass the salt.

Here's to you, Mrs Robinson

SUNDAY INDEPENDENT, 24 NOVEMBER 2002

I HAVE TO CONFESS, and I suppose this is as good a place as any to do my confessing. My confession is this: I have of late, I know not why, been troubled by curious dreams. I say "curious", but I am being discreet. These dreams are more than curious – they cause me to wake in the night, trembling and mopping myself and reaching for a glass of water. There is pleasure involved in these dreams, but they are guilty pleasures. They are not the sorts of pleasures you would want to tell your mother.

The sum and essence of my problem – the nub, you might say – is Anne Robinson. Oh go on, you know Anne Robinson. Anne Robinson is the Torquemada of Trivia, the Grand Inquisitor of the Intellect. Anne Robinson is a torturer, a tyrant, a short, female, bespectacled, red-headed Idi Amin of the airwaves. God, I love that woman.

Anne Robinson presents *The Weakest Link* (BBC Prime, DStv, weekdays, 7.05pm) in much the same way that Daisy de Melker presented her husband with his morning coffee. But unlike Daisy de Melker, Anne Robinson doesn't smile. It would be fair to say that Anne Robinson is sarcastic, but only if you agree that it would be fair to say that Ronnie Biggs had no respect for the law, or that the shark in *Jaws* had pointy teeth and he showed them pearly white. In Anne Robinson's hands, sarcasm is an artistic medium. It is expressive, it is aesthetic and it causes you to question your assumptions about the world, which is apparently what contemporary artists understand to be the principal purpose of art. Anne Robinson's sarcasm, indeed, could win the Turner Prize. Come to think of it, that would be a bright day for contemporary art, when you consider the sort of threadbare balderdash that *does* win the Turner Prize.

The Weakest Link is an English question-and-answer game show in which a procession of spotty Brits take turns to quail and crumble beneath the gimlet gaze of Anne Robinson. ("Do you even know what a gimlet is?" Anne Robinson asked me in my dream last night. "Er … uh … it is a small tool that bores things, isn't it?" I stammered. "And does that description fit anyone else in this room, would you say?" said Anne Robinson. I blushed and lowered my head in a kind of furious ecstasy of abasement.)

Anne Robinson's greatest asset, besides the ability to convince you she is wearing leather thighboots and a riding crop beneath her black ankle-length coat, is a talent for making you believe she knows all the answers to all the questions. Anne Robinson, you would swear, is omniscient and omnipotent, and she knows when you've been naughty, and she knows when you've been nice. When you answer incorrectly, she looks at you with such mingled disappointment and contempt that you feel – yea, verily, you *feel* – that your coming chastisement is proper and deserved and you only wish she would find it in herself to punish you a little longer.

"Roy, what do you do for a living?" Anne Robinson asked a portly fellow on the show this week.

"I'm a comedian, Anne," he replied bravely.

"Really?" said Anne, with a voice that could be used to perform keyhole surgery. "Are you a professional comedian, Roy, or do you mean your friends think that you are a bit of a card down at the pub?"

Roy swallowed heavily. "No, no, I'm a professional," he said gamely.

"So people pay you to be funny, do they, Roy? You must be very funny indeed. Tell us a joke."

Roy did not want to tell a joke. Roy would rather have performed an emergency appendectomy on himself using his own teeth than tell a joke at that moment. But when Anne Robinson speaks, strong men bend the knee. Roy told a joke. I could scarcely hear the joke, I was in such agonies of masculine sympathy. Anne Robinson listened to Roy's joke. Her face was as the face of Pharaoh Akhenaten on a mural in the Luxor necropolis. The Pharaoh Akhenaten was not remembered by antiquity for his sense of humour, particularly in necropolises.

"Roy," said Anne Robinson.

Roy shuffled his feet and dropped his eyes. "Yes, Anne," said Roy.

"Do you know any *funny* jokes, Roy?" said Anne Robinson.

Oh, how she haunts my dreams. Night after night she returns, her stiletto heels clacking on my floor and across my chest, mouth pursed with the inward pleasure of kindness withheld, asking me questions, always questions, questions that torment and mock, questions with no answers. "If it's called *Business* Class," she demands, "why do they allow babies in?" and "Where is the reflexology pressure point for feet?" and "Do hot cakes really sell better than other sorts of cakes?"

And when I cannot reply, oh what awful scenes there do follow. Such scenes as I cannot describe, lest your parrot read the lining of its cage and be irredeemably corrupted. Needless to say, I am concerned. I haven't had such dreams since those dark days in the early eighties when I was visited nightly by the lady from the Morkels adverts. Do you remember her? I can't explain it either. I can only remind myself of the story that many of the male members of Margaret Thatcher's cabinet, and indeed her political opponents, reported erotic dreams about the Boss. Consider that, and join me in turning my face towards the heavens and asking, in a trembling voice, "Ye gods! What horrors lurk in the heart of men?"

While we strive each day to walk the straight and narrow path, through the meadows and the broad and sunlit uplands, alas our darker drives are not ours to command. Oh, we men are beasts. We deserve to be punished.

On stage with Jerry Springer

SUNDAY INDEPENDENT, 19 JANUARY 2003

H AVE YOU EVER wondered how the producers of Jerry Springer's American show lure their guests on air? I have. Every episode features some or other variety of grinning hillbilly who has contacted the show in order to air his or her toothless atrocities, and each of those stories entails bringing into the studio some ungrinning hillbillies, the artless victims of those atrocities, who have no idea why they are there. I am not myself a hillbilly, toothed or otherwise, so I have never really understood precisely why a man would say to his wife, "Sure, honey, I'll be a guest with you on *The Jerry Springer Show*. Won't tell me what it's about, eh? No problem. Say, why are we bringing granddad and the vacuum cleaner with us?"

Surely, I have always thought, the producers must use some other cunning strategem to lure the witless on stage. And then this week, sitting in the Green Room backstage at Jerry Springer's South African show, drinking complimentary vodka through a straw while waiting to be called for make-up, a terrible thought occurred to me. What if their cunning strategem is to phone and say: "We would like you to be a guest on Jerry's chat show. No, no, not that show, the other one. The *respectable* one."

The thought made me wobble a little at the knees. I scoured my memory for indiscretions and the kind of harmless youthful eccentricities you pay witnesses to keep quiet about. I didn't fancy the prospect of bounding on stage to be confronted with a Greek chorus of bad memories pointing their fingers at me while the audience hissed and checked its dictionaries to get a clearer picture of my perversions. I didn't want to spend the rest of my life with smart alecs making barnyard sounds whenever I entered a room.

Jerry Springer's Saturday Night (M-Net, Saturdays, after the movie) is Jerry Springer's other show. Unlike his American series, it has no truck with adulterers, paedophiles, incestuous love triangles and foot fetishists. No, wait, that's not true – rather, the adulterers, paedophiles, incestuous love triangles and foot fetishists with which it has truck don't actually admit to it. The idea of the show is that Jerry interviews local celebrities of interest. Hands up who can spot the fatal flaw in that idea.

For some weeks now I have felt immensely sorry for Jerry Springer. Imagine flying 25 hours out of Chicago once a month to interview Heinz Winkler or Amore Vittone. No really – imagine it. Speaking to Heinz Winkler must be something like sticking your head inside an empty washing machine and murmuring phrases in Esperanto. Except after five minutes of interviewing Heinz Winkler, you would want to turn the washing machine on. With your head still inside.

Some weeks ago I watched Jerry interviewing a radio DJ named Nicole Fox. What questions can you think of to ask radio DJ Nicole Fox? Me neither. Neither could Jerry. The interview consisted of Jerry gallantly saying "You don't have a face for radio," and radio DJ Nicole Fox agreeing between cackles of the kind of laughter that terrified the Munchkins when they heard it swooping overhead. Sometimes she would cackle even when Jerry hadn't said anything. "Gee," I remember saying aloud to my bourbon, "how deep are they going to have to reach for guests? I hope there is someone leaning over that barrel with mighty long arms."

Apparently their arms are like the tentacles of a giant squid, because last night there I was, sweating in front of the cameras, trying to remember which is my best side, or whether I even have a best side, and cursing those extra helpings of Christmas pudding. I was on screen for 10 minutes, which means three hours idling in the Green Room beforehand, hoovering up the buffet and playing "I-spy" with the other guests. My heart sank when I arrived to find Mark Banks, resplendent on the waiting-room sofa, wearing a shirt shiny and green and ornate, like a Muslim Christmas tree. You don't want to be on the same show as Mark Banks. Mark Banks is very funny, and a funny guest makes other guests look dull. If you're a guest, you want to avoid Mark Banks as a rabid dog avoids his water bowl. You want to be on a show with, say, Heinz Winkler or radio DJ Nicole Fox.

During an ad break, Tobie Cronjé and I stripped down and oiled up and engaged in a bout of Greco-Roman wrestling to decide who would have to go on directly after Mark Banks. Tobie was surprisingly powerful and had several painful grappling moves, but I am proud to announce that the correspondent for your quality Sunday newspaper won through. Panic lent strength to my headlock.

In the end it was all very jolly backstage, after the vodka kicked in. I met a group of pleasant young men calling themselves the Sons of Trout, who I imagine are some manner of religious cult, but very polite with it. There was a blonde woman named Wes-Lee who claimed to be some manner of singer. "So, what do you do?" we asked each other simultaneously.

The interview passed in a blur and a stammer and a hot tick-tock. I was pleased to note that there were no Tennessee mountain folk on stage accusing me of impregnating their goats or their trailer vans, but less pleased to notice the collective sigh of disappointment from the audience when I emerged. I think they had been expecting Simon Gear.

Afterwards the producers patted me kindly on the shoulders. "Never mind," they said, "you did your best."

After the show a member of the audience sidled up and asked me for an autograph. "Certainly," I said, beaming graciously, taking up a pen with a flourish.

"Not yours. Jerry's," said the audience member. He looked at me narrowly. "What's your name again?"

Big Brother Iraq

SUNDAY INDEPENDENT, 23 MARCH 2003

'As I speak to you, every part of my body is entirely sealed!" said Emma in the northern Kuwaiti desert. I couldn't be sure it was true – Sky News' coverage of the war in the Gulf, while impressively thorough, couldn't take us *that* far into the heart of the campaign.

Emma was a frightening sight – in her head-to-toe charcoal-lined camouflage protective suit and her weirdly anachronistic gas mask, she resembled some sort of paramilitary Womble. Throughout the day, whenever we crossed to the troops in northern Kuwait, Emma was either struggling into her protective gear or wriggling from it, the cold and fearful sound of the gas-alert siren or – almost indistinguishable – the all-clear in the background. On one occasion we crossed over to find that Emma had taken refuge in the bunker. The camera, fixed on its tripod, impassively showed distant men running, shouting, affixing their gas masks, kicking up small clouds of desert sand. For a terrible, terrible moment before sanity reasserted itself I leant closer to the screen, hoping something exciting might be about to happen. For that dreadful moment I forgot I was watching a war. It was as though I were watching *Big Brother Iraq*.

The 24-hour multi-channel coverage of operations in Iraq is even more surreal than coverage of the Gulf War in 1991. The various international news channels this time were better prepared, with journalists on the front lines, on aircraft carriers, attached to infantry units and tank divisions. The news-gathering and news-transmission operations are as carefully planned and executed as the military procedures themselves. What's worse, with 10 years of Reality TV conditioning the way we experience real life and television – and real life on television – it becomes increasingly difficult not to treat the coverage as another species of entertainment, an unfolding saga with twists and turns and unexpected surprises.

Since Thursday morning the war has been playing itself out in our living rooms like an elaborate drama series, complete with theme music and credits and titles and celebrity guests and constant scrolling updates on the story so far. Strangely, having reporters there on the ground, speaking into the microphone with one hand blocking an ear against the noise of a Cobra helicopter gunship passing overhead, saying things like "There has been a fire-fight on the outskirts of Basra, just a few kilometres from here", somehow does not make the war more real. It makes it seem like any other Reality show. We have seen so much on television pretending to be real, these last years, that nothing on television feels real any more.

Once again, Sky News has edged out the competition at CNN and BBC World in the battle of the broadcasters. While the others lapse occasionally into logos and channel idents and – CNN's speciality – inserts explaining just how they have managed to set up their cameras and where the broadcasting unit is located, Sky's coverage – or "intelligence", I suppose you would say – has all the depth and variety you expect from modern war coverage. Plus, there is the quirky pleasure of hearing the Sky reporters refer to the "Dee-Em-Zed", instead of the Americans' "Dee-Em-Zee".

I made some slight attempt to watch the local channels, but I was defeated. When I crossed over to e.tv, some local worthy was explaining to Debra Patta how the working classes of South Africa were going to bring the Bush regime to its knees by "boycotting American movies and American oil". Over on SABC3, we were talking to Rene Horne, live in Baghdad. "It's very tense here," said Rene Horne, half a day after the first missiles started landing in Baghdad. "Almost like a war zone."

When the war first started I was jumping from one channel to the next – like the multi-camera views in the *Big Brother* house – but now I seldom budge from Sky. Oh yes, when men in distant parts are killing each other, I demand nothing but the best.

Intimations of mortuaries

SUNDAY INDEPENDENT, 6 APRIL 2003

I DO HOPE YOU can read this column today – if the writing is too faint and spidery and trails away, I can only offer my apologies and the assurance that it won't go on forever. I am getting older, you see, and my hand is not as firm nor as steady as once it was. Today is my birthday, and at my back I have the distinct impression that I hear the snorts and whinnies and muffled hoofbeats of time's winged chariot drawing near. Either that, or the neighbour has made up with her boyfriend again.

And yet I am not downcast. Age creeps up on one, like a Gurkha in the jungles of Malaya, belly-down in the tropical ferns and a kukri between his teeth, but not everything that stirs in the night is an assassin. I am in good spirits today. I greet the advancing world with a smile and a whistle and I offer it a sip of my drink. The rest of the year is for worrying; on your birthday you deserve a break.

In the run-up to my birthday, I must confess, my mind has been turning to matters of mortality. Last Monday I tuned in to *Six Feet Under* (e.tv, Mondays, 9pm), to see what insights I could glean. *Six Feet Under* – a sort of quirky American drama series set in a family mortuary – is gathering some sort of international cult momentum. It is billed as a black comedy because it has dead people in it and because it has moments of idiosyncrasy. Idiosyncrasy is what people without humour offer when they want to be amusing but they don't want to crack one-liners or tell jokes.

The show is written by Alan Ball, who won an Oscar for writing *American Beauty*. I was never that impressed with the script for *American Beauty*. That famous scene in which the gawky teenage boy shows Thora Birch the video-tape of a plastic packet blowing in the wind only worked for me because that is precisely the kind of self-conscious, inarticulate groping for an arresting point of view that is characteristic of gawky teenage boys who have spent too much time on their own, and most of that time hoping that they are in some way special. (I say "they", though of course I mean "we".) "There is so much beauty in the world," says the gawky teenage boy mistily, looking at the footage of the plastic bag, "I don't know if I can take it."

I would be far more impressed by the scene if I could shake the nagging suspicion that Allan Ball intends us to take the gawky teenage boy and his plastic bag seriously. Certainly audiences around the world did take it seriously, and loved it, but that is not always the writer's fault. In this case, though, I think the writer was with his audience all the way. There is a lumbering, over-obvious earnestness about the story and its so-called twists which, if it isn't a case of ultra-ultra-refined satire, are so dull as to paralyse the brain.

I have the same feeling with *Six Feet Under*. It is a series about people straining to make sense of their lives against the perpetual dark backcloth of death. As are we all. But – aha! – the show takes place in a funeral parlour. See! Death is all around us! The death, I can't shake the feeling, is there in the way that Death or Sin or Virtue appeared in medieval morality plays – to spell itself out so obviously that even the most chuckleheaded viewer can't miss the point. Even worse, in this particular version of black comedy, the dead people provide all the blackness and all the comedy, and that is really why the show does not work for me.

The comic vision, and especially the black comic vision, is one that – if it is genuine – permeates the entire story and its characterisations. It has many forms and avatars, depending on whose vision it is, but one of its consistent qualities is a sense of the ridiculous that comes of human beings' attempts to take themselves and their doings seriously.

I say "seriously", but really I mean "earnestly" or "self-importantly". It is possible to be simultaneously comic and serious; it is possible to perceive absurdity while believing that one's relationship with absurdity is a matter that has meaning. *Six Feet Under* is not black comedy, it is a drama series that regards itself with a great deal of self-importance.

Death is in the script simply to provide macabre gags and to provide the silvering on the mirrors in which the characters endlessly examine themselves in a series of interminable monologues posing as conversations. There is a thumping predictability, as though it were written by a gifted teenager who still has the gifted teenager's blight of imagining that he is the first to have discovered the tortured minutiae of hormonal existentialism.

Six Feet Under is not bad television. Indeed, it is because it is good television that I have taken it sufficiently seriously to figure out why I don't like it. There is pleasure in that. Of course, bad television has its own pleasures – they are fugitive pleasures but none the less welcome. This is the 300th column I have written in this newspaper about the variegated pleasures of watching television, and I thank you for reading them. I don't imagine you have read all 300 – not even I have read all 300, and my mother certainly hasn't – but every bit helps. I can't imagine that I shall write another 300 columns – there are younger television viewers out there with sharper eyes and tongues and newfangled palmtops in which to take their notes, rather than a tatty notebook and a leaking biro. But I have enjoyed being here, and if you will have me, I shall stick around a little longer yet.

Never mind Willy – free Harry

SUNDAY INDEPENDENT, 29 JUNE 2003

P RINCE WILLIAM TURNED 21 this week, which didn't really come as a surprise. It had to happen sooner or later, and this was as good a week as any. To mark the occasion, M-Net screened *The Reluctant Royal*, a documentary about, well, Will. How reluctant is Will? He is so reluctant he didn't appear in the documentary at all, except in file footage and old clips of him as a jolly toddler, all kitted out in stripy jersey and tiny red shorts. It was quite sweet to see – I had forgotten how much Prince William, aged four, looked like Simon Gear, aged now.

Despite not having an actual prince to talk to, the documentary did all it could. What it could do was footage of fringe. Oh, he has a mighty fringe, does William. We saw the fringe from all angles. We saw it from above, from the side, from the other side. We didn't see it from a Will's eye-view, of course, because Will is very reluctant. His reluctance extends to cameras being strapped to his forehead.

So there was no Will-cam, but it was an impressive fringe, if you like fringes. It was the kind of fringe I spent years envying as a schoolboy. All the cool kids in Durban had fringes like that – they hung down and you could look through them, and the cool kids could flick them back with a toss of the head. The really cool kids could stick out their lower lips and blow upwards, and the fringe would levitate. I never had such a fringe. My hair was of the wrong sort. It waved when it should have flopped. It had too much relationship with gravity. That is one of the reasons I resent Oprah. Whenever she says: "You can be anything you want to be", I always want to reply: "Oh yeah? Well, I want to have a fringe like Prince William's. Or like Stuart Wright, who sat two desks down in Mr Nupen's history class."

There were times when the documentary succeeded in its primary task: winning our sympathy for the reluctant prince. It is not really in my nature to have much fellow-feeling for some tall, rich, befringed future king. Seldom do I think of William and sigh aloud, "Poor bugger." Rarely do I look up from the muddle and murk of my life and think: "Could be worse. At least I'm not heir to the throne of Windsor." But perhaps I should, because it can't be all fun. A moment in the show brought that home.

There was old footage of Diana on holiday in the Caribbean with her young sons. They were splashing at the sea's edge, laughing, happy together. The water was blue and the sun danced on the surface and made their fringes shine like electrum. "Not such a bad life," I thought.

At that moment the camera pulled back to a wider angle. There, perched like strange beaked birds behind a line drawn in the sand perhaps 15 metres from the family, were all the photographers of the world, four deep, jostling and leaning over each other, snapping and snapping and snapping. I looked at William again. "Poor bugger," I thought.

The show had its share of drama. "William is the Royal Family's last hope!" said the voice-over, sounding like Obi-Wan Kenobi discussing Luke Skywalker. "But first he must come to terms with his destiny!"

Epic stuff, but still I can't get that interested in him. He is just about as dull as I suppose a future king of England has to be. There is another character I find far more intriguing.

He is there in all the file footage of William, but instead of occupying centre screen, blond and radiant like a sun, he is a dark, brooding smudge at the edges, his mood unreadable, like a cloud gathering but not yet large enough to threaten. Harry has the makings of a Shakespearean character: dark, inward, bearing an almost embarrassing resemblance to James Hewitt, orbiting ever on the fringes of the Windsor solar system.

While William wears chinos and simpers for the camera, I imagine Harry stalking the gardens thinking furious thoughts, brooding on his uncertain blood, absent-mindedly strangling baby birds and crushing small mammals beneath his heel. One day, like Mordred, he will leave the kingdom and raise a mighty army in exile, always dreaming of the day he will return … or perhaps it's just me.

2

Lifestyle

Of mice and morons

STYLE, SEPTEMBER 2000

HAVE YOU NOTICED how stupid the world is becoming? Well, not the world, exactly – the world, while not necessarily one's first choice as an after-dinner speaker, has come up with some nifty ideas in its time. Plate tectonics was a pretty shrewd manoeuvre, and the condensation cycle generally earns nods of approval in all the right circles. No, I mean the people who inhabit the world.

Stupidity is everywhere. It is the air we breathe. There are, of course, many shades of the stupid. I don't mean the recognisable stupidity of drooling, slack-jawed incomprehension, although, as anyone who has ever watched SABC1 will tell you, there is plenty of that shuffling around. Far more depressing is the stupidity that disguises itself as thought, that talks so glibly and eloquently – indeed, that never stops talking. How powerful is this species of stupidity? It is so powerful it has invented a genre of literature that actually makes people more stupid for having read it.

I was rictally grinning my way through a dinner party recently, when conversation turned, like a deflating boerewors on a suburban braai, to the subject of self-help. For some reason those beyond help are always talking about self-help. They can't help themselves. A young lady of doubtful provenance dipped into her handbag and hauled out a glossy paperback. "Read this!" she commanded. "It will change your life. It contains the lost wisdom of the ancient Mayans." The book was called *The Avocado Prophecies* or *Footprints of the Toucans* or some such horsefeathers and flapdoodle. I fixed her with an eye both cold and unaccommodating. I have no patience with the cultural anthropology of loserdom.

Any curling potpourri of antiquated mysticism is celebrated nowadays, provided it can be attributed to the Incas or the Etruscans or some other culture that has disappeared with scarcely a trace. Besides celebrating communal cocaine use and the social merits of human sacrifice, what can the Mayans teach us now? How to be invaded by a rag-tag bunch of Spanish ruffians? If those ancient cultures were so damned clever, where are they now? Eh? Pyramids and maps of the stars are all very well, but they might have found the wheel a touch more useful in the long run.

Anthropological mysticism is but one rickety arm of the genre of quick-fire self-help. To sell an idea today, you simply have to tell people it will change their lives, and tell them it won't be hard. It's not stupid for people to believe in something better, but it is a very modern stupidity to believe it will come easy. The fashion for mainstream mysticism is not a swing away from religion as such, but away from systems of belief that require rigour and application.

Hence the popularity of faraway cultures – they don't have to make sense. In fact it's better that they don't. Modern folk are so hostile to thought, we'll put our faith in anything, provided it's not rational. With alternative medicine it's the alternative that attracts, not the medicine. No doubt sundry roots and tubers and suchlike have useful healing properties, but the way people go on you'd think that dangling crystals and painting your bedroom puce is guaranteed to work, for no other reason than that it hasn't been subjected to clinical testing.

The more non-rational a self-help book pretends to be, the more certain it is to succeed. We prefer anecdote and analogy to case studies and evidence. Invent a snappy metaphor and the crowds will flock. Consider the latest best-seller in the field: *Who Moved my Cheese?* by one Dr Spencer Johnson. It bills itself, and I'm not making this up, as the parable of four characters who live in a maze. Their lives are dedicated to the pursuit of, ahem, cheese. Apparently they like cheese. Two characters are mice named "Sniff" and "Scurry". Two are miniature people named "Hem" and "Haw". There's more, but I can't bring myself to utter it. Yet is this any more preposterous than a book titled *60 Ways to Make Your Life Amazing*? I doubt it.

And for all this hogwash and hoo-hah, are people noticeably wiser, kinder or more interesting dinner-party guests? They are not. I say to hell with this obsession with the real you. If you want the world to be a better place, don't try to be more true to yourself – try to be more polite. Say please and thank you, teach your children not to interrupt adults while they're talking, wear a jacket to dinner. Sod self-discovery, bring back manners. Imagine a day when every self-help book is replaced by a manual of common etiquette. Now there's a world I could live in.

Operation Copulation

MARKETING MIX, SEPTEMBER 2000

THERE ARE MANY ways to spice up a flagging marriage but I wouldn't have thought that visiting Brackenfell was one of them. Brackenfell, in case you've never had the pleasure of driving past it at high speed while murmuring a spell to ward off evil spirits, is a dismal suburb in the north of Cape Town. Until recently, the best thing you could say about Brackenfell is that it's neither Salt River nor Woodstock. Actually, that is still the best thing you can say about it. That is no longer, however, the most interesting thing you can say about Brackenfell, because recently Brackenfell was announced as being the lucky beneficiary of Cape Town's newest and boldest marketing initiative.

When it comes to marketing, you have to take your hat off to Cape Town, and not merely to shoo it away. Cape Town is more ready and willing to sell itself than any large town you've ever met. Cape Town is the Hansie Cronjé of seaside settlements.

It doesn't miss a trick: the last time I arrived at Cape Town airport I was handed a book of coupons, redeemable against the price of my next visit.

Above all, Cape Town's strategy is broad. In recent times, it has sold itself internationally as the only place to be if you are (a) a homosexual sex tourist, (b) interested in sleeping with under-aged girls, (c) an admirer of Earl Spencer, (d) a money launderer or (e) a real-estate speculator. Or, indeed, any combination of the above. But the Brackenfell venture is a stroke of uncommon genius.

Brackenfell is the proposed site of a new multi-million-rand lodge, to be built in anticipation of a surge in swingers' tours. It will offer adult entertainment, on-call sex therapists and communal spa-baths. What is a swingers' tour, you ask, trembling? According to a recent report, one Robin Pike is advertising Cape Town as the ideal destination for international wife-swapping safaris. Allegedly, up to 100 British and German couples each month are queuing to come south and make whoopee with someone else's spouse. Projected revenue is more than R60 million a year, which explains why the scheme has been given the thumbs-up from Satour and the Ministry of Tourism.

I must confess the idea startles me. The notion that our husbands and wives are a marketable natural resource will take some getting used to. The realisation that the Big 5 now includes Mrs Katz from down the hall, frankly, leaves me dizzy. The obvious obstacle to the scheme is that old South African bugaboo – racial intolerance. Having canvassed the fellows down at the Chalk 'n Cue, I can sadly report that many a lad who would do his patriotic duty in the cause of tourism with Mr and Mrs Hamburg or the Von Stuttgarts would draw the line at his own better half in the clutches of an Englishman.

Still, there appear to be enough takers for the proposition to be viable: Johannesburg apparently has 6000 registered swingers, Cape Town a stately 2000 and Durban, ever keen to get in on the action, boasts a game 1000. Personally, I suspect that Johannesburg has a good deal more than 6000 but most of them don't realise they're swinging. They just think they work for an advertising agency.

There are obvious questions: How does one go about registering as a swinger? Must you pay a subscription fee? Is there a board of swinging directors? What constitutes a quorum at a swingers' AGM? And who provides the refreshments afterwards? Above all, what are the benefits of being a registered swinger? Discounts on bulk purchases of paper towels and red-tinted light-bulbs upon presentation of a valid membership card? Special family rates at participating love shacks and motels? Frequent-flyer miles? There is so much to think about.

Even more boggling to the mind is the question of what scheme Cape Town will dream up to top this one. Brazil has already cornered the market in organ transplant tourism, and Indonesia has surely had the last word in hostage chic. In the marketing stakes, cities are like sharks. When they stop moving, they die. Just ask Tripoli, or Vladivostok – all the open marriages in the world won't save them now.

The foolish will always be with us

STYLE, NOVEMBER 2000

EVERYBODY, IT SOMETIMES seems, is trying to give up something. Some people are trying to give up the second helping of ice cream, some are trying to give up Internet porn, some people – alas, not enough – are trying to give up saying the phrase "Don't go there". I can only encourage more good citizens to join the fight against "Don't *even* go there!" Wear ribbons pinned to your shirts, get yourself a hotline – we need to stamp out the scourge. It is not hip. It doesn't make you sound like Queen Latifah or Jennifer Lopez. It makes you sound like Mrs Huxtable on *The Cosby Show*.

And don't get me started on the habit – so enthusiastically championed by Shaleen Surtie-Richards, that sounding leviathan of the linguistic deep – of exclaiming "Hel-*lo*!" It's hard to explain precisely what "Hel-*lo*!" means, although you would recognise it if you heard it. It is generally uttered in a sort of sarcastic Californian accent, and it is intended to indicate your vast fund of common sense and finger-snapping street-smarts: "People tell me I'm a good conversationalist. Hel-*lo*! I knew that!" It is the modern version of the word "Duh!", and it is so annoying it can make a grown man weep.

The worst thing about such lapses of good sense is that they are not confined solely to imbeciles. The people who say these things aren't only the kind of folk who wear stretch-pants beyond the age of 24, or who collect the soundtracks of Andrew Lloyd Webber's musicals, or who name their children Jarrod or Savannah, or who have their own talk shows on television. Some of them are in every way decent, likeable, unexceptionable individuals who suddenly, for no clear reason, lapse into the worst failure of taste.

It is a common phenomenon. Consider the perfectly sensible man, earning a good living, surrounded by a loving family, who one morning wakes up and decides to grow a moustache. Consider Mike Haysman's hairstyle. Consider the otherwise professional businesswoman, responsible and well-regarded by her peers, who takes it into her head that a cellphone that rings with the title track of *The Good, the Bad and the Ugly* is both quirky and entertaining.

There is no word in English that adequately describes these unpredictable social atrocities, so I have had to borrow one from the Italians. The word I have selected is *culacino*. Strictly speaking, it refers to the mark that is left by a wet glass placed on a table, but I like the sound of it anyway. A *culacino* can crop up anywhere. It can be a thing: a *Best of Queen* CD lurking in a music collection, a Jack Kerouac paperback, a ponytail, a pendant with your name written in hieroglyphics, a patchwork leather jacket. A *culacino* can be an action: ordering a Jack Daniel's and Coca-Cola, or telling a tale at the dinner table that involves your sexual habits during the 18 months when you were single. Worst of all, though, a *culacino* is an indelible Freudian slip, a moment of madness offering an insight past the civilised mask, into the terrible beigeness of the human heart.

The reason I raise all this is that a good friend of mine is considering ordering personalised licence plates. It is a source of tremendous anxiety. Can I still be the friend of a man with personalised licence plates? If so, do I run the risk of one day waking and thinking to myself, "I know, I'll get myself a licence plate with *Untitled* written on it. That'll be cool!?"

Let's get this straight: personalised licence plates are the worst kind of *culacino*. They are bumper stickers that cost R3000. They are fluffy Garfield toys stuck to the rear window with plastic suction cups. The kind of man who would have a personalised licence plate is the kind of man who would carry a plastic Porsche keyring. I say "man" but I am being unfair – you can bet your last glue-on fingernail that Felicia has a set of personalised plates.

Appalling as the very notion is, worse is the kind of guff that people select for their plates. 007 – there's an original thought. 140MPH – ooh, you devil. The new generation of personal plates specialise in words, allowing middle-aged men to call themselves STUD or PYTHON on national roads. Even more dire is when they take the opportunity to make private jokes with their pals. I saw one sad specimen with a plate proudly announcing: LUNCH. Was he a pizza deliveryman specialising in midday service? Was he a dyslexic member of the Ku Klux Klan? Had BREAKFAST already been taken? Who cares. Yep, buddy, that was worth every cent of R3000. It saved you having to find a T-shirt saying TOSSER.

In the sharks' den

OUT THERE, FEBRUARY 2001

A SMALL GIRL PRESSED her face against the window and screamed. I knew she was screaming, although I could hear no sound. She looked like Edvard Munch's little sister, though tinged with a deeper shade of blue.

I looked at another window and there was another small girl, also screaming. I felt obscurely pleased. I haven't made girls emote like that since the time I shoved a shuttlecock down my trousers and sang "It's not unusual" in a Welsh accent at the Sunday School talent contest. (I was, lest the *Carte Blanche* team come knocking at my door, 10 years old myself.)

Now, as then, the girls were screaming in terror. It puzzled me. As far as I could remember, I had left my shuttlecock at home. I turned. A 12-foot shark was moving towards me, eyes small and dark like cigarette burns in a wooden table, mouth jagged and ajar like a kitchen drawer overstuffed with cutlery. I backed away, air-tank rattling against the glass of the window, the air of my exhalation escaping in a great cloud of cowardly bubbles.

I wished I could reach through the glass for one of those small girls and hold her out in front of me. Or better, I wished Clint Lishman were there. You don't know Clint Lishman. He was the little boy who beat me into second place in the Sunday School talent contest with his musical teaspoons routine.

I'm not sure precisely what prompted me to scuba-dive in the predator tank of the Two Oceans Aquarium. Perhaps it was the prospect of having to spend a whole weekend in Cape Town. Perhaps it was the fact that I had to write another column this month. For a modest fee, the aquarium takes divers on an escorted 30-minute tour of the tank. The escort is a charming young lady carrying a thin wooden stick.

Sitting on the platform above the tank, preparing to enter, I had eyed the thin wooden stick with some suspicion. "That's it, eh?" I'd murmured. "That's it," she'd confirmed. "A thin wooden stick, hmm?" I'd ventured. "As you say," she'd agreed, "it is a stick that is thin and wooden."

It is a meaningful moment in a coward's life to slip off a platform into an enclosed space containing predators with teeth. All the more so when protected only by a slip of a lass with a thin wooden stick and a nasty sense of humour. My breath came quickly as we sank through the dappled blue; I patted the pockets of my wetsuit for a cigarette.

Water has its own spatial demands. It's not enough to look over your shoulder for approaching sharks; you must also check beneath and above you. It is a large tank, but well stocked. There is a large rock structure, and around it circle yellowtail and turtles, dories and dogfish and a vast stingray, easily two metres across. But my attention was taken with the five ragged toothed sharks of imposing size and mien. They are vast and impossibly silent. There is something terrible yet familiar about them, like the shadows of your own mind, or the stirrings of a bad dream before you've quite fallen asleep.

Familiarity brings comfort. They avoid humans, as wild animals do. Occasionally one or more becomes curious, but I find a firm prod with a thin wooden stick does the trick. When the big boy backed me up against the glass, I pushed him away with my hand, politely but firmly, as though I were a dieter and he a second helping of sticky pudding.

All the same, I felt heroic and terribly manly, like Sean Connery in *Thunderball*, or Nick Nolte in *The Deep*. I turned to the small girls to give them a rugged thumbs-up, but the attention spans of children these days are shameful. They had already wandered off to look at the sea urchins.

Men are from bars

STYLE, MAY 2001

I AM ASKED MANY annoying questions. We are all asked many annoying questions. Most questions, if you stop to think about them, are annoying, which is probably why so few people stop to think about them, either when asking or answering. There are many varieties of annoying question. "Is everything all right with your meal, folks?" is common enough, as is "He's not in his office, would you like to hold?" The magazine columnist has his own cross to bear. He must endure "Why don't you look as young in real life as you do in your photograph?" and "Why do the bubbles in a glass of champagne always go from the bottom up, even when the glass is upside down?" and "How tall is Clare O'Donoghue?"

There are some questions that simply cannot be resolved. For instance, I genuinely have no idea how many roads a man must walk down before you can call him a man, and I have even less idea why an entire generation of hippies should consider the wind to be a good place to look for the answer. These riddles arise in many guises. An annoying question I have been much asked over the years is: "What do you men talk about when you get together?" It happened again this morning.

Many women have tried to crack the mysteries of male bonding, but we have proved tougher than the DNA double helix; more wily than the human genome. The secret of male bonding has proved impenetrable to outside intelligence, simply because the secret of male bonding is precisely the same as the secret of men themselves: there is no secret. Women never quite believe this. "Nothing," they say to themselves, "can be quite that inert. There must be something beneath the surface."

Ladies, take it from me: men are simple. We are not Rubik's cubes. We are more like hula hoops or pet rocks. When you ask, in that adorable way, "What are you thinking about?" and we reply, "Oh, nothing," it's not because we are too lazy or stupid to think up an endearing lie ("Um, I was just wondering whether I would experience the symptoms of a sympathetic pregnancy when one day you are with child, honey?"). Well, it is because we are too lazy or stupid to think up an endearing lie, but it's also because we want to tell you the truth. There is, almost without fail, nothing going on inside.

I sometimes catch myself at odd moments of the day and realise that I have thought about nothing and had no discernible emotion for several hours – sometimes weeks – in a row. Does it make me feel null and void? Somehow incomplete? Hell, no. I generally pull out a footstool and try to squeeze in a couple more hours while the going's good. I have lost track of the number of times successive partners have yelled at me: "Hunger does not count as an emotion!"

But this is not the whole truth. Of course we do, every so often, feel things, and that is when male bonding truly comes into its own. Here is a manly truth not often uttered: sometimes we do open our hearts to our mates in the bar and speak the dark fears and tender secrets of our fledgling souls, and we do so more easily than we would with our lady-folk. We do it there because we feel safer. Also because we've been drinking, but mainly because we feel safer.

Gather close, ladies, for what I am about to say is an important key to grasping the perverse simplicity of the male heart: the reason we feel safer talking to our mates is that we know that deep down they don't care. They care for us, of course, but they aren't going to think too long about our problems, and they're not going to raise the subject when everyone's sober. They won't think it odd and hurtful when the matter is never raised again, and they certainly won't expect it to be woven into the texture of everyday life and ongoing relationships. There are no consequences, and if there is anything in this world that appeals to the deepest part of a man, it is an act without consequences.

The male method of empathy when hearing a sad story is to top it with an even sadder story of your own. And that is as it should be. But such interchanges are blessed rare. For the most part, what men talk about when you're not around is pretty much the same as what they talk about when you are, only with fewer words. Often we scarcely talk at all. It doesn't really matter what we say; it's just nice to know that no one's really listening.

Sometimes a car is only a car

STYLE, JUNE 2001

I AM NOT REALLY a man. No, it's true, and it's time the truth came out: I am not really a man. It's not that I've been trying to hide it from you; I didn't know it myself until this morning. There I was, flipping through the pages of a glossy women's magazine, as one does when doing penance for sins committed and yet to come, when I came across one of those snappy polls that always purport to be the product of months of careful psychometric testing, but which were really dreamed up by a junior office worker over her lunch break. Are you a man? the magazine yelled, or perhaps shrilled. "Take our test and find out!"

The thinking, evidently, is that if you are really a man, you will be able to place a tick next to each of these cunningly devised questions. Shrugging, as one does with a monkey on one's shoulder, I took the test. There was the usual penetrative material ("Do you have a Y chromosome?"; "Do you have an Adam's apple?"; "Are your buttons on the right-hand side of your shirt?"), and a couple of a more stylish bent ("Can you make a martini?"; "Do you dislike any movie featuring an unshaven Frenchman and the women he loves?"). I was merrily chugging through, dispensing ticks like a tap-dancing water buffalo, when I came across Question 17(a): "Is your car more important than your girlfriend?" Questions 17 (b) and (c) were of similar inflection: "Do you spend more time with your car than your family?"; "Would you rather own an Italian sports car than a full head of hair?" and suchlike guff.

I ground to a halt. The truth is that I can't be a man, because I genuinely don't give a toss about cars. I sit in bars and listen to men around me talking about cars, and I wish I were at a baby shower or a press conference. I wouldn't know an Audi TT from a kick in the trousers. I don't even know if I'm spelling "TT" correctly.

If you'd ever seen my car you'd appreciate what I'm saying. My car is not a pretty sight. It's small and scuffed and other cars have driven into it. Come to that, I have driven it into other cars. My car is twisted and ugly. I leave it unlocked with the window rolled down, and nothing happens to it, because thieves are afraid of my car. They see it and say to themselves: "Oo-er." They're scared that, if they enter my car, they'll be attacked by wolves, or find that it's a time machine, much bigger inside than outside, that will whisk them away to Pluto, or to a South Carolina bayou. It isn't money or principle that makes me drive such a car; it's that I can't be bothered to do anything about it.

When people joshingly insult my car, as they do, they frame their merry banter as though my car were an extension of me. "Ho ho," they say, "things must be tough in the column-writing business" or "Darrel, Darrel, you're too young to give up on life." I find it puzzling.

My car – let me make this clear – is not an extension of me. My books, on the other hand, are an extension of me, but no one ever comes around and says: "Oh, Raymond Chandler, eh? That's a bit downmarket, isn't it? Surely you can afford to upgrade to Umberto Eco by now?"

Don't get me wrong – I understand the attraction of driving a powerful car. Like any man, I want to drive the Aston Martin in *Goldfinger*, especially if it will help me with Pussy Galore. But I do know that driving it won't turn me into Sean Connery.

Besides which, I can't be fussed to learn the mechanics of the ejector seat. (I had a car with an ejector seat when I was younger, of course, but it was no good on dates. I would become all fingers and thumbs and accidentally eject my date ahead of schedule. Premature ejection is a heavy burden for a young man to carry.)

So I'm afraid I don't understand the fascination with owning the most expensive car in the office. I already have a personality, and it came free (though not easy) and didn't need to be paid off over five years, with ruinous insurance premiums.

I suppose it's a fair trade-off – no one is going to steal my car, and no one is going to steal the personalities of those guys with their white BMWs. Of course, I understand that cars mean something mystical to women as well. Women – not all women, just the type I don't like – seem to feel that a man who owns a nice car is a good bet as husband and father to their children. I am not really surprised. In the animal world, female baboons feel the same way about the male baboon with the bluest bottom. It makes the same kind of sense.

Whose line is it, anyway?

STYLE, SEPTEMBER 2001

I AM NOT A fuddy-duddy. (Although, I suppose, anyone who would voluntarily use the word "fuddy-duddy" in public is demonstrating some marked signs of fuddiness, not to mention more than a whiff of duddidom.) I am, in the main, an open-minded sort of fellow. The darkling byways of human behaviour may sometimes sadden me, but they no longer have the power to shock.

Indeed, I have myself known a wild night or two. Why, there was the time when I was hitch-hiking to Grahamstown and I was picked up by two Rhodes students of indeterminate gender carrying a five-litre vat of Kool-aid ... but you don't want to hear about that. Suffice it to say that I still wake of a morning, screaming "The sheep is on fire! The sheep is on fire!"

So understand that I am not being more than necessarily curmudgeonly when I say: Haven't we gotten over this whole drug thing yet? Seriously, it was fun when we were kids – okay, it's still fun – but we're adults now. Aren't we meant to have some, some ... oh, what's the word? ... reminds me of a song by Aretha Franklin ... *dignity*, that's it. I'm not even talking about the sad cases of a certain age who pull their stretchy T-shirts over their rounded bellies and go paddling out into the world of children with a couple of Ecstasy pills in the coin compartment of their wallets. Their idea of dignity is to make a point of never being the *first* person to pull off their stretchy T-shirt and wave it around above their heads.

Not much better, though, are the processions of grown-ups who come trotting back to the dinner table from the bathroom, sniffing generously and suddenly eager to discuss the last three episodes of *Survivor*, or Kant's idea of the sublime, or the great idea they've had for opening a new store that is a clothing boutique but also a place where you can buy organic vegetables and sushi. "Everyone likes sushi," said my neighbour at the dinner table recently, her eyes rotating in opposite directions.

"I don't," I said. We looked at each other blankly, which is as it should be. I considered adding my feelings on the subject of organic vegetables and indeed clothing boutiques, but the moment had passed.

It's not that I don't understand the special pleasures of slipping off with an illegal substance and a credit card and the same rolled up hundred-dollar note you have been carrying around ever since you went on holiday to New York in 1993. It's fun and naughty and all those things to which we as adults cling, in the forlorn hope of ensuring that there is some small corner of us that will be forever young. But it soon becomes a little tatty, frankly. It's possible to overrate the feel-good factor of crouching in a damp cubicle, bringing your face closer to the porcelain of a public toilet than your mother ever imagined in her fond dreams of your future, for no better purpose than to ingest a questionable powder only recently excavated from the small intestine of a large Nigerian.

There is nothing really glamorous about it, is there? Tiptoeing off to the men's room with an entourage of adoring cadgers and slow-eyed party veterans isn't exactly going to whisk you away to the Oscars or to the whitewashed hotel balcony in the south of France. Especially not with the quality of drugs available locally. Learn from the discomfort of my old pal Donald, who as a youth on holiday in Cape Town tried a short snifter of a Schedule A narcotic that had been liberally, not to say vindictively, and we would add amusingly, mixed with an industrial strength laxative. He spent the next three days in a variety of public bathrooms around the Cape, though not with five of his closest friends. From this he learned to avoid drugs, and Cape Town.

There are many good reasons to frown upon drugs. They encourage drug dealers, for one. They cause you to forget where you left your car keys, for another. For a third thing, they make sure you only realise that you've misplaced your car keys after you've somehow managed to drive home.

Most compelling argument for me, though, is that drugs diminish dinner-party conversation. There is more of it, but that more adds up to so much less. Haven't we all had that uncomfortable experience of arriving at a dinner where a thoughtful host has filled the salt cellar with cocaine, but forgotten to tell you because he's still looking for his car keys, and the next thing you know, you're chattering away about, um, well, I can't remember what it was we were talking about, and anyway my tongue's a little numb, but while we're on the subject, I've though about something even more interesting – let's talk about me!

Don't call me, baby

STYLE, OCTOBER 2001

I DO NOT HAVE children. I have never had children, although I did once have the mumps, and on several occasions I have had house guests. I don't know if you have ever had house guests. On the whole I preferred the mumps. Mumps may cause a certain amount of physical discomfort and even temporary disfigurement, but they never say: "I wonder what's on the other channel?" or "So what are we doing tomorrow?"

At any rate, I have had better luck avoiding children than I have avoiding house guests. I avoid children the way sensible folk avoid an in-flight meal, or Mark Gillman. In the main, it is easy to avoid children. They are smaller than you and cannot run as fast, and if worse comes to worst and you are forced to fight, you can count on your greater readiness to punch dirty. Still, increasingly I am finding myself thrust into the proximity of infants.

I have long been of the opinion that aeroplanes should be divided into three classes: Business, Economy and Infant. My proposals are still tentative, but at present I conceive of Infant class as a lead-lined canister somewhere in the hold.

I'm always irate when I'm told that I cannot bring a second piece of hand-baggage onto the plane with me. The last time it happened, I pointed at some Russian-looking woman brushing wisps of hair out of her face. "But look at her!" I complained. "She's carrying two pieces of luggage!" "One of those is a baby, sir," said the steward firmly. For some reason, women carrying babies onto aeroplanes look Russian to me. I don't know why. "But my hand-baggage isn't going to scream and discharge fluids," I yelled. "It'll just sit there under my seat! No one will even know it's there! Tell me true – wouldn't you rather have my stylish hand-valise with retractable handle on your plane than that squirming mass of barely differentiated epithelial cells?" But as you will know if you have ever tried to rage against the monstrous regimen of infants, it was to no avail.

Babies are everywhere these days. Worse, babies are where I am whenever I go into a public place. Babies have become the new accessory. They are what

Alsatian dogs were to Capetonians a few years ago: people just can't seem to go out to a restaurant without them. Happily, I have not as yet noticed any babies with red ethnic-print bandannas knotted around their necks, but that is a very small mercy indeed.

What's more, nowadays I can't even fight back by lighting a cigarette and pointedly exhaling into the push-pram that some simpering Russian woman has parked next to my table. That's what the new smoking regulations are for! To make restaurants more baby-friendly! It's an outrage. The only reason I took up smoking in the first place was that I happened to notice a packet with the warning sign: "Caution: smoking is harmful to children." *Aha, I thought. All I need is a nicotine habit and no right-thinking parents will bring their bundles of mewing fluids anywhere near me. My life will be shorter, but infinitely more elegant.*

Still, although my sworn enmity to other people's children holds as firm as ever, I am slowly coming round to the notion that one of my own might not be the end of the world, one day when self-cleaning infant-wear has been invented. I sat down this morning and drew up a list of the things that children have going for them. The list is surprisingly impressive. For instance:

- Children are almost always small of stature, which makes them useful for getting to those hard-to-reach places in the home.
- Children make very desirable Scrabble opponents, being both easy to beat and fun to cheat.
- Children on the whole ask far better questions than adults. "Why is the sky blue?" and "Why does mommy wear different clothes to you?" are on the whole more likely to receive a favourable response than "Where is your column?" or "Why haven't you called?"

Children have other recommendations. Seldom do you find them wearing too much aftershave; only rarely do they pluck up the courage to make unnatural sexual requests; they are never of the opinion that you behave too childishly.

So I am gradually softening towards the wee folk, but I warn you, new parents of the nation: do not take this as a sign of weakness. Do not consider that open seat next to me as an invitation to sit down with your malodorous gurgler. Be cautioned: I have a packet of Stuyvesants, and I'm not afraid to use them.

Sealed with a kiss

STYLE, JANUARY 2002

S AY, WHEN LAST did you receive a love letter? I don't mean one of those insinuating SMS messages with misspelt words and no capital letters that a low class of person likes to send from bars in the early hours of the morning. Nor do I mean one of those dreary e-mail messages that arrive on your work desk and are supposed to make you think "Oh, how thoughtful!" when really they are just three lines and one of those faces created by typing a certain sequence of punctuation marks.

No, I mean a genuine, old-fashioned, handwritten love letter, sealed in an envelope with your name written on the front. Remember how your heart raced and your hands trembled! Remember that feeling, very much like swooning, when you saw your name written by the hand – the very hand! – of the one you love? Ah, the giddy, almost disbelieving joy of holding the letter and knowing that this very paper had been held by your beloved, that this paper has been marked by the indelible scrawls and squiggles of his or her love for you. It is a real object, an object that has physically travelled from them to you, not a screen that at the touch of a button will become a balance sheet or a mailbox or a magazine column. It is a letter of love, and can be nothing else.

Of all the things I miss from an earlier age – telegrams, say, and drive-ins and dressing for dinner and doctors that make house calls – I think it is the demise of the love letter that most impoverishes our modern lives. My infatuation started early. When I was 12 Shelly Whitfield gave me a love letter. Actually Shelley Whitfield didn't give it to me – she gave it to Joanna Thurley to give to me. Or was it Marge Golightly? I forget. But I have not forgotten that letter.

I carried it away, hot in the pocket of my school shirt, burning against my boyish breast, until I could open it behind the scoreboard on the cricket field. Shelley Whitfield must have borrowed her mother's lipstick as well as raiding her stationery drawer, because the outside of the envelope was patterned with Shelley's crimson lip-prints. I couldn't breathe as I held it in my hand. For weeks – ah, who am I kidding? – for years to come I studied that envelope and those lip-prints, examining the pattern of folds and swirls and cracks and valleys immortalised in lipstick. I blushed at the scarlet intimacy. Today, if I close my eyes and sit quietly, I can still remember the mingled scent of lipstick and paper, and it makes the breath catch in my throat.

I wrote back to Shelley Whitfield as passionately as I could, although that lark of applying lip-prints in boot polish didn't really have the desired results. Today, if I close my eyes and sit quietly, I can still taste school shoe. It ended of course, as all such passions must end. The differences were too great between us. She liked Bonnie Tyler and I liked Joan Jett and the Blackhearts. Besides, I was too shy ever actually to speak to her. Whenever we bumped into each other at the bicycle racks of a morning and she said "Hello", as she sometimes did, I would stammer and splutter and ring my bell to cover my confusion. Then I would snap her bra straps and run away. Did I but know it, that would not be the last relationship to end because of a lack of communication.

But that letter made an indelible impression on me. I cherish all the love letters I have ever sent or received. The love letter is erotic and poignant in a way that e-mails and telephone calls never can be. The love letter is about waiting and longing and delay, about calling up your beloved in your mind like a ghost. And that, really, is the best part, isn't it? There is a ninth-century Arabic poem by the medieval Zarif Al-Washsa that sighs:

To love is to kiss, in your mind, a hand or arm
or to send letters whose spells are stronger than witchcraft.
Love is nothing but this; when lovers sleep together, love perishes.

I can't say I encourage too fanatical an adherence to that last part, but Al-Washsa reminds us of a fine truth. I urge you: send a love letter to the one you love. Write it by hand. Send it today. Moisten the envelope flap with your tears of longing, or joy, or repentance. Bring some of the magic back. Write that letter.

Survival of the fittest

STYLE, MARCH 2002

I BELIEVE IN KEEPING FIT. I do. But the difference between me and the gaggle of earnest citizens in tracksuit pants who go filing into aerobics sessions and spinning classes, or who shuffle through the streets in the early morning hours like a string of crumpled washing looking for a line, togged out in sweatbands and running shoes and the facial expressions of St Sebastian being pierced by arrows, is that I understand what being fit means. I have read my Darwin.

They survive best, Charles Darwin told us, who are fittest for their environment. He was a canny one, that Darwin. I have given the matter some thought, and for the life of me I cannot imagine the situation in which my urban environment will demand survival skills involving pedalling a stationary bicycle while a frightening-looking stranger blows a whistle at me. Ditto jogging. I can understand that, centuries ago, the ability to run from Durban to Pietermaritzburg could conceivably have given you the edge over your neighbour, who might have to *walk* from Durban to Pietermaritzburg, but frankly today I just don't see that being the case. Even with the state of public transport nowadays, you can usually make some sort of plan involving wheels and an engine.

But I do not shirk my responsibilities. Every day I perform exercises to keep fit for my environment. Wrist rotations keep me limber both for handling a steering wheel and signing credit card slips; programmes of slow and regular breathing prepare me for standing in queues at the supermarket check-out. Ocular stamina training enables me to keep my eyes fixed on the numbers in a public elevator, without ever having to make eye-contact with strangers. I have learnt to drink hard liquor without falling to the ground and hurting myself.

Still, there are those that cling to their outmoded faith in physical tone and cardiovascular robustness. Take President Bush, for instance. No really, take him. In January the world sniggered to read of his brush with death. Apparently while seated on the sofa, watching football on television, the defender of the free world choked on a pretzel and pitched face-first on the floor. His personal physician later issued a statement blaming not the pretzel but "the president's overly strenuous work-out regime". Quite so. Bush may be well conditioned for plodding along a treadmill, but modern man is more likely to find himself sitting on a sofa watching a football match than he is to find himself plodding along a treadmill. For an urban survivalist such as myself that sofa would have offered no peril. And without bragging, I am fairly confident I would have known what to do with that pretzel.

At least the exercise industry in America recognises the need to diversify fitness training to accommodate the various challenges of the modern world. The Crunch gym chain has long offered aerobics classes in such specialised disciplines as Gospel Moves (should you find yourself in a Rhema church without a clear run for the exit), Recreational Hopscotch (should you be challenged to a duel by a pack of 12-year-old girls) and Circus Sports (should you, uh ... oh, I don't know). Their newest offering is a class in – I'm not making this up – Cardio Striptease.

The idea behind these exotica, I suppose, is to keep punters interested. The brochure for Cardio Striptease promises "an hour of erotic movement, culminating in a 25-minute stripathon". Whether or not the spandex actually leaves the body I cannot ascertain, but consider if you dare the vision of a troop of bouncing soccer moms thrusting pelvises and tweaking imaginary nipple caps and twirling leg-warmers above their heads. Now consider the kind of paunchy male villain in shiny shorts queuing up to join the class. Oh, the humanity.

There are other new ideas in aerobics. Bhangra Dancing offers a fun-filled workout as you master the traditional dance of the Sikhs; Poledancing is Cardio Striptease with, well, a pole. In some gyms poles are provided. Others make poles available at discount prices. Perhaps most alarming is Cycle Karaoke, which is described as "singing while spinning". I can see how such a class might be useful for eager young actors auditioning for Andrew Lloyd Webber's new show, set against the timeless backdrop of the Tour de France, but for the rest of us it sounds like something very close to hell. (Mind you, so does Andrew Lloyd Webber's new show, set against the timeless backdrop of the Tour de France.)

So keep on training, ye exercise fans, and I'll keep practising how to sit on the couch and watch TV. If I should find myself having to strip all night to save my life, or dance to the death in a darkened Sikh alleyway, I may regret my decision. I'll take my chances.

No brains, please – we're hippies

SL, JUNE 2002

H IPPIES ANNOY ME. Seriously, I can't bear hippies. I don't even mean the kind that sit in Knysna beading their moccasins and calling their children organic names like Walnut or Thrush. Them I would shoot on sight if I had good enough eyesight and a long enough barrel to reach Knysna. Nor do I mean the sort that tattoo the Chinese pictograph for "Unclean" on their lower backs and stumble around on Sunday afternoons with beach sand on their bare feet, still humming whatever tune was last playing at their trance party and paying with daddy's credit card. No, I don't even mean them.

These days hippies come in all shapes and sizes. Some wear shoes. Some even have jobs that don't involve trying to persuade other people with jobs to hand over cash for some aesthetically displeasing item that has been grown, plucked or woven the night before. There are some hippies that are indistinguishable from normal folk. They look like us, they dress like us, they wash their hair with the same frequency, but sooner or later they give themselves away.

Hippies, in my book, are all those annoying critters out there who spout anti-human hogwash. I don't mean anti-people, mind. Hippies are keen on people. Not as keen as on whales, squirrels, seaweed and whatever small or large animal a macrobiotic creature might be (and if you know, please don't tell me), but keen nonetheless. No, I mean anti-human. Because the hippy inclination is to sniff at the very things that make us human.

Hippies rabbit on about love and harmony and oneness with all living things. Hogwash, I say (which is a hygienic process entirely wasted on our tasty friends the swine, and altogether more appropriate for hippies of the Cape Town variety). It is not human nature to seek oneness with all living things. Humans survived because we found a way to make sure our interests took priority over the interests of other living things. We eat 'em. We wear 'em. We milk them, whether they like it or not. We hitch ploughs to them and when they harm us, like tapeworms or germs or white ants in our floor-boards, we figure out ways to kill them.

If we couldn't do those things, we wouldn't be here. If the little furry mammals that we once were had had a genetic predisposition to trying to live in harmony with all living creatures, a sabre-toothed tiger would be writing this column for an audience of woolly mammoths. And that just wouldn't work. Woolly mammoths don't have opposable thumbs. How would you turn the pages? You're not going to pay good money just to stare at the cover all month.

We're never going to live in harmony with all living creatures, or even with each other. We're not made that way. We are made to seek advantage for ourselves and our families. I am not suggesting that wars are good and kicking animals is fine. I am saying that we must recognise what we are, and the best we can do is find practical ways to curb ourselves, rather than nonsense platitudes.

Fighting for peace is not always a contradiction in terms. We did it in 1939. We did it because we had to. And it worked. The hippies sang sappy songs decrying the Cold War and the nuclear race, but that worked too. The generals, it turns out, were *right*. There wasn't a Third World War between Russia and the West, and there will not be one. There is a message there: peace – even the limited peace of which we are capable – is not achieved by blowing each other kisses. It is achieved by enforcing treaties and no-fly-zones and inspections of nuclear facilities. It is achieved through boring, ugly things like politics. It's not pretty, and it's not hippy, but that's who we are.

Academy of flirting

CAPE TIMES, 12 JULY 2002

I AM ALWAYS LOOKING for ways to make money. It is a family characteristic. Mad Uncle Roy spent some months in various international courts trying to enforce his patent on the wheel, and Grampa Ned depleted the family fortune trying to popularise ferret-racing as a professional sport ("Cheaper than a dog; more fun than a horse" was his motto, though sadly not anyone else's).

Our ideas, admittedly, are not always good, but this time I have a winner. I am going to start a School of Flirting in Cape Town. That's right, a School of Flirting. Or perhaps I will call it an Academy of Flirting. Academies are sexier than schools.

My academy will teach people to flirt. Flirting is an art, and like all arts it exists to make life more bearable. It adds sparkle to your day, pep to your stride. Unexpected flirting is like a shot of tequila, except afterwards it doesn't cause you to shudder and make an unattractive face. At least, not if you've done it right. Flirting need not lead to anything – most often it doesn't. Usually it is not intended to. It is simply a slight dance to distant music, a *pas de deux* of possibility that leaves both parties feeling better about themselves and about the potential of life to surprise us. (I hope I need not add that flirting does not involve surprising your colleagues with hearty hugs and kisses. At all times when flirting, and indeed when doing anything intimate, it is important to keep the image of Peter Marais far from your mind.)

Cape Town urgently needs an Academy of Flirting. Flirting is not big in Cape Town. There are plenty of kids in short skirts and tight T-shirts with saucy messages on the front, but that is not flirting. There are plenty of drunken businessmen wearing blue shirts and yellow ties and red faces willing to buy you drinks at pseudo-Irish bars on week nights, but that is not flirting either.

Flirting is an adult thing, and it doesn't leer. It lies not in what is said, but in the spaces between. It is in that fine electric field that springs up between flirter and flirtee. (In the successful flirt, of course, flirter and flirtee take turns to change positions. If you know what I mean.)

The difficulty for my academy will be finding suitably qualified instructors. David Niven, say, or the younger Lauren Bacall. Personally, I am dead useless at flirting. When I try to flirt, I spend so much time thinking about what I should have just done that I forget what I should do next. A friend once tried to teach me. She had just returned from New York, where she had attended a Flirting Seminar. They have such things in New York. Frankly, they need them. New Yorkers are even worse at flirting than Capetonians. The difference is that New Yorkers are bad flirts because they are very busy. Capetonians are bad flirts because they don't really like people.

My friend ran me through the flirting rudiments: the eye contact, the slight pause before speaking, the twinkling eye. I tried it, but my eyes bulged like Homer Simpson's, and the slight pause before speaking made me resemble a Serbian war criminal listening to the translation in his earphones before deciding how to plead. "Why are you rolling your eyes?" demanded my friend.

"I'm trying to make them twinkle," I said.

"You're frightening me," she said. "It's horrible. Stop it."

"I can't!" I cried. "Once you start twinkling, you can't just stop!"

So do come to my academy, dear reader. But don't take that seat in the back row, left corner. That's where I'll be sitting.

Nature is not our friend

SL, AUGUST 2002

N OW DON'T GET me wrong: I am not opposed to nature, precisely. That would be a foolish position to take. Nature has much to recommend it. Rainbows, for instance, are popular among those of a romantic bent, and who among us does not smile to hear the sound of the breeze stirring the high leaves of the sheltering tree, or the chirruping of the sentimental songbird? Ah, yes, these are lovely things, all part of nature's rich bounty. And you might add others: the o'er looming mountains, say, or the majestic clouds, or the delicate whorls of the wayside flower, or the playful leaping of our finny friends the dolphins.

I'm just saying that we can get a little carried away with nature. Nature is all very well in its place, but its place is over there, outside the city limits. Unless you are one of those irredeemable losers who packed up their checked flannel shirts in a cardboard suitcase and moved to the Knysna forest to make shoes out of bark, or you are reading this while cast away on a desert island in the wide salty wastes of the south Atlantic (in which case, my congratulations to whoever is in charge of this magazine's subscription services. That delivery-in-a-bottle idea is really paying off), you almost certainly live in the city. Or if not the city exactly, then some place like Port Elizabeth or Bloemfontein. And that means that you reap the benefits of civilisation, which is to say, the triumph of humanity over nature.

As much as city dwellers whine about the noise and the grime and the traffic, it is better than the alternative. The alternative was droughts and floods and sabre-toothed tigers and Apache raiding parties that carried off the womenfolk, and your uncle Jethro approaching you carrying a mallet and a pair of pliers if you complained about toothache. The city is the home of modern medicine and hot running water and lengthened life expectancy and meals that you don't have to hunt and shoot and pluck yourself. Plus, you go live in a cave on a mountainside and then try to get lucky with the ladies on a Saturday night. See how far you get.

But human beings are an ungrateful mob. Even as we lie in our hot baths or eat cornflakes with milk that still hasn't curdled even though it was extracted from the cow more than six hours ago, still there is a tendency to sneer at science and civilisation. People today will buy anything, provided it can somehow be implied that it has nothing to do with modern science.

The other day – as I was passing through my local pharmacy, something I like to do to keep up to date with the latest developments in self-medication – I noticed an advertisement for a herbal supplement. "Nature's caffeine!" declared the advertisement. Think about that for a moment. Where do these people imagine caffeine comes from? Do they think coffee is some kind of synthetic drug cooked up by a bunch of mad scientists in Berlin? It doesn't seem to matter. People see the word *natural* and they assume it must be better for you than something that doesn't have the word *natural* attached. If the cigarette companies had clear thinking PR departments, they would long ago have sold themselves as "Tobacco! Nature's Nicorette patch!"

Recently I had a dose of the flu and popped into the chemist to stock up on those products that I love so: pills and fizzy things that make you sleep and not hurt so much. Clutching these precious fruits of civilisation, I was making my way to my car when I bumped into someone I knew. She clucked and tutted at my purchases. "That stuff is bad for you," she sighed. "You should get a natural remedy."

She went on to mention one of those appalling garden potions: milkwort, or essence of frangipani, or hemlock, or something that once grew in some Knysna hippy's Wellington boot during the rainy season. "Natural, eh?" I said.

"Yes," she replied, "natural is better for you."

I glared at her and sniffed. "Has it occurred to you," I asked, "that influenza is natural. Tumours, thrombosis, cataracts, snakebites ... these things are all natural. I want what is not natural. I want to be healthy all the time. I want to live longer than I would in nature. Human beings made these drugs," I shook the packet, "and human beings know more about what is good for human beings than nature ever did." I sneezed, and shook my fist at the skies. "Nature," I told her, "is not our friend."

You would do well to remember that, dear readers. Sip your wheatgrass and decry modern farming methods if you must, but when the Apache raiders start circling, don't come crying to me.

The sound of one hand clapping

CAPE TIMES, 2 AUGUST 2002

'MASTURBATION IS THE thinking man's television," said someone once. I forget precisely who said it – it wasn't Woody Allen, and I would be very much surprised to learn that it was William Shakespeare. I think we can rule out Emily Brontë, although I doubt the sentiment would have been far from her heart. I am also not sure that was precisely the quote. It may have been "Television is the unthinking man's masturbation," although I doubt it.

I am not sure I entirely endorse the sentiment. Television lasts longer, for one thing, and has more variety (especially if you have satellite) and can be operated by remote control. Still, masturbation has its own charms.

Masturbation has been on my mind lately. You may not consider that masturbation is a fit subject of conversation in a respectable organ that may fall into the unscrupulous hands of small children, but if you think that small children need to learn about masturbation from a daily newspaper, yours was a very dull childhood indeed. I am however aware – indeed, I am frequently reminded by certain members of the public – that this column finds its best use lining the birdcages of the peninsula, so if you find that next week Polly's demands are of a nature more clamorous and unnatural than a cuttlefish and a cracker, I suppose you will have to blame me.

There has been something of a hubbub and brouhaha in recent weeks because two of those critters on *Big Brother* – a man and a woman – are apparently in the habit of pleasing themselves loudly and with abandon in a variety of locations, including the jacuzzi, which is just about what I would expect of a jacuzzi. I have a phobia about jacuzzis. I have never so much as dandled a toe in a jacuzzi. I always have the awful suspicion that five minutes before I arrived, someone had been pleasing themselves loudly and with abandon in that jacuzzi. Even the word "jacuzzi" makes me uncomfortable. It sounds like the surname of a pimp in the old quarter of Napoli.

But I digress. I am not surprised that housemates should be making recourse to the comfort of the hand. Frankly I expected more would. When I first saw them I remember uttering a sentence on the subject that began with the words, "What a bunch of". But while there are occasions in which masturbation is clearly inappropriate – in public, say, or while preparing the main course at your dinner party – I would suggest that today it is a practice to be actively encouraged. Instead of being frowned upon as the resort of the lonely and the teenaged and the married, masturbation should be celebrated as a positive sexual option that is safe, as well as easy and convenient.

Oh, there are many good things to say about masturbation. No one ever became resentful because they masturbated, then didn't call themselves the next day. No one ever performed an unnatural act on themselves without their consent. Plus, you never have to fake a headache. If you're not in the mood, well, it really isn't an issue. But mainly it is safe. No one ever made themselves pregnant or gave themselves a disease. I am not suggesting you sit your children down and tell them about masturbating. That is just creepy. Besides, they already know. I am just suggesting that it would be better for all if masturbation were more purposefully embraced as a leisure option. It is not often my columns have a social message, but this one does: "Masturbators of the world, unite!" Although I suppose that might be defeating the purpose.

Here's to the ladies

CAPE TIMES, 8 AUGUST 2002

S AY, DID YOU know it's Women's Day tomorrow? No, don't roll your eyes like that, Women's Day is important. *Women* are important, if you want my opinion on it. If it weren't for women, we would all be men, and that is just not a fate worth considering.

Imagine a world without women. I mean a world other than certain bars in Somerset Road. If we were all men, no one would ever stop to ask for directions, so when we became lost in our cars we would just drive around in circles forever, scowling at the street signs. Over enough time, the whole world would be on the roads, just driving and driving, everyone growing old looking for wherever it is he was originally going. Imagine the traffic jam. Imagine the road rage. It would be the end of life as we know it. This is how the world would end: not with a bang but with a bunch of guys braining each other with hockey sticks.

Women are important for many other reasons too. If it weren't for women, no one would ever make their beds. Is there a man in the world who would make his bed in the morning if he were left to his own devices? I don't know why women consider the made bed to be such a symbol of all that is good about civilisation, but they do. Women are about as likely to leave their home with the bed unmade as we are likely to leave the bar with some beer left in the glass. What would the world be like if no one made their bed? Would the fabric of society unravel? Would the mask fall from our savage faces? I don't know, and thanks to women, I will never have to find out.

Women single-handedly keep the crockery industry in business. If there were no women, who would bother with saucers? Who would buy a sugar bowl, much less use it for holding sugar? Even dinner plates wouldn't survive without women. If the cardboard box didn't leak while it was being delivered, I always say, there is no call to remove the pizza from it now.

Oh, I like women for many reasons. They buy more books than men do. Admittedly, they mainly buy *The Naked Chef* and inspiring Oprah book-club choices about women who overcome personal hardship or the kidnapping of their children, but that is better than nothing. If it weren't for women, our book stores would sell nothing at all besides the memoirs of American CEOs, and weak parables about corporate change. No, women are great. They smell better than men, provided they do not happen to be carrying a baby or a cat, and they live longer than men do. Especially those rural Frenchwomen. The oldest women in the world always seems to be living in the French countryside. Bless them. If I weren't able to say, "There is a 120-year-old woman in rural France who has spent her entire life smoking and drinking," I would have no defence for my lifestyle whatsoever.

Good for women, I say. They get the thumbs-up from me. Ladies, I wish you a good Women's Day tomorrow. I am not entirely sure what women do on Women's Day, just as I am not entirely sure what women do between the time they say "Okay, I'm ready to go" and the time they are actually ready to go, but that is none of my business. Whatever you gals will be doing tomorrow, you deserve to enjoy it. Here's to you.

The penis

CAPE TIMES, 30 AUGUST 2002

IT IS A peculiar thing, the penis. Oh yes it is, and don't pretend you haven't noticed. I don't ordinarily much think about the penis – like the hidden shafts and sealed chambers of an Egyptian pyramid, I consider it a mystery best left unprobed – but recently I found myself in a situation in which I could scarce avoid the damn thing. Everywhere I turned, there was a penis. Penises jiggled and bobbled around me like a field of wheat after a long dry season.

Where was I, you ask with narrowed eyes? Was I in the forest with a band of painted men carrying tom-toms and trying to reconnect with their inner selves? Was I in the casting offices of a popular daily South African soap opera? None of the above (or, in a way, all of the above). I was in the changing room of a local gym.

Under normal circumstances I am not much by way of a gym-goer, but I had lost a bet and … oh, it's a long story. It is tricky, being in the men's locker-room, because you just can't stop yourself inspecting the fittings and appliances. There I was, surrounded by the naked male form in its various incarnations and configurations, and I don't mind telling you I was fascinated.

Obviously I have seen a penis before. Everyone takes a sidelong glance at the fellow beside you in the men's room, but that is just idle curiosity, and from that angle you aren't doing much more than absent-mindedly comparing size. But there in the locker-room you are exposed to the bewildering range of styles and shapes that constitute the irregular legion of the male member. Frankly, ladies – and some gentlemen – I don't know how you do it.

Under any circumstances the penis is not one of nature's showcases. Unlike the fiery sunset, say, or snapshots of the noble whale sporting in the salty brine, the penis is unlikely to be included in Mother Nature's collected portfolio of "My Best Work". Still, I can tell you after my day of research, there are some that pass muster, provided your aesthetic criteria are not too rigorous. Neatness and symmetry and a sense of your proper place will get you far in this world. But ye gods there are some infernal works out there.

I don't want to be too graphic, but let me just say that there are stranger things between the thighs of men than are dreamed of in our philosophies. One particularly misshapen corner of the room resembled nothing so much as a convention of those kiddy-party clowns who specialise in tying elongated balloons into humorous shapes. With my own eyes I spotted at least two dachshunds, several Loch Ness monsters and one weirdly lifelike rendition of Darren Scott.

It was a harrowing afternoon, and it left me with a renewed respect for the sheer audacity of phallocentric patriarchy. Well done, men. Any group with the cheek to construct an entire system of myth and value around such frankly unpromising raw material deserves all the unfair advantages it can lay its hands on. But mainly I was left with a profound appreciation for the heterosexual women of the world. You – yes, you – are our real heroes. Oh, how sorely at times you must be tempted to buy yourself a shapeless denim jacket and a pool cue and a spiky haircut and move to Observatory. How you can even look us in the eye without bursting out laughing is beyond me. I am mystified but eternally grateful. Here's to you again, ladies. And thank you.

Nothing but fear itself

CAPE TIMES, 13 SEPTEMBER 2002

Boo! NO, NO, wait, don't be scared, it's only me. Sorry, I was just fooling around. I didn't mean to give you such a fright. Please come back. I won't do it again, promise.

Gee, why are you so jumpy today? I hope it doesn't have anything to do with Friday the thirteenth.

None of your medieval superstitions here, if you please. I like to think of this column as a small corner of enlightenment in the general Dark Age that is our daily lot. We are all free-thinkers round this neck of the paper. We spill salt with impunity round here. We step on cracks in the sidewalk with a song on our lips, we walk under ladders with scarcely an upward glance. I don't remember that a black cat has ever actually crossed my path – I always seem to be heading in the same direction as the black cats I meet, which suggests that I am either doing something right or something very wrong – but if one ever did, I can confidently claim I would hardly turn a hair.

Besides, Friday the thirteenth has never been especially unlucky for me. Quite the contrary. It was a Friday the thirteenth back in 1982, I remember, when Shelley Whitfield first sent a note with Heidi Tydlesley to tell me that she liked me. Ah, first love! Nine unimaginable days of passion and bliss in the sultry Durban summer, before she left me for Steven Kenton. I still can't shake the feeling I could have made it last longer if only I had worked up the nerve to actually speak to her … oh, but never mind that now. My point is that foolish superstitions never helped anyone.

There are people so afraid of today's date that they refuse to leave their beds all day, which will certainly prove unlucky should the house catch fire. There are others – triskeidecaphobics, if you want the fancy word – who have a morbid fear of the number thirteen itself. It makes no sense, but phobias seldom do. There are as many phobias as there are people to be afraid. Most phobias have names – "chrematophobia", for instance, is the unreasonable fear of money. So is "working for a newspaper".

But there are many other phobias, far more reasonable in these troubled modern times, that do not have names. There should be a word, for instance, for:

- the nagging fear that you have just sent a saucy SMS to the wrong number;
- the whispering fear that everyone else is at a party to which you were not invited;
- the gnawing fear that mullets really are coming back in fashion;
- the choking fear that at any moment old friends from out of town might ask if they can come and stay with you for a couple of days;
- the lingering fear that you may already have met Mr or Ms Right, but you were too busy thinking about lunch to recognise them at the time;
- the lonely fear that you are the only man in the whole world who doesn't see what the big deal is about Anna Kournikova;
- the slow fear that maybe, one day, despite your best efforts and your deepest convictions, you really will die after all, just like everyone else.

No sir, it is not true that we have nothing to fear but fear itself. To those with eyes to see, there are plenty of other things to worry about.

People of the book

CAPE TIMES, 11 OCTOBER 2002

G EE, IT MUST be fun being a novelist in South Africa. I say that, but I don't really mean it. I am being sarcastic. I don't like being sarcastic – sarcasm is a quality in print which, like sincerity, must be carefully handled if it is not to be extremely unattractive. I apologise for my sarcasm, but I was driven to it by an experience earlier this week. (Incidentally, it will gratify those Cape Town patriots who have been sending me misspelt hand-scrawled faxes yelling "Cape Town – luv it or leaf it!" to learn that this was not a Cape Town experience.)

I was in Johannesburg for the Alan Paton Book Awards, at which cash prizes are awarded for the best South African fiction and non-fiction of the past year. It is a rare joy to see a writer receiving money for something other than ad slogans or giving good service at a restaurant. The fiction award went to Ivan Vladislavic for his novel *The Restless Supermarket*. I was pleased because I know Ivan Vladislavic to be a good writer, and I was mildly ashamed not to have read the book.

Later in the week I trotted out to the nearest branch of a major book chain to buy a copy. They did not have a copy. Nor did the next branch I tried. "Have you sold out because of the sudden rush of interest?" I asked.

"No," said the lout behind the till with the Metallica T-shirt and the earring in his eyebrow, "we just haven't ordered any."

At the third branch I was feeling testy. "Do you have *The Restless Supermarket* by Ivan Vladislavic?" I asked.

A shaven youth eyed me blankly. "That's a strange name," he said.

"Yes," I agreed, "it is."

"What's it about?" said the shaven youth.

"I don't know," I replied. "I haven't read it yet. I was hoping I might read the copy I am trying to purchase from you."

"Huh," said the shaven youth helpfully. "I wonder. So, is the author Russian?"

"No," I said through narrow lips. "He may well prove to be of Eastern European descent, but he is South African, he lives two blocks away, and his book has just won a major literary award."

"Huh," said the youth. "Cool. No, nothing in stock." He paused a moment in what passed for thought. "It must be cool to win a big literary prize, hey."

"Yes," I said, "it must make the world of difference to your sales."

I was being sarcastic again. I don't know Ivan Vladislavic, but I felt angry on his behalf. It must be difficult enough being a novelist in a society in which the majority of the few people who do buy books only seem to pop in once a year for the latest Naked Chef – you might expect a prize-winner to get a little extra help. I have seen next to nothing in the national media about *The Restless Supermarket*. I haven't seen it advertised. I haven't even seen it on sale. It is not this or that person's fault – it is the mood of a society that doesn't much care about its writers or its writing. If that is our mood, then I suppose we must be happy with the general quality of the writing in our magazines and newspapers and with watching *Big Okes* and *Mr Bones*, and with the fact that our best talents turn to advertising or producing corporate videos. We must be happy, but sometimes it turns me a little sarcastic.

Another sniper column

CAPE TIMES, 8 NOVEMBER 2002

I THINK THE DANGER has passed that I shall ever be a sniper. There was a time when the thought would have been an appealing one, but I have a job now and I can afford DStv and the occasional family-sized pizza all to myself, so I just don't have that burning resentment at the world any more.

Anyway, I was never really cut out to be a serial-killer sniper. No head for heights, for one thing. I would imagine that a sniper would have to be capable of scaling tall buildings and book depositories and suchlike, if he wanted to be the best sniper he could be – and why else would you become a sniper? Plus, I have never been a big fan of random murder. If you are going to be a serial killer, I would suggest a more focused approach. If I were about to set off on a career as public enemy number one, with all the attendant risks of capture and social embarrassment that ensue, I would make sure I was at least killing people I really wanted to kill. People who drive slowly in the fast lane, for instance, or people who use the phrase "Don't go there", or who employ the word "stunning" as an adjective to describe anything besides a blow to the head. If I were still young and disaffected, no one would again be able to say, "That was a stunning salad" without looking uneasily over their shoulders.

Please understand, I am under no delusion that society is ready to embrace the discriminating serial killer, but if I were a sniper and confining myself to picking off people who forward jokes by e-mail, or men who wear open-toed shoes at night, or Jamie Oliver, then at least when the fevered dreams visit in the tortured solitary hours I would be able to console myself that I have been making the world a better place.

It will be some time before the Americans stop talking about the Washington sniper. You would think with the number of serial killers at work in America they would have learnt not to overreact by now, but you would be wrong. I was still smiling at the report of the Washington DC mayor's office advising the local citizens not to walk in a straight line while the sniper was at large, but rather to weave down the street (how would traffic officers issue on-the-spot sobriety tests? "Excuse me, sir, would you kindly zigzag on either side of that white line."), when I read the latest cautionary warning.

Some specialist in such matters laments that the sniper might have been stopped before he sniped, had his friends and relatives only paid attention to the subtle warning signs. The subtle warning signs in this case came when he announced he was going to buy a rifle and shoot people. Apparently even once the snipings had started, and someone offered this information and the *name* of the sniper, it still took the Washington police several weeks and bodies before they considered him worth investigating, which should make you feel a little better about our own police force.

But the report went on to say that people should be alert for other warning signs. The public is encouraged to report individuals who show signs of depression or anger, who make threats and who display suicidal tendencies. Now really. Christmas is almost upon us. Christmas is the season of depression, anger and suicide. If you use those criteria to arrest people, there will be scarcely a family in the country left sitting around the turkey.

Good fences make good neighbours

CAPE TIMES, 15 NOVEMBER 2002

I DON'T MIND TELLING you, I'm becoming a little nervous. I live, you see, in what is called a "quiet neighbourhood". I do not know who my neighbours are, and ordinarily that is precisely the way I like it. Not for me the Mediterranean exuberance of the bustling street, the merry housewives gabbing over the backyard fence, the tousle-haired urchins popping round to borrow a cup of sugar. For me, neighbours are like relatives – you can't choose 'em, you have to have 'em, but the wise man keeps contact with the blighters to the bare minimum.

I cherish the quietness of my neighbourhood, but of late it has begun to trouble me. Why is it so quiet? Why don't I ever see my neighbours leaving for work in the morning, for instance? I raised this issue with my friend Chunko. "I think you will find," said Chunko, "that most people leave for work at some time of the morning prior to eleven o'clock."

"So?" I said.

"So you are still asleep," said Chunko.

It makes sense, I suppose, but I am not soothed. If the statistics are anything to go by, the fact that I am seldom made aware of my neighbours probably means that I am living in a community of serial killers, sex offenders and fugitive international revolutionaries. Besides the excitement of discovering last week that James Kilgore, the last member of the Symbionese Liberation Army, has been living in Claremont, I was most struck by the comments of his neighbours. "He was such a quiet man," they said. "We would never have guessed."

I briefly lived in Claremont myself, in the days when I was a disgruntled university student, and I am compelled to confess that I would not be surprised to find a good deal more international villains hiding out there. There is a kind of simmering menace that hangs over Claremont, an unnatural stillness in the heat of the summer mornings that would be just the ticket for a Josef

Mengele, say, or a Jack the Ripper living out the final years of his long retirement. Whispers have it that Robert Mugabe has a safe house tucked away somewhere above the railway line. Or perhaps I only remember Claremont that way because I spent most of my disgruntled student mornings fending off the kind of hangovers that make the world seem an altogether sinister place. Who can say?

But Kilgore's neighbours' comments were food for thought. Admittedly, you would probably *expect* an international fugitive to keep a low profile, rather than run up SLA banners on a home-made flagpole and play the *Internationale* on a trumpet each morning and offer night classes to explain precisely what "Symbionese" means. All the same, it is always, as neighbours around the world are quick to tell reporters, the quiet ones you have to watch.

Jeffrey Dahmer? Quiet. Fred and Rosemary West? Even more quiet. OJ Simpson? Seldom had loud parties. So don't complain about the people across the road that play rap music all night and occasionally throw beer bottles at each other on the front lawn. At least you know they are not sex-killer cannibals or plotting the violent overthrow of the state, or Lord Lucan. You may not have peace and quiet, but you have peace of mind. Now you will have to excuse me. I have bought a drum kit and a tuba, and each night from now on I am going to teach myself to play them. It's the only polite thing to do. I don't want the neighbours to worry.

Bag to the future

STYLE, DECEMBER 2002

I'M NOT, AS you might know, a trendsetter. I can't pretend: I am no friend of the trend. I don't know one end of a trend from another. When I am told that beige is the new brown, or that old is the new new, or that socks worn with sandals are big in Europe this season, I can but shrug. Trends do not rouse me to strong emotions. Well, there was the occasion when someone announced in my presence that the mullet was coming back as an acceptable hairstyle so I killed him and hid his body in the woods before he could tell anyone else. Those were strong emotions, I suppose. But for the most part, I care little for the malicious oddities of the world of fashion.

So you will understand that I carry my man's bag not in order to resemble David Beckham, but in order to carry things. That's right, you heard me: my man's bag. A man's bag, in case you have never seen one, is a rather sporty-looking accessory, designed to hold things. Bigger than a pocket, smaller than a knapsack, the man's bag slings over one shoulder, cunningly freeing the hands for important everyday functions, like helping yourself to food at a cocktail party, or shaking hands with yourself, or shooing away small children. The man's bag, I am compelled to admit, might bear a superficial resemblance to a handbag, but there is one vital difference: it is *not* a handbag. It is a bag for men. It is, as I say, a *man's* bag, and more than that, it is *my* bag and no matter what snide comments and sarcastic wolf whistles and complimentary wine spritzers I may receive, I am proud of it.

It is rather a handsome and masculine man's bag, if you must know. It has "Puma" written on the side, and I have always found pumas to be very hand-some and masculine beasts. Leopards I find handsome but a little effeminate. Something swishy about the tail, if you see what I mean. I am told that my man's bag is all the rage in New York at the moment, although come to think of it the star-spangled banner is also popular in New York at the moment, and so are firemen, not to mention dark nightclubs where men wearing leather masks beat each other with rubber sticks moulded in rude shapes, so I suppose that shouldn't count for much. Anyway, I carry my man's bag for practical reasons.

I lose things, you see. My patience, my temper and roulette, mainly, but also my cellphone and my wallet and especially my keys. I am a world-class key-loser. I lose keys as Tiger Woods plays golf, or as Tom Hanks' wife cries at Oscar ceremonies. No one is better at losing keys than me. Many people claim to be absent-minded, but I have them all beat. I will take on all corners in a key-losing competition. When it comes to misplacing important everyday items, I am unrivalled for speed, endurance and sheer creativity.

And so I started carrying a man's bag, and since then I have not lost a single item. At first, though, I thought I was going to lose my friends. My first day with the man's bag, I went off with a couple of hearty fellows to watch the Springboks play Australia at Ellis Park. They regarded me in heavy silence. "What is that?" they said.

"It is a man's bag," I replied, shrugging my shoulder to hitch up the strap.

There was another silence, and suddenly I was glad I was holding the tickets. "If anyone at the stadium asks," they said at last, "tell them your girlfriend is off buying the beer."

But South African men are not the boors that other South African men sometimes fear. Not a single man in Ellis Park threatened me with violence because of my man's bag. In fact, no man made a disparaging comment. I wish the same were true of the womenfolk. In the stadium I found myself beside a large fellow from some suburb where people conduct motor maintenance on their front lawns. He inspected my man's bag for a while and tugged contemplatively on his mullet. "What do you carry in there?" he said at last.

"Probably the same things you carry in the pockets of your blue cotton shorts," I replied.

"But with the bag your pockets don't bulge and things don't fall out," said my neighbour thoughtfully.

"Correct," I replied.

He turned to his wife. "Maybe I should get a bag like that,' he said. "I'm always losing my keys."

His wife leaned over to eye the merchandise. 'No," she said. "Do you want to look like a moffie?"

SMS SCKS

CAPE TIMES, 27 DECEMBER 2002

C AN SOMEONE TELL me – what is the deal with group SMSing? Really, it is beginning to annoy me.

It used to be an irksome but necessary chore of Christmastime – if you were one who went in for such things as Christmastime chores – to handwrite warm festive cards to friends and relatives and business acquaintances and people you met on holiday, and post them off in good time to arrive before Christmas day.

For the most part, admittedly, the cards were simply watercolours of robins or snowmen or apple-cheeked children deporting themselves like kittens with balls of wool, inside which you had scrawled "With love to the whole family" or some similar effusion of the heart in spidery handwriting with a blue ballpoint pen. People would line their cards on the mantlepiece or mount them on lengths of string and look at them with bloody-minded satisfaction on Christmas Eve as they sipped their brandy and waited for the kids to fall asleep. Christmas cards were a minimal exercise in civility.

To send a Christmas card, you needed actually to buy the object, write in it, envelope it, lick the flap, stamp, address and finally post it. It was an exercise that demanded an investment of time and effort. You may not especially like someone or choose to spend time with them, but the act of sending them a Christmas card was a way of expressing that they were not beyond the pale of your attention – that you still acknowledged them as being in the world and to an extent in your life. It was a kind of covenant between people; to be on someone's Christmas card list meant that – regardless of the state of relations between you – in their eyes you still qualified as a human being deserving of recognition, even if only once a year.

This is no longer the case. Not only is the Christmas card – with its hand-writing and its personalised name and address – scarcely sent any longer, but increasingly it is being replaced by the group SMS. Have you received a group SMS? On Christmas Eve and morn my telephone was athrob with them. This does not mean that I am popular and have many friends – this just means that my number is stored in an unconscionable number of cellphones.

It is not flattering to receive a group SMS saying "Wishing you a Christmas of love, light and hipness", and not merely because no one using the word "hipness" is a friend of mine. It is not flattering because it is not especially being sent to you. It is simultaneously being sent to everyone else in that person's cellphone, including their dermatologist, their tax guy and the AA emergency rescue operator. I received warm SMSes solicitous about my Yule season and the year ahead from people I could scarcely remember meeting. I received one from the ex-girlfriend of a one-time friend; I received one from a man in the music industry who is in the process of trying to sue me; and one from a local soap actress who has only ever previously used my number to send me threatening messages and late-night drunken promises to have my legs broken. Very few of the people who sent me Christmas wishes would have actively chosen to send me Christmas wishes, and that is hardly the thinking behind the Christmas wish, I wouldn't think.

Ah well, that's folks for you. Say, while I'm on the subject, how was your Christmas? Yes, yours. I do hope it was good. Yes, I do. Yes, I'm talking to you.

Another puzzling New Year

CAPE TIMES, 3 JANUARY 2003

WHAT WERE YOU doing on New Year's Eve? Were you? Really? Gosh. Wasn't it painful? No such high-jinks and shenanigans for me, I can tell you. I started the New Year as I intend to finish it: painstakingly piecing together the sundered bodies of ballerinas.

I don't know if this sounds peculiar to you, but I spent my New Year's Eve in a painful ecstasy of absorption, poring over the jumbled smudges of a 1500-piece jigsaw puzzle. The puzzle, not that it matters, was a reproduction of Edgar Degas' "Dance Class", or, if you are the sort of person who likes their jigsaw puzzle unwashed, eating a baguette and wearing a beret, "*Classe de Dans*". Oh, don't sneer – it was either that or the 2000-piece photograph of seven dalmations in a basket. It was the first jigsaw puzzle I have tackled in nigh 18 years, and it was just the thing for a thoughtful New Year's Eve.

You learn interesting things about yourself when you sit down to a dining-room table spread with cardboard pieces. I chose to do a jigsaw puzzle on New Year's Eve as a kind of gesture to myself. I wanted to greet the New Year, if not sober, exactly, then at least with some measure of self-possession. A jigsaw puzzle seemed perfect – I would spend the last evening of the year piecing together the bigger picture, putting things in their place, rediscovering the lessons of proportion and perspective, and at the end of it I would have made, with my own hands, an object both pleasing to contemplate and greater than the sum of its parts. "As with this jigsaw puzzle," I said to myself sternly on the Tuesday afternoon, settling down with a French painting and an even more French bottle of champagne, "so let it be with your life."

By midnight, as I reluctantly broke from my labours to stand outside and watch the flares from the ships and hear the distant roar of the hippies on the beach celebrating the New Year three minutes too early, the puzzle was still French but the champagne was long finished. So was that shaker of gin I keep tucked under the sofa for emergencies. My eyes were swimming with tiny specks of colour and the after-image of long-ago brush strokes. I was cursing Degas' enthusiasm for the colour green. What kind of a man paints the entire top-left corner green? And all the same colour green, at that. It must have made the painting go by more quickly, but what about the people doing the jigsaw puzzles, eh? What about them?

As I looked at the sky over Cape Town, I found myself thinking those deep and echoing thoughts that men and women have always thought, searching the heavens on New Year's Eve: "Cor, I'm glad I'm not doing a jigsaw puzzle of the Milky Way! That would take forever!"

Eventually I finished, with the sun risen and my eyes bleary and my back in spasm, and I stumbled to bed with a jigsaw hangover as bad as any I could have acquired from less salubrious pursuits. And I remembered, as I drifted off in an impressionistic swirl of green, that a jigsaw puzzle is not a very good metaphor for a life. In life you haven't the picture on the box to guide you, and in life there are very often pieces missing. But there is this similarity: in life as in jigsaw puzzles, it's easier and a lot more fun with someone helping you. And then I thought something else, but I can't remember what.

Valentine's Day

CAPE TIMES, 14 FEBRUARY 2003

O F ALL THE days of the year, Valentine's Day is far and away the least romantic. Mind you, it is possible that I only say that now because I have not yet reached the age when I have to choose the date on which to have my annual prostate examination. Come to think of it, when I *do* reach the age when I have to book my annual prostate examination, I am going to book it for Valentine's Day, so that the two least romantic days of the year can happen at the same time.

It is not easy to define what romance is, but I know just what it isn't. It isn't a duty forced on you by newspapers and shopping malls and a partner who will otherwise sulk and sigh and question your love. Romance, I think, has something to do with intimacy, and there is nothing intimate about sharing a date with every other couple so bereft of imagination and enterprise that they need to be told which day of the year they should be nice to each other. I dislike the publicness of Valentine's Day. To take your partner to dinner and sit in a restaurant with all those other couples proudly showing off that they are not spending this Valentine's Day without a partner, that is one step away from joining a cult and taking part in a mass wedding. Seriously – sending a Valentine card is like being a Moonie.

Even worse are the aesthetics of Valentine's Day. Red hearts and ribbons and cherubs and fuzzy stuffed Grizzlies holding little flags that say "I love you beary much" … that is how hell will be decorated. And if hell has a soundtrack audible above the screams of the tormented, it will be Celine Dion and Chris de Burgh and the rhythmic ka-ching of cash registers. No, to hell with Valentine's Day. You know who had the right idea about Valentine's Day? Al Capone. I am not necessarily suggesting that massacring your enemies with a tommy-gun is the way to celebrate Valentine's Day, but on a day of rampant sentiment, those sentiments are not furthest from my heart.

Nor do I object solely to the commercial aspect. Valentine's Day may be a rip-off, but it is no more of a rip-off than, say, going to a World Cup match and buying a beer. Just because they extort ten rand for the flimsy plastic beaker in which you receive your beer does not cause me to say, "There should be no World Cup." No, indeed. Nothing short of losing to New Zealand this weekend would make me say that.

In fact, on Valentine's Day a store-bought token of your dutiful affection is probably the best of a bunch of very bad deals. I recently heard of some loser whose idea of an imaginative Valentine gift is to fill a glass jar with slips of paper that he calls "Affection Cheques". Yes, he does. The idea is that whenever his beloved feels down, she can take a lucky dip from the jar and cash in her Affection Cheque: "Pay the bearer one hug", for instance, or "I'll do the dishes tonight". If I have to explain why I run outside and take deep breaths of fresh air whenever I imagine their relationship, you are probably in that relationship.

So no, I am not celebrating Valentine's Day. But there is something that I am celebrating today. I may even celebrate it with a few drinks. Today is Friday: now *that's* a day worth making a fuss over.

Another day, another dolour

CAPE TIMES, 4 APRIL 2003

OO-ER, I DON'T like this time of year. This time of year makes me distinctly uneasy. "April," said TS Eliot, "is the cruelest month," and now I know I why. (He also said, incidentally, that September is the funniest month and that February is the month most likely to buy you a drink if you're feeling down, but you never hear about that, do you? No, as usual, if it's not bad news, the media doesn't want to know about it.)

I noticed, as a result of my usual close scrutiny of the posters on lampposts, whence a world of information flows, that today is national Cleavage Day. Now if ever there has been a redundant day, more so even than national Workers' Day, it is surely Cleavage Day. I don't mean to sound all sensitive and feminist here, but I can say without fear of exaggeration that in my household *every* day is Cleavage Day. When it comes to consistent recognition and appreciation, I don't think the assembled cleavages around my neck of the woods have anything to complain about.

Still, Cleavage Day brings the same kind of dilemmas as Vagina Day did. What do you mean, you missed Vagina Day? Vagina Day and Cleavage Day are always at this time of year, and whenever they roll round I am stumped for the appropriate way to celebrate them. I am not big on commemorating every day that comes along – for instance, I allowed International Obsessive-Compulsive Disorder Day to come and go last year with scarcely a second thought – but I don't want to ignore V-day entirely because, well, the ladies down at the office can be very sensitive about these things. It's one thing boycotting Valentine's Day and Youth Day – as far as I am concerned Youth Day is entirely wasted on the young – but no matter how much they protest that Vagina Day is just a day like any other, deep down the ladies at work expect a little special attention.

But what? I don't even know what the correct Vagina Day greeting might be. "I wish you a happy Vagina Day" sounds inappropriate, "Merry Vagina Day" just comes across as sarcastic, and wild horses could not drag the words "Have a relaxed Vagina Day" from my lips. Last year I contented myself with sending thoughtful and decorative cards to the ladies in the office, but that just resulted in a written warning from management, and the reputation as someone you don't want to be alone with in the lift. It alarms me, I can tell you. It makes me want to hide indoors until sunset. Fortunately National Productivity Day isn't until sometime in October.

I don't know what to do about all these commemorative days, I really don't. There are just too many of them – we've scarcely finished with International Day of Respiratory Tract Disease when it's time for National Stutterers' Day. I am not making up any of these days, incidentally. A few years ago there were actually advice hotlines established for Stutterers' Day. I called one, being a man of social conscience, and also always keen on some good advice, but no matter how often I called, the lines were always engaged.

I am putting my foot down. No more days. International No-Smoking Day can expect short shrift from me, and I am going to try my best to get through International Erectile Disfunction Day without dwelling on it as much as I did last year. There is one day I do still mark, though. On Sunday it is my birthday. Happy birthday to me.

No nudes is good news

SPECTRASTYLE, 1 APRIL 2003

I AM ALARMED – YES, alarmed – by recent developments in the world of nudism. You may not be aware that there is such a thing as the world of nudism, but there is, and it is having developments. Primarily, judging by what I can glean from international news reports, nudism is on the increase. Nudism is surging. Nudism is, you might say, waxing, and that leaves me a little edgy.

You will remember that nudism had a peak of popularity back in the sixties and seventies and even straggling on into the eighties. Hippies and exhibitionists and weirdos and Scandinavians were first responsible for popularising nudist beaches and nudist colonies and nude triathlons and similar peculiar exercises in nudeness. They claimed it was good for your health, as though anyone ever felt better for visiting a nudist beach and spending the next two weeks digging grains of sand from secret parts of the body. Fortunately in time people saw the perils of nudism – it leads, among other things, to Beau Brummel – and the fad waned.

That encouraged me, I can tell you. It made me think that perhaps humanity still has some residual shred of taste and good sense. In the overwhelming majority of cases, the human body is just not intended to be undressed in public. The invention of clothing is one of civilisation's finest moments – it is what separates us from the beasts of the field, and also from the Swedes. I may be a naked bachelor in the shaded safety of my own home, but I would not dream of unleashing my wobbly expanses upon the unsuspecting public. That would not only be unsightly, it would be downright uncivilised. It is one thing not being ashamed of having a belly like a VW Beetle, but it is quite another to inflict those visions upon others. Just as your right to swing your arm ends where my nose begins, Ngconde Balfour's right to wear skintight golf shirts should end where our line of sight begins.

It was Oprah Winfrey who first alerted me to the resurgence in clothlessness as a lifestyle choice. It was recently reported that Oprah is to celebrate her 50th birthday by having naked photographs taken. Naked photographs, I suppose I should add, of herself. When I heard that, I had to sit down and drink a glass of water until the world stopped spinning. Fortunately, Oprah is not intending to publish the pictures – they are apparently for the sole viewing pleasure of her lucky boyfriend Steadman – but still I am not sure I feel comfortable living in a world in which there exist nudie photographs of Oprah Winfrey.

Scarcely had I recovered from that shock when I read the news that an American travel agency is organising the world's first nudist flight. Castaways Travel has apparently chartered a Boeing 727 to Mexico for what has been described, with hardly a snicker, as a nudist package holiday. Everyone files on board as usual, but once the flight is in the air, passengers are encouraged to unbuckle and disrobe and enjoy the delights of pressurised nudity. Evidently staff will remain clothed – airline regulations wisely stipulate no nudity in the cockpit – and there will be no hot drinks or food served, to avoid scalding should there be spillage during turbulence. Still, I cannot begin to express what a worrying development this is. I become anxious on international flights as it is, without this new additional worry that I may have accidentally booked onto the wrong flight, and when the seatbelt lights are extinguished that balding sales rep in the seat beside me is going to sigh happily and start unzipping his trousers.

Nor is it just loony overseas types who are leading the comeback of the pale and wobbly bits on the public stage. Last year, as part of a strategy for wooing more Scandinavian tourists, members of the Port Elizabeth town council unveiled a proposal to establish an official nudist beach in the city. See? The insanity is spreading! No disrespect to readers from the Eastern Cape, but Port Elizabeth is simply not so aesthetically blessed that it can afford this risk. Take a walk downtown and look at your fellow pedestrians and ask yourself: "How many of these people would I like to see without their clothes on?" Do not be fooled, my friends – nudist beaches are not like paparazzi photographs from Cannes. Nudist beaches have real people, and real people should wear clothes.

Good people of South Africa, it is not too late. We can stop this madness before it takes root. Civilisation is in our hands. The next time you are invited to strip in public, say no. Just say no. If we set a good example, soon everyone will be doing it.

Flu is a tense of fly

CAPE TIMES, 18 APRIL 2003

F OR EVERY CLOUD there is a silver lining, as the poet once wrote, before rejecting it as a cliché. For many the cloud is the new SARS flu virus. Indeed, for many there is nothing good to say about SARS, but not for me. No sir, I use a smile as my umbrella. For all its obvious drawbacks – the sneezing, the shortness of breath, the involuntary dying – SARS has given me a ray of hope.

I have been impressed with the alacrity shown by our authorities in taking measures to nip SARS in the bud. Of course, they have a lot of alacrity to spare, considering how little they used up on AIDS, but still. Naturally, one man's alacrity is another man's opportunity. For many years now I have been wrestling with one of the thorniest problems of contemporary life: how to avoid economy class.

The economy-class section of an aeroplane has become to me as the headmaster's office was when I was a small boy, or as the dark space under the bed was when I was an even smaller boy – I fear it with all my mortal being. I sweat and itch and swoon when I think of having to go there. Fortunately, not for the same reasons – I don't actually think some enormous child-devouring crocodile of darkness will swallow me, nor do I really anticipate that I will be sexually interfered with by my headmaster in economy class – but there are horrors back there that make me quite shrill with terror.

Babies; fat people with arms the size of legs trying to share your armrest; babies; junior businessmen who smell of Axe deodorant and read self-help books; *babies* – these are the sorts of wretches and villains with whom no civilised individual should have to share personal space, yet in economy class they are thrust upon you as plagues of boils and locusts were thrust upon the ancient citizens of Egypt. Short of actually shelling out the hard cash to join the sports administrators on the other side of the blue curtain, however, there has been nothing one could do about it. Until SARS.

I have hit upon a cunning wheeze to lift myself out of purgatory, the next time I travel any sort of distance in economy class. I will tell you but you can't use it yourself, or they will soon rumble us, those airline swines. It was with a certain interest that I read the reports of passengers boarding flights, buckling up, then beginning to snuffle and croak and ostentatiously blow their nose on the hems of stewardesses' skirts. "Are you all right, sir?" ask the stewardesses, backing away.

"Well," say the passengers, "yes, although I seem to have suddenly come down with the symptoms of flu, not to mention unusual respiratory complications. Do I feel hot to you?"

"Have you been to Asia recently, sir?" the flight crew ask, wrapping their faces in the blue curtain.

"Well," say the wily passengers, "no, although I did eat at the Mai Lai Oriental Barbeque joint a few days ago."

Without further ado they are swept away from the assembled fiends and atrocities of economy class and are quarantined in blissful seclusion at the rear of the aircraft in a curtained cubicle. For the rest of the flight they do not have to see, hear or breathe the body odour of another human being. To be sure, you have a certain amount of inconvenient medical examination to endure when you arrive, but that, my friends, is a small price to pay. Book me a seat. I am ready to go travelling.

Home of the free ride

CAPE TIMES, 25 APRIL 2003

GOD BLESS AMERICA. Every time I open the newspaper I see something else that makes me realise afresh how true it is that America is the land of opportunity. "Bring me your poor huddled masses," says the Statue of Liberty, "and I will teach them how to make money by suing people."

I have already in these pages saluted the legal nous and financial acumen of one Gregory Rhymes, a roly-poly Yankee teenager who brought suit against McDonald's for allegedly selling him several thousand greasy hamburgers over the years without once – not once! – telling him that if your diet consists almost exclusively of greasy hamburgers, you may very well not keep your slim, boyish figure. Big Greg is rivalled in my esteem only by the legendary Stella Rimsky, who set the aspirational benchmark for klutzes and dunderheads everywhere by earning a large sum of money after protesting to the court that McDonald's takeaway coffee is unpleasantly hot when poured over your lap instead of the more usual method of transporting it in a polystyrene cup.

But there is a new hero. Join me in applauding Ms Geremie Hoff, 56, of St Louis, Missouri, who this month won nearly R50 000 and a free blow-wave after she sued her hair salon for giving her a bad haircut. Ah, America! When Ms Hoff's parents and grandparents arrived on the overcrowded transport ship from the Old Country, bowed by poverty, oppressed by the lank hair and unflattering cuts that were the unhappy lot of the European peasantry, how little they could have dreamed that one day their daughter would grow up to turn personal grooming into a civil rights issue. They must be so proud.

According to testimony, Ms Hoff took herself off to the salon to have her hair straightened. Later that night, clumps of her hair came loose, and the resulting bald spots made her feel "depressed and reclusive". She sued for emotional distress, depression, counselling costs and lost income. Lost income? How did a patchy head lose the huffy Ms Hoff her income? Was she a photographic model? Was she one of those circus trapeze artists who dangle themselves from the high-wire by her hair? Did she make a living impersonating Lady Godiva at upmarket cocktail parties? No, she was a part-time tour guide, but she resigned after her traumatic hair experience. People just don't trust information from people with bad hair.

"Say, Stanley, what's that building over there?"

"The tour guide said that's the St Louis municipal suntan parlour and library, honey."

"What does she know? She has a patch of loose hair."

It is an extraordinary thing, the extent to which it has become a modern principle not only accepted but actively embraced by law that if something goes wrong, it must be someone's fault, and that money will ease the pain. No one really becomes depressed and reclusive and quits their job because of a bad haircut. Look at Gwen Gill – she still pitches up for work every day. Bad haircuts are acts of god, like hurricanes and tidal waves and lightning strikes. Bad things happen in the world – they happen to everyone and sometimes they happen to us. That's just the world, and only a fool takes the world personally.

No, whatever is troubling Ms Hoff, I suspect it is something that runs altogether deeper and will last a lot longer than her loosened hair, and I very much doubt whether the money – any amount of money – will make the slightest difference.

Confessions of a bad son

CAPE TIMES, 9 MAY 2003

I AM A BAD SON. No, I am. I am not proud of it, but I must face facts. Not once, in all my years of having a mother – which is most of them – have I given a good Mother's Day present. I have tried, but I am just no good at it.

It all began with a double-album of *Olivia Newton-John's Greatest Hits, Volume Two*, and it hasn't improved. I was maybe 10, and all day I roamed the shopping centre, jingling the money in my pocket, looking for a suitable present. I forget where the money came from – almost certainly my mother – but I remember standing staring at the rows of perfume bottles in the cosmetics section of the department store, wondering how anyone could tell them apart, too shy to ask the big ladies with the very red lips at the counter. Finally one of the ladies spritzed me with perfume and they all laughed and I ran away and bought *Olivia Newton-John's Greatest Hits, Volume Two*.

My mother had never given any indication that she was a fan of Olivia Newton-John. We did not, for instance, have *Olivia Newton-John's Greatest Hits, Volume One*. I can't honestly say that I had ever heard an Olivia Newton-John song, although I knew she had been in a movie called *Grease*, which a lot of older kids had seen and my father hated because it had John Travolta in it. "John Revolter," he used to say, and chuckle. Still, I thought Olivia Newton-John looked pretty on the cover, it came with a poster, so if she didn't like the songs, she would at least have something to pin on the wall.

My mother accepted her double gift of Olivia Newton-John with great excitement and gratitude, and I think she may even have played it once, because I remember my father saying, "What's all that yowling?" and my mother saying, "Shhh, it's my present."

The next year I was determined to buy perfume, like good sons buy their mothers. I went to the perfume counter and studied the bottles. I still couldn't tell them apart by smelling them, but I bought the one with the most exciting name. "That's very popular," said the lady with the bright red lips, wrapping my perfume.

So I gave it to my mother, and it was received with great excitement and gratitude, but afterwards my Aunt Rosemary took me aside and said: "Darrel, you're 11 now. You are old enough to know some things. And one of those things is that you must never, never, never again buy a woman *You're the Fire* perfume."

There have been other attempts: the gold chain that turned her neck green; the T-shirt that announced "World's Best Mom"; the fluffy Garfield with suction pads on his paws to attach to the back window of the car. If you were to pile up all the gifts I gave when I was a child, it would look like the props wardrobe for Jerry Springer's American show. Adult efforts haven't been much better: the complete collection of potted cactuses of the world; the tickets on a so-called pleasure cruise that turned out to feature Margaret and Ferdinand from *Big Brother* as special celebrity hosts. Through it all she has reacted with great excitement and gratitude – except, obviously, the cruise that turned out to have Margaret and Ferdinand as special celebrity hosts. After that she said: "Really, dear, all I want is a telephone call. Please."

If you are a mom, bless you. Sons are not always good at thank-yous. But thank you. Happy Mother's Day.

Somewhere over the rainbow

CAPE TIMES, 30 MAY 2003

I HAVE BEEN PLANNING a holiday. Even the most diligent and workaholic columnist needs from time to time to breathe that sweet, sweet air that is not clogged by the miasma of deadlines, and to stretch and yawn and shut his eyes far from the crash and rattle of outraged readers' letters hitting his doorstep. Why outraged readers can't just write their letters on regular paper like everyone else, I'll never know.

So I have of late been perusing travel brochures. Ah, but the world is pretty in travel brochures. Everywhere at the far end of a long-distance flight, it seems, is nothing but one long, empty palm-lined beach, or an endless succession of noble and ancient ruins, proud and deserted, lit by the gentle golden light of sunset. I would like to live in a travel brochure, or at least travel in one. Nowhere in travel brochures are there queues of unhappy people waiting for a delayed flight; nowhere in travel brochures are there vast Americans with shirts like shower curtains and backsides like an Engen garage, shouldering past you to rub their bellies against the Mona Lisa. In travel brochures the only people you ever see are happy locals, ready to offer you a tasty drink in half a hollow pineapple, or cool strangers in evening dresses with a glint in their eye to suggest passionate assignations behind the curtains at the Vienna Opera House.

Sometimes I think the best part of travelling is the part before you leave, when you can imagine a perfectly framed world of edited highlights. Of course, the canny traveller knows that this is just a dream. "Travel" and "travail" (meaning "painful or laborious effort") were in Middle English precisely the same word, with the same meaning. I'm not sure that things have changed all that much.

Still, it is a beautiful dream. Whose heart is so flinty they didn't sigh to recently read of one Koichiro Takata, a 22-year-old ophthalmology student from Japan, who was so disappointed by his holiday in Kashmir that he tried to commit suicide? The fact that Mr Takata chose Kashmir for his dream holiday – presumably edging out such rival fun spots as Kabul and Mosul and Khartoum – should probably tell us something about his judgement, but I felt a strong pang of sympathetic recognition when he announced from his Kashmiri hospital bed: "This place does not look like my travel brochures. This is not the Kashmir I read about. I feel hurt."

It seems that, upon landing in Kashmir, Mr Takata became anxious about the armed soldiers patrolling the streets, feeling they detracted from the natural beauty of the place. Apparently there were no camouflaged gunmen in any of his travel brochures. Unable to stand the disappointment a second longer, Mr Takata produced a pair of scissors and started stabbing himself in the chest. I myself have at times been tempted to produce a pair of scissors and stab my travel agent, not to mention the person sitting next to me on the flight, but I have always stopped short of turning the clippers on myself. I suppose my sense of personal honour is just not as powerful as Mr Takata's. The Kashmiri Tourism Authority declined to comment, which is probably sensible.

Mr Takata has since made a full recovery, and says he will not be dissuaded from future travelling. Bless you, Mr Takata, for continuing to be a dreamer. The world needs dreamers, but if you ever make it to Cape Town, I sincerely hope there isn't a cloud covering the mountain on the day you arrive.

3
Sport

Losers in sport

BUSINESS DAY, 1 OCTOBER 1999

THIS MAY SEEM UNLIKELY, but something Craig Jamieson said recently made me pause to think. Interviewed on television, the former Natal rugby captain reminisced about the province's famous first-ever Currie Cup final victory in 1990.

"It was a tight game," he recalled fondly, "but then Theo van Rensburg missed a tackle and gave us the title." I winced in sympathy with Theo, who was no doubt at that moment frozen in horror, braai tongs in hand, *wors* half-turned, his mates all pretending to find something fascinating to read in the newspaper.

But then an image floated into my head: it is the final minute of a home test against France, South Africa one point behind. Theo steps up to take a kick almost directly in front of the poles. Like a great soggy baguette, the ball wobbles wide. Dizzy from a memory I had successfully repressed for the better part of a decade, I felt my sympathy for Theo van Rensburg evaporate. "Serves the loser bastard right," I snarled.

One of the fundamental truths of sport is that, regardless of talent or training, some sportsmen are winners, some are losers, and there is nothing anyone can do about it. Indeed, the athletes we take most enthusiastically to our hearts are those who parlay unexceptional gifts into the stuff of greatness. The World Cup squad of 1995 is an obvious case: a modest team with all the flair of a pair of stovepipe jeans, but when it came down to it, Stransky's drop went through, and Mehrtens' went wide.

Consider Gerrie Coetzee, one of the most gifted heavyweights of the post-Larry Holmes era, who contrived to lose first to a drug addict and then to Frank Bruno, himself a confirmed loser and an Englishman to boot. Baby Jake Matlala, by contrast – a man knee-high to Martin Locke, with a punch like a slap from Glenn Hicks – is a multiple world champion. Baby Jake is a winner, Gerrie was a loser.

The most obvious breed of loser is the Choker. Wayne Ferreira and Elana

Meyer are champions in this breed, and they say their prayers to St Zola Budd of the Order of Perpetual Fourth Place. They are classic chokers – extravagantly talented, but blessed with the mental toughness of a punnet of Denny's button mushrooms. To them BMT is a sandwich with bacon, mayonnaise and tomato. Their careers are as predictable as a Hugh Bladen commentary: when the heat is on, when they are in a position to make that single step to greatness, they wilt like Steve Hofmeyr being handed a condom.

South African chokers – from Kevin Curren to Okkert Brits – is a favourite topic with my friend Phillip, especially after the fourth beer. His explanation – simple, yet sound – is that so many South Africans choke on the big stage because they had maids making their beds when they were kids. They are soft, pampered, cut off from the consequences of their actions: if they spill Nesquik on the sheets, by the next time they get into bed everything will be smooth and clean and snuggly. There is always an excuse, someone to blame, a reason for not doing the dirty work themselves. You would think that someone with Wayne's complexion or Elana's voice would know something about overcoming hardships, but no – they would rather dream up a hamstring injury and hobble off into that hazy, humourless middle distance reserved for sulkers and chokers. They should be struck firmly and frequently with a blunt object – preferably Hugh Bladen – and taken to a training camp for the South African paralympic team to be taught a few hard truths about grit, guts and gratitude.

There is of course another breed – the Unlucky Loser, whose AGMs are chaired by that Job in cricket flannels, Andrew Hudson. If you are an Unlucky Loser, you can have so much talent and temperament that it is running down your leg onto the pitch, but things still will not go your way. A cover drive will rebound off a passing seagull onto your stumps; an earthquake will trip you up while starting off for a sharp single. Unlucky Losers are nice guys, for the most part, but you would not want to be on an aeroplane with them.

By contrast, consider Mark Boucher, who is that most glorious sporting treasure – a lucky player. He will drop the straight balls that miss the bat, and snag the impossible catches; his eyes-shut slog six will win the match. We need that sort of luck at least as much as ability. If our team is ever again to reach the World Cup final, it will be due to training and tactics and even talent. If we are ever again to win, however, it will only be because, when it truly matters, we are not Losers.

Rugby World Cup 1999:
Being a supporter

BUSINESS DAY, 8 OCTOBER 1999

I DON'T KNOW IF you have noticed, but suddenly there are a lot more Springbok supporters than there were a week ago. I bumped into a colleague on Monday morning. "Hey, hey," he said, giving me a strange wiggle of the eyebrows, "the Boks are looking good for the finals."

I looked at him with some confusion. "But weren't you saying on Friday that we have no chance?" I asked.

"Hey, no man, we're on track. Mallett's got the right plan." He breezed off down the corridor, happy in his own punditry. It was the first of many such conversations this week. It is most peculiar. In recent times a positive word about the team was as rare as a modest word from Geoffrey Boycott, but one decent result in the opening game and all of a sudden the flags are flying again. It is a staggering turnabout; by the time we beat England in the quarter-finals, critics of Nick Mallett will be as rare as former supporters of apartheid.

Last season, when the Springboks were chasing the record for consecutive test victories, everybody was a fan. The expert gentlemen of the press were calling Mallett "Saint Nick"; bars were packed on Saturday afternoons. Then we started losing.

Suddenly Mallett was the worst coach since John Williams; suddenly people started saying, "I'm not going to wake up early for the game" or "I'm playing golf on Saturday." Frown at them, and they would say, "What's the point? We're going to lose anyway." The point, of course, is that supporting a team means supporting them through bad times as well as good. It is sharing the bad times that makes us deserve the good times, and makes those good times that much sweeter.

Amid the fluffy memories of face paint and Francois Pienaar and jumbo jets in '95, it is easy to forget that before the opening match against Australia the prevailing mood was one of pessimism at worst, resigned good will at best. Nor is such fickleness confined to the playing field. We were all pleased to share in the warm and fuzzy good times of the '94 elections, all quick to claim Nelson Mandela as our own, happy to paint ourselves as stripes in Desmond Tutu's Rainbow Nation. Then, at the first knock-back, at the first dip of the rand or lurch of the ship, we throw up our hands and whine at dinner parties and talk darkly about leaving for – oh, the irony – New Zealand. We are, I am sorry to say, fair-weather fans.

I am not decrying our right to criticise and complain. One of the great joys of sport is that it is the only arena in which we are every one of us experts. But the right of complaint should be balanced by the duty of commitment. Without commitment we are not supporters, merely fans, and fans are a dime a dozen. Remember all those phantoms who suddenly emerged before the '95 final with enthusiastic opinions about how to stop Jonah Lomu or what position Mark Andrews should be playing? Where were they six months before, when the All Blacks were trampling us in rainy Carisbrooke at 4am?

It is often said (although perhaps only by me) that every rugby nation has the team it deserves. We should give thanks that one of the glories of being South African is that we so frequently have a team so much better than we deserve.

Woman beats man

BUSINESS DAY, 15 OCTOBER 1999

WHEN I WAS 12 years old, Caron Beasely challenged me to arm-wrestle. She was a small girl, was Caron Beasely, and sickly. She carried an asthma pump, and in some places her skin was so pale you could see her circulatory system. Taking all these factors into account, plus the fact that she was only 10, I accepted.

When I say that I still wake in the night, my right hand clenched like Mike Lipkin's, blindly screaming Caron Beasely's name, you will gather what the outcome was. From that day, I was firmly of the opinion that in the field of physical sports, men and women should not mix.

I am still of that opinion, though for different reasons. On Saturday night Seattle saw the first officially sanctioned professional boxing match between a man and a woman, and a sorry sight it must have been. Margaret McGregor scored a unanimous points decision over one Loi Chow, a jockey whose two previous experiences of the square ring had left him face-down in the resin with the distant sound of galloping hoofs in his head.

It is reported that when Chow received his first combination of blows to the head, he responded by bouncing away, smiling and doing not much else. In real life that is called chivalry; in the ring it is called maintaining a perfect record of defeats. But Chow's disgrace was in accepting the fight, not in losing it. Afterwards he declared: "I don't think I got whipped. I hit her with a couple of good shots." That may be the saddest sporting quote you will ever hear outside of a Springbok press conference.

Apparently the occasion was not a commercial success, which means we will be spared the sight of Chow demanding a rematch over 1800m with riding crop and blinkers. Whatever the bout was – and it resembled more strongly a circus sideshow, the bearded lady taking on Tickey the clown for your viewing pleasure – it was not sport. I do not enjoy all-female boxing matches either, incidentally, but that is for reasons of taste and aesthetics and values that are these days disgracefully old-fashioned and (am I allowed to admit this in a national newspaper?) perhaps even sexist.

My objection to this match is very different. The principle of boxing is that it is a violent match-up of equals in a confined space – the purest distillation of the gladiatorial impulse. While this is a principle frequently violated in the raddled world of professional boxing – witness Mike Tyson versus Peter McNeeley – it is at least the sustaining myth. There can never, and in a civilised world could never, be a match-up between a man and a woman equal in expertise and experience. Simply, it would result in a terrible beating. It is a biological truth that in our legalistic society we are quick to forget – being equal does not mean being the same.

This does not preclude mixed participation in non-physical sports, of course, although I can't help noticing that the South African team for the 1999 World Scrabble Championships in Melbourne is an all-male affair. This, I suspect, is attributable more to common sense than strength of intellect. Team member Trevor Hovelmeier was quoted as saying that to play at international level, players need to memorise all 5140 four-letter words that exist in the English language. What intelligent woman is going to spend valuable time acquainting herself with the fact that *kino* is a dark red resin obtained from an Indian leguminous tree, or *xyst* is a training area for Greek athletes? That is the kind of thing that men do. It is no coincidence that trainspotting and batting averages were male inventions.

There is another good reason for discouraging inter-gender athletic contests. Serena Williams, that most uncouth of tennis professionals, recently applied to be wild-carded into a men's tournament. I tell you, it has me worried. There is only one male professional who you can be sure will find a way of losing to a 17-year-old girl, and haven't Wayne Ferreira's friends and family suffered enough already?

Rugby World Cup 1999: Why we dislike the English

BUSINESS DAY, 22 OCTOBER 1999

'IF WE LOSE to England on Sunday," said Sad Henry, down at the Chalk 'n Cue, "I am going to quit my job and become a full-time alcoholic." We were not much troubled by this threat. Sad Henry has quit his job in order to become a full-time alcoholic on at least four occasions since 1992, but Sad Henry has expensive taste in alcohol, and it does not take him long to realise that in order to be a full-time alcoholic he needs at least a part-time job. Ideally Sad Henry should have a job that combines the two, but Percy Sonn has already taken it.

Still, we understood Sad Henry's anxiety. Of all possible ways to go out of the World Cup, losing to England ranks even lower than having the entire team expelled for being discovered at a private sauna party jointly hosted by Elton John and George Michael. There is not a country in the world to whom I would less like to lose, not even New Zealand. If we find the All Blacks unpalatable, it is largely because they remind us too much of ourselves. Sometimes New Zealand and South Africa sound like nothing so much as a pair of society matrons who have arrived at a party and discovered that they are both wearing the same dress. But to lose to England is not just infuriating, it is disgraceful.

One of my happiest rugby memories was Danie Gerber's inside swerve past Dusty Hare to score during the 1984 tour by John Scott's Englishmen, but that moment of almost transcendental pleasure was superseded by Jonah Lomu wiping the soil from his studs on Mike "Pussy" Catt's chest at Newlands in 1995. Who does not smile to remember the English cricket team losing to Mashonaland, or being bowled out for something like 24 by Curtley Ambrose on a flat pitch? Who is not, in their heart of hearts, looking forward to the spectacle of the English soccer team lining up to face another penalty shoot-out in a major tournament?

The delight in tormenting the Poms is the common bond uniting the southern superpowers. During the NZ–England pool match in this World Cup, Wayne Graham, a Kiwi commentator who makes Bill Lawry's cricket ravings sound like the measured wisdom of Solomon, took an especial liking to Lomu's try: "Yes! Yes! He's showing them a thing or two! They mispronounce his name over here! Yes, they do! They call him Low-mu! But he's shoving it down the face of the lofty English!"

Graham had to be hauled off for an emergency sponge bath, but South African hearts, even as they quailed before the spectacle of Big Jonah in full flight, could not help a twinge of pleasure. It was easy to forget that handing off Jeremy Guscott is only slightly more impressive than side-stepping a tackle bag; the pleasure lay entirely in watching someone, well, shoving it down the collective English face.

It is hard to account for such vehemence of feeling. Perhaps it is the shared shame of having once been ruled by a people who, by all recent evidence, are such a shower of unmitigated losers. There was a newspaper report this week. "English men," it declared, "are closet pork-pie addicts!"

Apparently the pasty-faced, pastry-loving Brits secretively scoff their meaty treats before they get home, lest the wife get wind of it. Not bad enough that they are a people whose idea of a good time is a pork pie, but they cannot even stand up and eat them at home with a straight back and chin held high. Is it any wonder that Sad Henry is so troubled? The English are the secret shadow of weakness that lurks within all of us, but that we so forcefully suppress. To lose on Sunday would be to face that unspeakable shadow. Fortunately, we are not going to lose.

South African sport needs new songs

BUSINESS DAY, 12 NOVEMBER 1999

A T A CERTAIN moment during the most recent test match, a number of the regulars down at the Chalk 'n Cue linked arms and raised their voices in song. "Olé!" we sang, "Olé, olé, olé!" Then, fearing that this was not sufficient adequately to express our enthusiasm, we added: "Olé!" and "Olé!" Not to drag out the anecdote, let me say that we repeated this lyric several times. We finished well satisfied, but of course Porky Withers, the local gin-soak, had to pipe up with his usual *"Nog 'n Olé!"* We ignored him sternly. Porky Withers never knows when enough is enough.

Later in the match, forgetting that we were supposed to be setting Porky Withers an example, we began singing again. "Olé!" we harmonised, "Olé, olé, o—" An elderly lady tapped me on the shoulder, none too gently. "Excuse me," she said, in a tone that verged on the brusque, "but don't you know any other songs?"

We pondered that, while Karl the barman fetched the next round. South Africans, it dawned on us, are woefully short of stirring anthems to sing during sport. Which is surprising, given that Leon Schuster made enough money out of "Hier Kommie Bokke" to retire to Knysna, a happy event for him, though an unfortunate setback to the Knysna elephant-breeding programme. We gave it a try, but it just didn't take, somehow. We could get out "Hier Kommie Bokke" just fine, but it always fell apart during the line that goes "Laa-lalalalalala".

Someone pointed out that PJ Powers has a career based exclusively around singing at World Cup ceremonies, but some of life's mysteries are best left unexplored. We settled, finally, on "Shosholoza", one of the most powerful of the world's sporting anthems. It cannot but lift the performances of the athletes and indeed the spectators. We need to resurrect "Shosholoza" for our major events, we all agreed, but mostly we need to learn the words properly. Those mumbled lines between the first chorus and the second where we lower our eyes and try to approximate the sounds are simply embarrassing.

A problem with "Shosholoza" is that it is rather harmonically complex for a sporting song, which is to say, a song intended to be sung while drinking heavily. There is a point where the two vocal lines overlap, and where the pitch of the voice changes, and coordinating that is a lot to expect of the lads in Kings Park, working their way through their second pocket of spiked oranges. If you have ever seen those two sunburnt fools wearing watermelons on their heads trying to start a Mexican wave on the Saturday afternoon of a Newlands cricket test, you will understand the need for simplicity. Watching a grown man trying to stand up and sit down at the same time is not a pretty sight.

Singability is the key here. Chelsea supporters in the UK are fond of launching into "One man went to mow, went to mow a meadow", not because of the allusive resonance of the lyrics, but because it is next to impossible to forget the words, no matter how many pints you have inhaled before the match. You also do not have to know when to stop. You never have to stop.

Most sporting anthems are similarly bereft of meaningful history. Liverpool's moving "You'll Never Walk Alone" is simply a song lifted from the cheesy old musical *Carousel*. It might have been "Memories" from *Cats*, had history been crueller.

The Twickenham anthem, "Swing Low, Sweet Chariot" is an old slavery spiritual from the American south. It was first sung at Twickenham not in support of the emancipationist movement, but light-heartedly on the occasion that Chris Oti, a player of Nigerian descent, scored a hat-trick of tries. Appropriately enough for the Twickenham crowd, it is an ode to death relieving the singer of this earthly misery.

We in South Africa need to bolster our repertoire of drinking songs that are clean enough to sing in public. So go on, enter the Bad Sport, Worse Singer competition. Submit your nominations for potential stadium favourites today. The winner will receive Leon Schuster. That's right, Leon Schuster. You can have him, really, We don't want him any more.

A celebration of cricket

BUSINESS DAY, 25 NOVEMBER 1999

H ARK! THE DISTANT THWACK of leather on willow! The soft patter like rain on an English summer resort of applause at the start of play! The slow creak and crack and ka-pow of Allan Donald's ligaments! If you listen closely, you can hear the low rumble of Darryl Cullinan brooding. It can only mean that cricket is here, and if all is not exactly right with the world, then it is at least not all wrong.

When finally I shuffle off this mortal coil, bury me on a grass embankment – if you can find one at an SA test venue – with a clear view of the scoreboard, in easy range of the man selling the draught beer in the big plastic cups, and know that I will be facing my own private timeless test with a sigh and a smile and lazy howzat. For as long as there are 22 grown men in white flannels (as well as two umpires and a third to watch the television replays) prepared to spend five days in painstaking pursuit of a phantasm, wrapped in a memory, swaddled in a dream, then all is not lost, for I will know there is still place in the world for the fine and the foolish and the noble pursuit of the pointless.

Cricket is the game that most closely approximates life – it seems long but is deceptively short; it is circular and repetitive but moves to an inexorable end; it is just but not always fair; it follows a system of tightly woven logic, playing itself out in a charmed circle of glorious absurdity.

Perhaps the highest praise for the game of cricket is that the Americans so thoroughly fail to understand it. For cricket, bless it, is by all reasonable standards an exercise in madness. It is ludicrous, and that is the point, for "ludicrous" literally means "done in sport" or "playing the game". And playing the game is what we still like to pretend that cricket is all about. This season England returns to South Africa for a tour, and there is a pleasing symmetry that they should return for the centenary of their hitherto most significant tussle with the home team. Even in the midst of bloody warfare, cricket played its role as a measure of civilised madness.

During the early stages of the Anglo-Boer War, the British in Mafeking were besieged by the Boers (commanded, then as now, by one General Cronjé). In April 1900 Veldkornet Sarel Eloff, a grandson of Paul Kruger, sent a note through the lines to Robert Baden-Powell, commander of the Mafeking garrison:

> *I see that your men play cricket on Sundays. If you would allow my men to join in, it would be very agreeable to me. Wishing you a pleasant day, I remain your obliging friend,*
>
> *S Eloff*

Baden-Powell, with a wily evasiveness alas unavailable to Nasser Hussain, declined, but you can but sigh for a time when cricket provided such a bond between civilised men. Perhaps it is simply spring fever talking, but I have never looked forward to a summer with keener pleasure. Ah, to be at the Wanderers, now that spring and England are here.

Sporting sex

BUSINESS DAY, 27 JANUARY 2000

ALAS, IT IS the way of the world that with each fresh advance of science, there must follow a wave of ethical quibbles hard upon it. So it is with the latest development in sport. Sex before the big match, announced *New Scientist* magazine late last year, is a good idea.

Of course, that was not news to me – I always recommend getting sex out of the way before the game starts. Bitter experience has taught me that it is no use trying to squeeze it in, if you will pardon the expression, during the slow-mo replays and beer ads. For that to work, you need a very understanding partner or at least a hand that has not just been holding an icy cold lager. You also need the ability to accelerate from a standing start to the finish line in less time than it takes an Aussie referee to blow a penalty against the Springboks.

In any case, for the sake of your performance as well as your peace of mind, it is best to discharge your, well, your romantic responsibilities before Hugh Bladen or Trevor Quirk start speaking. Believe me, you do not want to be startled mid-innings by Trevor's dulcet tones. That way impotence lies.

Apparently, though, if *New Scientist* is to be believed, it is also a good idea for the athletes to have an early kick-off. One Emmanuele Jannini of the University of L'Aquilla has released findings that confirm what Ian Botham, James Small and the entire French rugby team have been trying to tell us for years: pre-match sex enhances on-field performance. Evidently orgasm stimulates the production of testosterone, which gives athletes the edge in sports requiring the controlled exercise of aggression.

There are few players who can have failed to notice that playing well in the match increases your chance of getting lucky afterwards, but having the converse scientifically proven is a startling breakthrough.

Knowing how scientifically minded the SA cricket team is, it is surely only a matter of time before each player has his own individualised data base, plotting the nookie/runs-scored ratio, or the heavy petting/dot balls coefficient. Just as important as fitness training will be lessons in pick-up lines and attractive hairstyles – once Mornantau Hayward has lost that seven-rand-rentboy puff-and-peroxide look, his strike rate on and off the field can only improve. Derek Crookes? Well, perhaps it would be kinder not to mention Derek Crookes.

And this is where the question of ethics creeps in. It is one thing knowing how to improve your team's performance, but quite another to implement official policies. At what stage will local rugby teams be justified in sending out a nationwide call for patriotic lasses and – do not kid yourself – lads to lend a Vaselined hand in preparing the squads for competition? ("Do you give a toss for your country? Come prove it at Newlands, Saturday 2.30pm.")

And at what stage will testosterone production become a mandatory training measure? After a slump in form will the management take a player aside, press upon him a stack of saucy magazines and a box of Kleenex and frogmarch him to the nearest empty cubicle? Will wives have to co-sign contracts, guaranteeing their availability and co-operation during the season? Will they submit themselves to refresher courses, fitness training and technique workshops? It is an uncertain future into which science is leading us.

Finally, and most worrying, if sex before the game is so advantageous, what about sex during the game? I am quite sure that team physiotherapists, currently in charge of rub-downs and heat treatments, will not take kindly to any untoward enlargement of their job descriptions, but the possibilities are distinctly unsettling. I do not care to think too deeply on the prospect of the Springboks trooping off at half-time, 20 points down against the All Blacks, to be greeted by an irate Nick Mallett and Alan Solomons: "Boys, you're lacking aggression out there. Split up into pairs and do that exercise we demonstrated last week!"

Tyson 2000

BUSINESS DAY, 3 FEBRUARY 2000

HOW STRONG IS Mike Tyson? Why, he is so strong he does not even need to hit you. The wind speed of his gloves windmilling above your head is enough to knock you down.

The more I watch Tyson's recent fights, the more convinced I am that I have chosen the wrong career. I am sure with a little training I could last two rounds of not being hit by Mike Tyson. Just last week I was not hit by Larry Holmes, and I cannot begin to count the number of times I have not been hit by George Foreman. And let me tell you, George Foreman does not hit you a whole lot harder than Tyson does not hit you.

Last Saturday Iron Mike dropped Julius "Dead-weight" Francis five times in five minutes with a series of cuffs and waves and an unprovoked cuddle, leading me to suspect that the chief objection to his fighting in Britain had been raised not by women's rights activists but by Equity, the British actors' union.

Tyson at least knew his lines and had rehearsed his moves; it was such a shamefully ham-fisted performance from Francis that both Tyson and his current overlord Shelley Finkel were scrambling after the fight to insist that Tyson had knocked him out with a body blow. It was a necessary subterfuge. Even Stevie Wonder, seated at ringside behind David "I wear the pants in this house" Beckham, could see that Tyson had missed with the punches to Francis's head. The fight was the least convincing piece of sporting theatre since the Pakistani cricket team played Kenya, yet there is no denying that when Tyson fights he generates a primal excitement.

Tyson's aura was built 15 years ago, based equally on his ferocious fighting ability, and his hype as the baddest man on the planet. In a curious irony, today it is the talent that is over-hyped, whereas my fear is that Tyson may be badder than we realise.

Tyson has been beaten by every quality boxer he has fought. Even our own Francois Botha, as fearsome as a tub of yoghurt, nearly put him away.

Like Graham Hick on a flat pitch, Tyson can bully the weak and mediocre, but he folds against quality. He remains a drawcard purely because of his reputation for unpredictability and uncommon violence.

Tyson, truthfully, is not right in the head. He was not healthy when he went into prison, and if anything he is worse now. It is questionable whether he should be allowed to walk the streets. Listen carefully to one of his interviews – this is not a man feigning badness, but someone in tenuous and decidedly sporadic contact with what you and I call reality.

It has become a cliché to say that our interest in Tyson is similar to the urge to rubberneck when passing a car crash, but the tragedy of it is that on some level, we do not believe it is real. On some level we believe the blood and the piece of ear and the swearing and baby-talk are all hype and make-believe. We no longer blink when Julius Francis comes over all swagger and strut at the press conference, only to dive like Jacques Cousteau on the night, because we have come to accept that boxing is showbiz. Shows like WWF wrestling and even those poxy Gladiators have blurred the line between sport and play-acting to such an extent that we expect melodrama and plot twists; we almost expect real-life sport to appear scripted.

The more pantomimish Tyson appears, the more likely we are to accept it. It is a telling fact that Tyson was invited to join the WWF wrestling circus, but was ultimately regarded as not sufficiently stable to be a regular. When it comes to being a psycho, Tyson is too real to pretend, and yet he is too cartoonish for us to truly recognise what we are looking at. Tyson is a symptom of the devaluing of the real, and he may yet be its biggest victim.

When we finally get bored with Tyson we will switch channels, but Tyson confused, uncontrolled and becoming rapidly more so is stuck with himself. I hope I am wrong, but I have a feeling, with Mike Tyson, the worst is yet to come.

Clichés, champions and Baby Jake

BUSINESS DAY, 24 FEBRUARY 2000

S PORT WRITERS ARE not the sole purveyors of the cliché. The cliché is common wherever people speak without first troubling to think. That is to say, the cliché is very common indeed.

Sometimes a cliché can be a cliché before it has even been around long enough to become popularly recognised. I recently met an Internet consultant, for instance, who scratched his beard and told me that the secret of his profession is: "I think outside the box." I did not know exactly what that meant, but I knew I would not be able to sleep nights unless I immediately stamped on his instep and punched him in the throat.

But sports writers and commentators do appear to swaddle themselves rather more conspicuously than most in the fluffy bathrobe of hackneyed phrase and received wisdom. There are three reasons for this.

Firstly, sport writers tend to allow themselves to be persuaded that what they write about is unimportant, frivolous, somehow of less value than politics or motor cars. Secondly, there is the mistaken assumption that sports fans are a slow-witted lot, made up of the kind of individual whose idea of international sophistication is drinking a Namibian beer while performing a Mexican wave, who becomes suspicious of writing that does more than tell the score and mention that Bafana Bafana need to guard against conceding an early goal. In such a dusty wasteland, writers and commentators like Andy Capostagno and Mike Haysman and John Robbie and Neil Manthorpe are like desert flowers with the dew still clinging to their petals. If you see what I mean.

Thirdly, I would suggest that clichés and phrases that say nothing by repeating the overly familiar are actually more noticeable in a sporting context than in any other. Sport, unlike politics or economics, is such a rich and varied field that any attempt to reduce it and fit it into a standard mould is doomed to squirming failure. When Hugh Bladen offers a commentary that could be effectively superimposed over any other game he has ever commented on, it says far more about Hugh Bladen than it does about the game.

Ordinarily, clichés merely irritate, and at worst muffle the clarity of the action. Occasionally, however, they are downright misleading. In the build-up to last weekend's "Night of the Legends", it became popular in the sports pages to say that Hawk Makepula and Baby Jake Matlala were fighting not merely for the world title, but also for the title of people's champion. Stuff and nonsense. The whole point of being a people's champion is that it is not transferable with an official title – otherwise you would just call him champion and have done with it.

Makepula won the fight, and won it well, but the decision was greeted with boos and disbelief. One local journalist wrote, across copy stained and speckled with his tears, that Makepula should not take his triumph as an indicator of his ability. Such are the emotions when a people's champion is defeated.

Makepula – an extraordinarily gifted fighter with remarkable accuracy of punch and a fine sense of the ring – may one day become people's champion in his own right, but for now he has to be content with champion of the world. If he does one day manage to lay the same claim to the hearts of The People (whoever they may be), he will be one of the lucky few South Africans to do so despite being blessed with luminous talent.

Baby Jake is the archetypal South African people's hero – a man cheerfully struggling in the face of adversity, overcoming desperate disadvantages (age; limited talent; being the only man that Martin Locke can pat on the head) and rising above himself through pluck, mental toughness and high work rate. We love our gifted winners, obviously – our Joosts and our Vuyani Bungus and our Penny Heynses – but it is the less gifted winners who claim their place in our myths and our dreams of ourselves.

Baby Jake will never lose his place in the South African psyche. For the greater part of the 1990s he was a parable of ourselves – he seemed to say that with hard work and good PR, the little guy can beat the world. That was what we most needed to hear.

Superstition in sport

BUSINESS DAY, 2 MARCH 2000

I T TOOK ME a long time to realise that other people have this power too. For years I shouldered the burden in silence, fancying it mine alone – this terrible power to win or lose sporting events, merely by the way I watch them.

Superstition is common in sport. This is probably because the world of sport is itself a charmed circle, separate from the laws of logic and humdrum causality that plague our workaday lives. It is a place of romance and dreams, of implausibilities and impossibilities, rewards and punishments that follow not the narrow rules of consequence, but grander principles that the mortal heart can only dimly comprehend. Sport is the business of the gods, and their ways are dusky. The bounce of the ball, the rub of the green – the fingers of the gods are upon all of them.

Many sportsmen, I know, have their own rituals. They have lucky socks, routines for getting kitted up, set routes for driving to the ground. But I do not so much care what the players do. The players are but pawns, cyphers at the mercy of more powerful force fields. And those force fields are directed by you and me at home. Well, me, anyway.

I only appreciated the full weight of my responsibility after South Africa's readmission to world sport. The 1992 Cricket World Cup, to be precise. Every match I watched at my friend Mark the Shark's house – those long dark hours of coffee and cigarettes – we won. Every match I watched at our friend Doctor Teddy's house – a charming experience, with plenty of finger snacks and liquor and chops on the Weber for breakfast – we lost. And not to teams that should have beaten us, either: New Zealand and Sri Lanka and, of all things, England.

That troubled me, but it was only a year or so later, sitting on Doctor Teddy's couch watching Theo van Rensburg, the biggest choker since Isadora Duncan's scarf, slicing a last-minute penalty at Ellis Park that would have beaten the French, that I suddenly realised what I was doing to the country

I love. Luck follows inscrutable rules and apparently I was breaking one of them. Came the 1995 Rugby World Cup, I avoided Doctor Teddy's home like the very plague. I do not think I need remind you of the result.

I am used to winning test matches for my nation, and I am resigned to receiving no credit. There is a chair I sit in when we need a wicket, a shirt I wear for matches against the All Blacks, another for matches against anyone else. But even I am not as passionate as a certain friend of mine in Cape Town.

A caution: The following anecdote will illustrate the reach and stamina of one fan's superstition, but it is not for small children or ladies of delicate sensibility. If you fall into either category, kindly avert your gaze for the next 200 words. Very well: it was the early 1990s, and it was cricket season. In the pub after a one-day international, I ran into a fellow named Jeremy, who looked unusually gaunt and hollow-eyed. "Tired?" I asked.

He sighed weakly. "Tim Shaw," he said.

The story was gruesome. Lanky left-arm spinner Tim Shaw was enjoying a rare appearance in the SA team. Jeremy, with one eye on the game, was relaxing at home and had taken to – there is no more polite way of saying this – pleasuring himself. It was a tense match, SA had posted a low score, the opposition were scoring freely. Then Tim Shaw came on, and immediately bowled a maiden. Jeremy stopped pleasuring himself. Shaw's next delivery was pulled for four. Jeremy started again. Dot ball. Jeremy realised what he had to do.

"I didn't stop till he stopped," said Jeremy. "He bowled all 10 overs on the trot. With a drinks break in between."

"And from the other end?" I asked.

Jeremy shuddered. "Fanie de Villiers. I don't want to talk about it."

Nor did I. And you have my word, I never will again.

The day after Hansie was accused

BUSINESS DAY, 13 APRIL 2000

I F HANSIE CRONJÉ is guilty, we might as well all go home, tell our children there is no Father Christmas and start watching WWF wrestling. If Hansie Cronjé is guilty, I might as well be a lawyer.

In 1992 the SA cricket team were playing in the World Cup in Australia. The matches started shortly before midnight and carried on till the pearly half-light of coffee and alarm clocks. At the same time I was writing final law exams. On the morning SA were to play England in the semi-finals, I was scheduled to write a four-hour law exam. If the match ended on time, I would be able to make it from my friend Mark the Shark's house to campus (by taxi and on foot) to start writing.

I need scarcely remind you what happened that day. SA were batting second. First there was one rain delay, then there was another. "If you leave now," said Mark the Shark, "you can make it for the exam."

On the screen, Dave Richardson and Brian McMillan were squinting at the skies, willing it to stop raining. Peter Kirsten chewed his nails. In the background Hansie loomed darkly, his eyebrows knitted like cumulonimbus. I stayed.

We lost the match but I never regretted my decision. If I had left, I would not have deserved to feel a part of the team. I would not have been able to say, for the next eight years, "*We're* playing Australia tomorrow", rather than "*They're* playing Australia tomorrow".

During the eight years that have passed since – years I have spent happily not being a lawyer – Hansie has come to represent all that was good about feeling a part of South African cricket. As much as Fanie de Villers in the Sydney test of 1992, it was Hansie's miraculous pick-up, turn and throw from the boundary to run out Alan Border returning for a third that set up the SA win. It was the birth of Hansie's slog-sweep against Shane Warne in 1993 and 1994 that made us realise the fat boy did not walk on water. It was Hansie's bludgeoned 80-odd on the last day of the 1998 Centurion test match against Muralitheran and Sri Lanka that showed us how to win, and win well.

In my household, Hansie has become an untouchable: not in the Indian sense, but in the Elliot Ness, crime-busting incorruptible sense. If the other three are guilty it will be a source of shame; if Hansie is guilty, it will be a source of unimaginable pain. As I write this, we have had no further news. There is a news conference scheduled for tomorrow. If Hansie is guilty, neither South African sport nor the game of cricket will ever be quite the same again. Please, Hansie, say it isn't so.

Olympics 2000:
A lesson from chess

BUSINESS DAY, 15 SEPTEMBER 2000

THE SUPERSTARS OF the athletics world jetted in to Sydney this week, flexing their contracts and sponsorships, slipping on their zillion-rand running shoes, specially designed by evil-genius bio-nuclear technicians in top-secret subterranean lairs hidden inside the hollowed-out slopes of a Swiss Alp. Meanwhile, I sat on an aeroplane beside a young sportsman who will probably never make a cent from his sport, but who trembled with the kind of enthusiasm that burns like a torch.

I was flying from Lusaka to Johannesburg, and I had the privilege of being seated beside the Zambian youth chess champion, a handsome boy of 14 who stared at the clouds with wide eyes and saved his pine-scented moist towelette to take home to show his mother. He was in transit to a tournament in Uruguay, of all places, and he was so excited at being in an aeroplane that he could scarcely concentrate on the games. I insisted we play on a small magnetic chess set. With one eye and most of his mind directed out the window, he beat me two out of three games. The third ended in stalemate, largely because I swopped the pieces around while he was in the bathroom.

He was reading a thin pamphlet, handwritten and photocopied and stapled together. It was titled *Chess Etiquette*, and it gave instruction on how to be a courteous player: to shake hands before the game, to smile and congratulate your opponent if you lose, to thank him if you win. "Do not shout or cry," it commanded sternly. He sat with his eyes closed, repeating the words softly to himself, determined to forget nothing.

I told him he seemed an extremely polite young man, and that I did not think he had anything to worry about. He looked at me seriously and replied that no member of his family had ever travelled out of Zambia. He said: "My mother is proud that I am playing chess. But she says she will only be truly proud when I have returned and my coach tells her I have behaved myself well."

"Do you think you'll win?" I asked him. He just looked at me blankly and shrugged, as though the question had never cropped up before.

Over the next two weeks my hopes and thoughts will be with the South African team in Sydney, and I shall be rooting for gold with the loudest of them, but a large part of my heart will be with a small boy in Uruguay who still believes that honour weighs more than gold.

Of course, there will be no chess players at the Olympics. Nor will there be bridge players or snooker teams, despite impassioned representations by both codes. They have been rebuffed as not sufficiently Olympian. It seems at first glance to make sense – the Olympics are a celebration of physical achievement and excellence. *Higher, faster, stronger*, says the motto, not "Slower, and more thoughtful". It is not for nothing that there are no ancient Greek statues of naked men playing cards. Still, it is hard to tell quite what the qualifications for sporting status may be. What in the world makes synchronised swimming a sport? Why was tug-o-war considered a sport worthy of the Olympics between 1900 and 1920, and then not any more?

Once you start such questions, it is hard to stop. Why was cricket sufficiently Olympian to be played in the Paris games of 1900 (the Frenchies walking away with a proud silver medal), and not in the 100 years since? Ditto croquet, for that matter. Even golf had but two brief Olympic appearances, in 1900 and 1904, and now languishes in dignified Olympic isolation. It is all very peculiar.

But among all the great mysteries of sport qualification, there are some that defy all attempts at explanation. How did the Olympic organisers come to choose Town Planning as an Olympic event, between 1912 and 1948. Who thought it would be a good idea to include Musical Composition in 1928, 1936 and 1948? And if you were at the Athens games in 1896, please write and tell me: What in the world is the 100m Freestyle for Sailors?

Olympics 2000:
Perspective down under

BUSINESS DAY, 21 SEPTEMBER 2000

THERE IS SOMETHING soothing about watching the Olympic Games. It is disappointing, of course, that SA is taking such a caning on the medals table, but it is a gentle regret that I experience, not the agonies of personal investment. The psychic well-being of the nation is not on the line with each fresh event, and that is both an unfamiliar and a weirdly relaxing feeling.

That is not simply because most of our top athletes are trained and based overseas. (The drama of Penny Heyns failing to repeat her Atlanta double is really a showdown between her current training regime in Canada and her previous training regime in the USA. All we contributed was the flag.) Part of it is because the vastness of it all puts things in perspective. The stage is so big and there are so many players – rich ones like America and Australia, poor ones like Poland or Pakistan or us – that one's emotions take their proper places. It is right and proper that the joy of winning should be many times more intense than the disappointment of not winning. I imagine that this is what watching sport might once have felt like, before money and television and the manic compulsions of defensive nationalism.

All in all, Sydney is putting on a pretty good show. The opening ceremony was impressive and even entertaining, if you enjoy watching gangs of sexually ambiguous construction workers tap-dancing. As it happens, we do not, down at the Chalk 'n Cue, but we were kept happy by Keith Quinn and John MacBeth, the two Australian commentators. Keith and Johnno should be compulsory listening for every South African tempted to grumble about Quirk or Bladen.

"Those are construction workers," said Keith during an especially vigorous outbreak of dancing, "you can see their hard hats."

"That's right, Keith," agreed John, "construction workers built a lot in this country. They built the roads and the bridges."

Keith was not about to leave it at that. "They also built the buildings, John," he chipped in.

"That's right, Keith, they did," agreed John generously.

The ceremony had started with several dozen Australians on horseback. It was a time of strong emotions. How we laughed when Keith declared: "It is so appropriate that the ceremony should start with the sound of hoofs." How we cheered when the riders formed four perfect Olympic rings and one squiggly Olympic amoeba that wriggled and undulated before finally resolving itself into a kind of Olympic oval. How we nodded in grave agreement when John reminded us: "Horses were very important in the early days. They enabled people to travel further than if they were without horses."

I don't know if Keith and Johnno were the swimming commentators, but the best entertainment of the first week was waiting for the reaction as it became increasingly evident that Ian Thorpe was losing the 200m freestyle final. I have nothing against Ian Thorpe, who seems a nice enough lad, if a little big in the foot area. It was the Aussie triumphalism that was difficult to stomach. "He's the greatest thing in the water!" the commentators bellowed. "The Carl Lewis of the pool! No, faster than Carl Lewis! And such a humble boy!"

As he was beaten into silver by Pieter Hoogenband, I leaned closer to my screen. Would they lapse into silence? Would they apologise? They barely broke stride. "And Thorpie's the first to congratulate the Dutch swimmer! What a gentleman!"

Olympics 2000:
God needs an off-season too

BUSINESS DAY, 28 SEPTEMBER 2000

E VERY TIME A large aeroplane plunges into the sea or accidentally reverses into a tall building, someone pops up a few days later, eager to tell a reporter they were booked on that flight, and that only a nudge from the hand of a merciful and inscrutable God saved them from the big plunge.

"God put that traffic jam on the way to the airport to stop me catching that flight," they say, or: "If God hadn't given me a heart attack on Wednesday morning, I would have been flying on Wednesday evening."

I have a relative who flies frequently, and through a combination of bad timing and alcohol abuse, misses at least three out of every five flights. "God is keeping me from dying on those flights," she says.

"But those flights have all landed perfectly safely and on time," we point out.

"Yes, but one day they won't, and I'll have been saved," she insists, reaching for a miniature bottle of rum.

There is a family friend who each morning prays that the traffic lights on the way to work will all be green. "But what about people in the cross traffic?" I once asked. "Are they all sinners?"

She eyed me sternly. "One shouldn't presume to understand God's plans," she said.

I mention all this to illustrate in some small way my sense of wonder at the boundless capacity of certain individuals to persuade themselves that their god arranges the minute details of the universe to suit them. It is a form of humbleness that conceals a staggering vanity. "God's plan was that I swim this heat for Him today," said Penny Heyns after suffering the equivalent of a Concorde engine failure during the 200m breaststroke last week.

In His infinite subtlety, Penny was suggesting, God had woven a plan that required her to finish 20th in the qualifying rounds. After winning gold four years ago, rather less subtly, she declared God made her swim for His greater glory. Perhaps this time God made her swim just to show He knew how to lose gracefully.

My position, if I have not made it clear, is that I no more want to know details of an athlete's faith than I want to know who he or she votes for, or what movies they like watching. International sport is fraught enough without making it an arena for a kind of muscular jihad in which various denominations battle out a theology that seems to imply Jesus Christ is a swimmer and rugby player, the Prophet Mohammed plays squash and hockey, and the Buddha favours table tennis.

According to Joost van der Westhuizen's cosmogeny, his god was sufficiently exercised by his rugby career to make sure he won the Currie Cup, but only gave him third in the World Cup. More baffling, at least two SA athletes gave thanks to their god this week for allowing them to honour Him by finishing sixth and ninth respectively. Werner Botha – 800m – was perhaps the most puzzling: "I'm not disappointed," he beamed. "God willing, it wasn't my day."

Silver-medal swimmer Terence Parkin, by contrast, perhaps working on the principle that God helps those who help themselves to lucrative endorsement contracts, was rather more swift to talk about the motivating powers of his pre-race McDonald's burger. Maurice Greene spread his glory evenly and sometimes interchangeably between God and Nike.

It all makes me a little anxious. I begin to see evangelists everywhere. What was the deeper significance of Cathy Freeman's hooded bodysuit? Is she really an Amish sprinter, the hood a kind of aerodynamic bonnet? I suppose, though, that the Olympics are, of all athletic occasions, the right place for declarations of religious fervour. The original games, after all, had athletes competing for the glorification of the great god Zeus. That, plus the gold for winning, of course.

Paralympics

BUSINESS DAY, 2 NOVEMBER 2000

I AM NOT SURE what it says about us as a sporting nation that over the past four years our Olympic performance has subsided while our Paralympians have improved their medal haul by about 30 per cent. I am not sure that I want to think too deeply on the matter, although I do know that it will make me far less likely to curse and hurl unmerited threats at absent polio sufferers the next time I screech into a vacant parking bay, only to discover that taunting yellow wheelchair painted on the tarmac.

Ooh, they infuriate me, those yellow-painted wheelchairs, but I suppose it is all in a good cause. Walking an extra 500m with an armful of shopping is a small price to pay for an additional gold medal or two.

For the Paralympians to train and qualify and compete at the games is indeed a fine achievement and an example in endurance and fortitude to those of us who are too quick to grumble and whimper when we misplace the remote control and have to get up off the couch to change channels manually, but the coverage of the games provided the keen observer with other more profound lessons about human nature.

For a certain lazy kind of writer, it has been easy to eulogise the men and women of the Paralympics as models of moral rectitude, shining examples of all that we could or should be. The ideal of Olympic sportsmanship is long dead, and the sentimental tendency is to transfer that idealism onto the Paralympics.

If you are a one-legged shot-putter, or an armless butterfly swimmer, the suggestion goes, you are somehow necessarily lit by a purer and more noble flame. You are different in fundamental ways from a two-legged putter of the shot: you are more morally admirable. This is, of course, a patronising nonsense.

As the Paralympians themselves would be first to remind us, a human being with a physical disability is still a human being, subject to the same weaknesses and temptations as the rest of us. If anything, the Paralympics were riven with even more scandals and squabbles than the Olympics. The power-lifters demonstrated that theirs is a sport that, across the spectrum of physical challenges, attracts the kind of dimwit who cannot figure out how far in advance of the competition to stop taking performance-enhancing drugs. Similarly, scarcely an event went by without protests and accusations that this or that medallist was not quite as disabled as he or she was officially registered as being. There are subtle gradations of disability invisible to the naked eye, but evident to the partially sighted one.

My favourite cheating wheeze, though, is the practice of "boosting", in which, if newspapers are to be believed, athletes put their nether regions to excruciating torture in order that the body's release of adrenaline will boost their performances. This is obviously only feasible if one has no sensation below the waist, but some of the more grisly practices included nailing one's genitals to the wheelchair, twisting elastic bands around the testicles and blocking off catheters so that the bladder fills to capacity. Not the sort of thing you would expect to find Stephen Hawking doing while mulling over an especially tricky equation.

I found it all weirdly comforting. It reinforced what we all should already know: a person in a wheelchair is not a different kind of person from you or me; it is you or me in a wheelchair, just as courageous, cowardly and sneaky as we are, just as weak and strong as everyone else. Congratulations for the medals, Amakrokokroko. You made us proud.

Keep in character

BUSINESS DAY, 12 APRIL 2001

S OME YEARS AGO, when George Foreman came rumbling back from the gloom and darkness of sporting middle-age to become the oldest man to win the heavyweight boxing title, twenty-odd years after his Rumble in the Jungle with Muhammad Ali, he discovered that the world of sports was entirely changed.

As late as the 1970s, a sportsman's involvement in marketing and commerce seldom extended beyond wearing a particular sweatband, or perhaps posing for a still photograph for a magazine advertisement. Ali bent those rules, as he bent so many others, but even he was really only ever marketing himself. In the 1970s Foreman had the same dark, frightening charisma that Sonny Liston had a decade before. It was a charisma based on violence coupled with silence.

To read Norman Mailer's account, for instance, of the weeks leading up to the Rumble in the Jungle, or to watch *When We Were Kings*, the outstanding documentary of the fight, is to see the same picture: Ali dancing and clowning and preening in the foreground, like a parakeet or a poppinjay, trying to distract our attention and probably his own from the brooding shadow of Foreman, stalking the background like a muscular jungle panther. In the film there is a dazzling montage of the two training in Kinshasa. Ali is skipping, smiling, chattering, chanting rhymes, philosophising about the nature of prettiness. There are beaming people standing around; some are sipping what seems to be champagne.

This is intercut with Foreman standing alone before a heavy bag in a dimly lit room, feet apart and rooted to the ground. He looks neither up nor down, swinging body blow after body blow into the bag, blows that cause the fundament to shudder, like a man chopping down a redwood. Each punch, Mailer tells us in his book, could stave the hull of a whaleship.

Watching today, knowing what happened, I still cannot imagine how Foreman could lose, how he did not kill Muhammad Ali. Such was the power of Foreman's enigma, the force of his silence. He allowed us to invest him with our darkest fears and fantasies. He was like a principle of nature.

Then, when he returned, he discovered that sportsmen could make even more money out of the ring than in it. He became Smiling George, the cheeseburger spokesman. He appeared on chat shows and music videos. I had the misfortune to watch him star in his very own infomercial for George Foreman's patented fat-free cooking skillets, or some such. A grinning Foreman cracked jokes and demonstrated how to fry a steak that tastes good without making you worry at the weigh-in. It was a depressing turn of events. It always is when this fantasy world of sport, in which we invest so much of our human desire for archetypes, for grand narratives, for good and evil, for epic tales and truths and mythic characters, is revealed to be made up of nothing more than people with sporting ability.

I was reminded of George Foreman while watching a recent cricket test match from Antigua. One of the commentators was Sir Vivian Richards who, in his own way, was a Foreman of the cricket pitch. He swaggered out to bat with an arrogance that was hostile. He owned the ground, he bullied and brutalised anyone who lined themselves against him. You feared for the safety or at least the mental well-being of his opponents. He was like a man apart, not quite bound by mortal rules.

Yet there he was, chatting away with Mike Haysman, yapping sweet pleasantries, making silly jokes and giggling like a small girl. At one point he took time out to promote an Antiguan movie in which his brother is acting – some Caribbean blockbuster titled *The Sweetest Mango*. He was, it must be said, utterly charming, but this was not the force of nature I had grown up fearing. This was not the concentrated essence of cricketing thunder. I liked him, but another sporting archetype quietly crumbled away. Say what you like about Geoff Boycott, but at least he is always in character.

Persecution complex

BUSINESS DAY, 19 APRIL 2001

EVERY SO OFTEN I have occasion to find myself in the small hamlet of Parys. The small hamlet of Parys, while being neither as large nor as cosmopolitan as its namesake in France, and lacking such other typically French features as swanky restaurants and the Eiffel Tower, has many things going for it that the real Paris does not. For instance, there are almost no Frenchmen in Parys, and that is an advantage not to be sniffed at. Or indeed, to use a more typically Parisian response, sneered at, sniffed and spat at.

Whenever I am in Parys I visit a local watering hole rejoicing in the name of Heinie's. I have not met the eponymous Heinie, and if I am careful and lucky, I may never do so. Heinie's is a good place to absorb local colour and also to absorb beer.

This weekend I was there, watching the Bulls play the Reds. Ordinarily I avoid watching the Bulls play. I am not one of those fair-weather SA sports fans who only support a winning team, but watching the Bulls goes beyond the call of duty. Even Bulls fans do not watch Bulls games any more. It is too depressing. In medieval times, the equivalent would have been watching the village idiot beat himself repeatedly over the head with a stick. But there I was, and I am glad I was. It was worth watching if only for Joost van der Westhuizen, who is still in my book the best scrumhalf in SA and possibly the universe. He is as hard, predatory and downright miraculous as ever he was. Without him, the Bulls would have lost by 370 points.

It was also worth watching the game in order to be gifted a glimpse into the inner life of a hidden South Africa. A man sat himself down beside me. He wore large glasses and a wig he must have found in a Parys second-hand store. I think it had once been a lampshade, but the gent had trimmed it to resemble those limp, lank hairstyles favoured by European soccer players in the 1970s. The game began. It seemed clear to me, and I would have assumed to every sentient creature watching, that the Bulls were once more busily going about the business of beating themselves. More than that – they beat themselves mechanically, efficiently, like self-cleaning carpets of the future. As passes were spilt and players fell the wrong way in tackles, I groaned and buried my face in my hands. So did the gent with the wig, but gradually I realised that his lamentations were directed not at the quality of play, but the referee.

The worse the Bulls played, the more forceful he became. "The referee hates us," he spluttered in Afrikaans. "They sit in Australia and they say to their referees: *Whatever you do, don't let those boerseuns win.*"

I have always considered myself as enthusiastic a ref-basher as the next man, but now I realise that is only true if the next man is not sitting next to me in Heinie's bar. I do not know what psychic debt it would have cost that man and his pals to admit that a South African rugby team might simply not be good enough, but it was more than they were equipped to pay. It must be exhausting to have the unflagging conviction that every foreigner out there, every other person in the entire world, is engaged in a ceaseless conspiracy to make your life an individual misery. It is a burden that must make the shoulders sag.

Still, there are upsides. We watched the Stormers game that followed, and while my heart sang with the joy of it, my happiness had nothing on the man with the wig. He turned to me at the final whistle, a strange light glowing in his eyes. "They all try to beat us," he yelled, "but they can't. We are kings. There is nothing we can't do!"

Then he adjusted the lampshade on his head and went to the bar with shoulders held square.

Comrade Porky

BUSINESS DAY, 7 JUNE 2001

PORKY WITHERS IS in training for the Comrades marathon. You must understand the magnitude of that statement: the last time Porky Withers was seen moving at any pace faster than a contented stagger was when Big Bob Plummer accidentally zipped up Porky's tie in his briefcase and walked out the door.

But it's true: he has given up ordering a chaser with his breakfast beer, and Sad Henry caught a glimpse of Porky in tracksuit and running shoes just this morning, doing his warm-up stretches. "He was touching his knees," said Sad Henry with an impressed sort of voice.

Every afternoon we sit in the Chalk 'n Cue and watch Porky Withers come sagging past the plate-glass window. Every 40 minutes or so he reappears, looking yet purpler in the face, his knees buckling further, his torso dragging closer to the ground, his sweat band slipping lower and lower over his eyes. It takes him two hours to complete four laps. Do not imagine that Porky Withers is running around the neighbourhood – nay, not even around the block. He is running around the Chalk 'n Cue.

Getting fit will kill Porky Withers, we all agree as we watch Leon the barman carry Porky inside, lay him down on the bar and pour gin into his mouth, using a rolled-up newspaper as a funnel. Some people are just not fit to be fit.

The rest of us know our limitations: we are in training to be Comrades marathon tele-refs. To be a tele-ref is surely a passion smouldering in every SA sport watcher's bosom. We are all experts in our fields – being able to yell insults at the referee is almost a prerequisite to qualifying as an SA sport watcher. I once became an expert in curling, a peculiar northern hemisphere sport involving ice and flat weights with handles, after just four minutes of watching the Nagano Winter Olympics. You have not seen a sad sporting sight until you have seen a South African in grubby vest and white boxer shorts yelling advice at a bunch of Scandinavians in furry parkas on the other side of the world.

Most of us would reluctantly admit that we are probably not up to the rigours of actually running from one side of a rugby field to another or standing all day in the Calcutta sun and still being able to monitor every nuance of the tackle-ball rule or every infringement of the front-foot no-ball. Being a tele-ref, though, is a job that causes our very DNA to cry out in happy recognition. "Hell, yes! I can watch a slow-mo replay and tell you that the ball bounced this side of the line! That's a job I can do!"

The latest tele-ref is to monitor the Comrades marathon. It was announced this week that some highly trained individual will sit in front of a television set, no doubt keeping himself hydrated and with a dedicated team to massage his thighs, and watch 11 hours of coverage, keeping a crafty eye peeled for suspicious behaviour during the race. The object is obviously to try to nab the legion of dedicated Comrades cheats, although I suspect the definition of "suspicious behaviour" may have to be more clearly defined. In my book, running for 11 hours dressed up like a rhinoceros is sufficiently suspicious to be grounds for thorough psychiatric investigation, and you can imagine how delighted I was one year to recognise my investment broker trotting along in baby's diaper and bonnet, sucking on a dummy.

There will be other mobile referees on motorbikes, zooming between the runners and inspecting them for signs of being someone else, but I would guess that the tele-ref has the hardest job. If recent years are anything to go by, he or she will have to brave 11 hours of the commentary of Lindsay Waite – not a commitment to be undertaken lightly. Whoever the tele-ref may be, I hope they are up to the task. I wish all competitors well in the run-in to the big run-out, but always remember: there's more to life than health.

Kelehe's moving victory

BUSINESS DAY, 21 JUNE 2001

AFTER THE DROUGHT, a deluge. The sport came thick and fast this weekend. Television-watching muscles that had become soft through weeks of inactivity were made to stretch and ache as we reeled under the accumulative pleasures of having rugby, soccer and the Comrades marathon to digest in the space of two days. Of course, they were not undiluted pleasures. With renewed competition comes the shadow of defeat.

Happily, it was not defeat but the feet of Andrew Kelehe that kicked off the weekend. As stirring as it was to see the small man powering away from the Russians and surging into the stadium with all of SA riding on his shoulders, the moment of real beauty came as he crossed the finish line to be almost bowled over by his tearful wife Rose. Is there any dream that strikes a greater chord in the competitive heart of man than to have completed an epic trial in triumph, to be met with the wordlessly weeping joy and pride of the woman you love? It moved me to the quick.

At a stroke, Andrew Kelehe was Odysseus returning after 10 years on the wide and salty deep, and Rose was his Penelope. Who among us could hear her sobbing testimony without tremors of envy: "He is my husband," she told Trevor Quirk, "and he keeps doing the impossible. He can do anything." Is that not, deep down, what we all dream of one day hearing our wives and lovers say about us? I would guess Andrew will not be on washing-up duty in the Kelehe household for some while to come.

As much as I am puzzled and a little frightened by the very idea of long-distance road-running, Comrades is one of those great sporting spectacles. I feel about it the way I feel about test cricket: it is so magnificently pointless, so heroically futile that its very existence reminds us that humankind still gloriously struggles on in its senseless pursuit of happiness. We are odd creatures, thankfully, and Comrades shines like a beacon of oddness. No matter what is happening on the front page of the newspaper, I will be assured that all is still right with the world as long as there are 22 men still prepared to wear white flannels and chase a red leather ball for the better part of a week, or as long as there are pot-bellied men and women adorned with helium balloons who believe running from Durban and Maritzburg is a good idea. This is my article of faith: as long as Bruce Fordyce is still running Comrades, we are all going to be OK.

A day at Loftus

BUSINESS DAY, 2 AUGUST 2001

AH, AND WHAT a day it was. The afternoon was warm and bright, the air was so clear you could barely see it, and so thin that if you ran up the stairs to get to your seat, your lungs burnt as though they had been filled with braai-lighter fluid. Not that I attempted anything so foolishly energetic as running up the stairs to get to my seat.

Outside the stadium was the fine aroma of boerewors rolls and ketchup and expectation; inside was the stirring sight of men wearing green wigs and caps with Springbok horns and moustaches dyed with the colours of the South African flag. It was a grand day to be in Pretoria, and when the Springboks ran out, the roar of the Loftus crowd was enough to lift you off your chair and into the air, as though you were an empty chip packet borne aloft by the hot gust of men's hopes. I had never been to Loftus Versfeld before, and after last Saturday I may never go again. It can only ever be downhill from here.

I arrived with certain expectations of what a rugby test in Pretoria would be like, but I was surprised. The Loftus crowd is a curious one. Sure enough, as I arrived in the parking lot some beefy fellow in blue rugby shorts was unfurling a large old SA flag from the back of his bakkie. I paused to frown and tut, but as I watched he unfurled an equally large new SA flag, and walked happily toward the stadium with a flag in each hand.

It was an auspicious beginning. I found my seat on the grandstand and settled down to watch the curtain-raiser. Five rows in front of me, what I can only describe as a tour bus of Japanese rugby fans arrived. There were 17 or 18 of them, all wearing matching sunglasses and Springbok-green golf shirts and fanning themselves with official match programmes. My word – I couldn't help thinking – they do take these cultural tours literally nowadays. It was an unworthy thought. I felt even worse about thinking it when a mountainous fellow behind me, sipping from a two-litre Coke bottle that had been diluted with some sort of fiery liquor – call me a purveyor of stereotypes, but I am guessing brandy – stood up and called out in Afrikaans: "Excuse me, if you're looking for the Hong Kong Sevens, I think you may have taken a wrong turn off the N1."

The group looked at him blankly, but his friends did not. The mountainous fellow sat down with the contented air of someone expecting applause, but his friends were not amused. A furious war of Afrikaans words broke out behind me.

"What do you want to go and say something like that for?" demanded one hardly less mountainous friend. "That was just rude, and furthermore Hong Kong is in China, you dummy," said another. (You will forgive me if my translation from Afrikaans lacks something of the warmth and colour of the original. There were certain words spoken that simply cannot be translated into English. And should not be, even if they could.)

The first mountainous fellow tried to defend himself. "I was just joking," he said, "and they don't even speak the language."

But he was getting nowhere. I was beginning to feel uncomfortable. It was like having the Drakensberg range suddenly start quarrelling above you while you are out for a pleasant stroll in the country air. But the story had a happy resolution. Half an hour later, as I came staggering back from buying beer, I noticed the original mountainous fellow buying biltong from a vendor. He was shelling out R15 a packet for 17 or 18 packets. As I watched, he winched himself to his feet and trekked down the concrete stairs to the row of rugby fans. He handed them the biltong and made his apologies, then trudged back to his seat, still blushing beneath his whiskers.

"That's better," said one of his friends as he sat down again. "Now we can enjoy the game." Boy, did we ever.

Anna vs Amanda

BUSINESS DAY, 18 OCTOBER 2001

PERHAPS IT IS the times we live in, but nothing seems truly to surprise me any more. I can watch the SA cricket team swing from world-beaters to hit-and-hope chumps in the space of a week and it no longer strikes me as worthy of comment. I can watch some dope from *Big Brother* crop up on a sports talk show and it does not even raise my eyebrows. But even I was taken aback by the announcement that Anna Kournikova was being imported to play a series of big-buck exhibition matches against Amanda Coetzer. Now really.

If I have been following the story correctly, this means one short female tennis player who has never won a grand slam tournament will be playing one taller female tennis player who has never won a grand slam tournament, and millions of rands will be riding on the outcome. Well, count me out. There is something all wrong about this. Even if I were the kind of person to give a flying fulmination for the result of an exhibition event that is stripped of relevance in terms of WTA points and competitive context, I would want to see the local heroine up against the best, not some middle-of-the-range masher whose career highlights are all in her hair.

But that is the whole point, I suppose. It is not about the tennis. Kournikova has about as much to do with tennis as the WWF has to do with wrestling. The WWF coined a new term to describe their particular brand of populist flim-flam and flummery. They call themselves "sports entertainment", and that is what Kournikova is: a cheap gimmick using sport as nothing more than a sales window for presenting itself to the world.

She is like one of those Miss World contestants who have a special talent. ("Miss Uruguay will demonstrate how to juggle with hamsters, Miss Sweden will sing the theme song to *Ally McBeal* while drinking a glass of water, and the former Miss Moscow will show us that she has a darn decent game of tennis.")

Come to think of it, I suppose it is necessary for Anna Kournikova to play exhibition matches. If she were to limit herself to the WTA circuit she would not play sufficient games for her sponsors to get their money's worth. One game a tournament does not add up to many games over the year.

Even aside from the obvious insult to the spirit of sport, I'm not sure what all the fuss is about. She is a pretty enough girl, but no more so than a zillion other professional models (which is really all she is). What do we think will happen? That she will suddenly decide to play topless? That she will celebrate each point won in a tie-break by making out with a ballboy while we watch? It's tragic. Ogle if you like, my friends, but when one day a women's pressure group demands a quota system of good-looking men wearing skimpy shorts in the Springbok tight five, remember you have only yourselves to blame.

A premier bore

BUSINESS DAY, 9 MAY 2002

I HAVE NEVER UNDERSTOOD people who do not understand sport. I occasionally envy them, mind you. Not being passionately involved in the physical and athletic fortunes of more or less random gangs of strangers must ease a great burden on your time, not to mention the state of your nerves and the depth of your emotional reserves. I think it must be a tremendous relief to know that for the next several months your sense of self and your outlook on the world will be determined by factors less impersonal than the bounce of a ball or whether Breyton Paulse gets a chance to run in space.

Much as I envy those people, though, I have never understood them. I am baffled by men who are capable of ambling through a Saturday afternoon without so much as a thought to the match – who can, indeed, pause at a television and peer politely at the score and make genial conversation like "Ah, good, Monty must have his kicking boots on" or "Tsk, tsk, another bad day at the office" before wandering off to have tea with their wives or wash their cars or whatever the hell these people do when the match is on.

As much as I sometimes envy them, on other occasions (mainly when SA is winning) I feel profoundly sorry for them. They are missing out on an entire dimension of life – a world of drama and comedy, of pathos and bathos and the incomparable rush of unmediated emotion that is available nowhere else with such regularity and such immediacy. Sport gives you the opportunity to gasp at greatness, to wince at small tragedies, to sigh at dreams achieved and chances let slip, to throb and thrum with larger emotions than are available in the humdrum everyday. Not to have sport in your life strikes me as just as sad as never having read powerful literature, or never having been moved by music to an urge other than to dance, or never having been lost, however briefly, in the deep pleasures of a fine painting.

And yet there are those who feel these things about me. Because in fact there is one sense in which I am not so far removed from those without sport.

It is like this: I do not care about English football. With the best will in the world, last weekend I could not give a flying bicycle kick through a rolling doughnut for whether Chelsea beat Arsenal or Arsenal beat Chelsea to win the FA Cup. I can barely tell Chelsea from Arsenal. They are both based in London, both fanatically supported by tribes of oiks and yahoos, and both comprised in the main of players who scarcely speak English, let alone hail from the clubs' traditional geographic precincts.

Admittedly, I am not a soccer fan at all. Soccer does not move me. I do watch the occasional Bafana Bafana match, and there will certainly be moments during the World Cup when I find myself watching South Korea tangling with Lichtenstein or some similar postage-stamp nation, but that is just another way of saying I am not a soccer fan. Watching World Cups and the occasional international does not qualify you as a fan. But, even if I were a soccer fan, this strange (white) SA passion for the English Premier League leaves me flummoxed.

I cannot fathom why a friend of mine is plunged into the blue mopes whenever Leeds lose. Whence an allegiance with Leeds? My friend has never so much as been to Leeds (which perhaps explains how he can maintain his enthusiasm for the dump). None of his relatives hail from Leeds (or if they do he wisely does not admit it).

I know others who will wear scarves and sing songs in praise of such socio-political obscurities as Sheffield Wednesday, Watford and Hull. I listen to their vast and intricate and, to me, entirely empty language of English football fandom, and I can only frown and shrug and take myself off to do something useful.

And my friends look at me and sigh and they say: "Isn't it sad? He is missing out on so much."

Players without passion
are like Danie-less dreams

BUSINESS DAY, 23 MAY 2002

IN 1995, IN the week or so before the biggest month of my life so far, I was bothered by a persistent dream. In this dream I am sitting in the locker-room at Newlands, one sock on, the other still in my hand, my boots beside me. From outside I hear an unearthly noise, a rumbling, swelling drone, as though a swarm of bees the size of mastodons were descending.

But it is not a swarm of bees the size of mastodons. It is the sound of the world in anticipation. It is the sound of the whole of SA leaning forward, rubbing its hands, stamping its feet. I am wearing a Springbok jersey, and as I sit there blinking in the half-light, I realise that I am in the South African team to run out in the opening match of the World Cup.

In my dream, as I sit there in the locker-room, berating myself for not having kept in shape, cursing that pack of cigarettes last weekend, I am gripped by at least as much excitement as fear. In my dream I know that I am in no condition to play international rugby – I am scarcely in condition to play with a rubber duck in the bath – but I am tingling with the possibility that I will be able to do something, that I will be on hand to take the pass or put my body in the way of Timmy Horan or do something to help us win.

Danie Gerber is my centre partner. He looks at me appraisingly. "I think you had better go to second centre," he says.

"I think you had better hang onto the ball in the backline moves," I say.

He nods and pats my shoulder. "Don't worry," he says, "we'll get through this." And then we run out of the dim locker-room and into the sudden white light, and that is where I always woke up.

After the World Cup started and we won the first match, albeit without the help of Danie and me, I stopped having that dream, but to this day I remember the almost unbearable mix of fear and elation when I realised I was about to run out in green and gold in front of my nation. This week

Percy Montgomery withdrew from the Springbok set-up in order to go play club rugby in Wales. I know that Percy Montgomery has been a Springbok many times before, and so the feeling is dulled and the novelty has worn off, but I still think he is a pale shadow of a man for turning his back on the Springbok jersey. I understand that money is important. Believe me, I do. But it is still just money and there is no cheque in the world so large and with sufficient zeroes that I would swap it for that feeling I had back in 1995 – even if it was just a feeling in a dream.

The death of Hansie

BUSINESS DAY, 5 JUNE 2002

THE DEATH OF Hansie Cronjé matters. Watching the television tributes – all slow-mo replays and sad strings and freeze frames – I felt my throat tighten and heart sigh. I felt myself remembering my own favourite moments of Hansie.

I remembered the time he took five wickets in a one-day match against India, when I had drawn his name as my player in our regular drinking game over at Chunko's house. I had to drink every time Hansie's name was mentioned by the commentators. Hansie had never really bowled in a one-day match before, so I fancied myself safe. I had to work the next morning. You would be surprised how many times a player gets mentioned by the commentators when he is a non-regular bowler taking a five-for in a one-day international.

I remembered being at Centurion when he struck the second fastest test 50 ever, to win a match against Sri Lanka that Muttiah Muralitheran seemed to be claiming. I remembered sitting and watching on television as he slogged Shane Warne into cow corner, and turning and saying to Chunko: "Thank god Hansie is South African."

I watched the television tributes and I felt profoundly sad. Hansie was one of those public figures who truly are public figures, because he *meant* something to each of us. He symbolised values and fears and beliefs and points of pride and points of shame. The sadness I felt was in the waste of his legacy. For nearly 10 years he had made me proud to be South African, he had given me faith and hope and belief in something, and he carried a burden of expectation that no human being could ever truly bear. Which is why I was never – and will never be – able to forgive him for falling. The anger and sorrow he caused me was as disproportionate as the pride and joy he had brought.

As someone who mattered to us, what he did mattered more than what you or I do. It is not fair, but it is what happens to public figures. If they live in our dreams, and our dreams of ourselves, their lives become more than the lives of real people. They become the stuff of drama and tragedy and symbolism, like figures in Greek legend who fly too close to the sun. Hansie fell from his pedestal, and then this week he fell – far too literally – from the sky. Hansie Cronjé was more than a real person, but he was also a real person, and the real person's life is over. We must mourn that, but we should not forget the full story of Hansie Cronjé. In his failings as well as his successes, he meant something. In death as well as life, he matters.

A new sports hero

BUSINESS DAY, 11 JULY 2002

I HAVE A NEW sports hero. He is, in fact, a hero for the modern times. Not only is he a true all-rounder, participating in an impressive range of events, but he embodies many of the old-fashioned values of sport itself. In these soulless, professional times, such is his love of his craft that he actually pays to participate, and in doing so, he shakes up the sanitised, pre-packaged formulae to which spectator sports have been subjected since the dominance of television programming and modern sponsorship demands.

His name is Mark Roberts, but you would know him better as that guy who streaked across Centre Court at Wimbledon last Sunday, performed a naked barrel-roll over the net and was bustled away, waving to an appreciative crowd. Mark Roberts was the most entertaining part of the men's final. And if I were the brains trust behind international men's tennis I would consider putting him on permanent retainer.

But Mark Roberts' sporting talents are too broad to confine him to the tennis tramlines. Mark has risen like a pink spectre at more than 150 sporting events, but he reserves his stand-out performances for the football pitch. He has popped up at the Champions League final (where he apparently dribbled upfield and slipped one past Bayern Leverkusen's goalie, the perfectly named Hans-Jorg Butt), and also at last year's FA Cup final, where alas he was denied the opportunity to complete the double by getting one over Nicky Butt. Whether David Seaman was equal to his shooting is unfortunately unrecorded.

Mark is a dedicated athlete. He is in sufficiently good shape that his appearances are greeted with a hearty hooray from the crowds, rather than the appalled silence that would follow the unkitted performance of, say, me. More than this, he has apparently paid out more than R30 000 in fines over the years, in pursuit of his athletic ambitions. From the delighted expressions on the faces of the crowd on Sunday, they would have been happy to have a quick whip around and pay this latest fine. You could almost feel the sense of the anticlimax when they had to get back to Lleyton Hewitt and David What's-his-name.

I was half hoping for Mark to come freewheeling out in the Tour de France this week, but no such luck. Spokes and bicycle chains, I suppose, are not the streaker's friends. Not to mention those sudden gear changes.

I know this sort of thing is not really to be encouraged – and when it is drunk men with moustaches running onto the rugby field while play is in progress, it is to be deplored – but Mark chooses his moments between spells of play, and he is such a consummate professional that I cannot but warm to him. Sometimes it is a relief to find that there is still space in professional sport in which something may happen that has not been planned and approved by the corporates.

Rugby's day of shame

BUSINESS DAY, 15 AUGUST 2002

PIETER VAN ZYL is on everybody's lips, if you will pardon the expression. No matter what else happened in the world of sport this past week, the principal topic of conversation was Pieter van Zyl, the man in the tatty jersey who waddled onto the field during the match on Saturday to put the hurt on referee Dave McHugh.

Pieter van Zyl was too good, or bad, to be true. If the Australian Rugby Union had wanted to hire someone to besmirch the name of South Africa and had sent down to central casting for a likely candidate, they could not have dredged up a more perfect stereotype than Pieter van Zyl. The Australians would have been as pleased with him as the JFK conspirators were when they found Lee Harvey Oswald.

I think a good deal of the embarrassment we felt on Saturday was not as much caused by the pitch invasion as it was by the very sight of Van Zyl being manhandled off the park in his faded Springbok jersey with "Bokke" on the back, hiking up over a belly the size and shape of a volkstaat, his face a pudgy smudge of belligerent incomprehension. The heart sank to see him, the way the hearts of French people must sink to see caricatures of a Frenchman in a stripy shirt and beret, chewing a garlic clove and twirling his moustache and saying "Ooh-la-la".

But cliché though he was, and as much as you would hesitate to invent such an obvious character for a novel or a screenplay, it is possible to see Pieter van Zyl as a powerful symbol of the political dilemma of old white SA.

There is no doubt that Pieter van Zyl was frustrated by the ref. We were all frustrated by the ref. The game was blown with more even-handedness and consistency than any of the other Springbok games during this Tri-Nations tournament, but we were still hamstrung by two McHugh decisions of unparalleled awfulness that brought about a 14-point swing in the result of the match. The All Blacks received no such decisions, nor have the opposing team in any of the Tri-Nations matches involving the Springboks. I wish a South African had not run onto the field to assault a match official, but I cannot honestly say that deep in my heart I am sorry to see pain inflicted on one of these referees. Let them get back some of the pain they have been inflicting on me. Given the right circumstances – mainly, without several hundred thousand witnesses – I would have been sorely tempted to do the same thing. My chief regret is that it was not Stuart Dickinson.

Still, the forces that pulled Pieter van Zyl onto that field like tectonic plates slowly pulling Madagascar free of Gondawanaland ran deeper than rugby. They were the frustration and bitterness of a decade of waning power, a decade of increasing helplessness and impotence. Pieter van Zyl felt short-changed by history, he has felt short-changed by history for some time now, and on Saturday, damn it all, he was not going to take it any more. There on Saturday, sitting in King's Park, something inside Pieter van Zyl snapped, and he went waddling into that bright sunlight to wrest back his own destiny from a world lined against him.

I do not mean to overstate the case, but it is truly said that sport – and especially rugby – is a conduit and a conductor for the powerful emotions that run through us. Pieter van Zyl's frustrations found a focal point in a game of rugby and in the figure of the referee. There is something inside me that whispers that it is perhaps fortunate that they found the precise outlet they did. It is a shame for rugby, but it may be a good thing for society. If he wasn't running onto a rugby pitch, he may have been doing something altogether more frightening. There are many Pieter van Zyls in this country. Let us hope they all watch sport.

With supporters like these,
who needs opposition?

BUSINESS DAY, 22 AUGUST 2002

I WAS AT THE STADIUM on Saturday, in the open stand, for the Tri-Nations match between South Africa and Australia. It was my first test at Ellis Park, and as the sun sank over the Highveld and Werner Greeff burst through to bring more than 60 000 spectators to their feet, there was nowhere in the world I would rather have been. And yet I will think twice before returning. It is awful to spoil with unhappy thoughts what was such a magical day, but on Saturday I had a glimpse into something that has long puzzled me.

For some years, and especially this season, I have been wondering why the Australians and New Zealanders dislike us so much. Obviously I am no great fan of your average Aussie or Kiwi, and nothing makes me happier than seeing a pair of slumped shoulders in a gold or black rugby jersey at the final whistle (unless it be a pair of slumped shoulders in an England jersey), but that is really just a jokey rivalry. The antipathy the Antipodeans feel for us seems to be quietly genuine. On Saturday at the stadium I took a look at some of the people around me, and I realised that if these are the South Africans to whom the international rugby fraternity are most frequently exposed, you can scarcely blame them for not liking us. I felt ashamed to be wearing the same colour green as some of those people.

It is not just the bozos that pelted the Australians with bottles after their third try, and it was not just the cretin who tried to rush the field and tipped head-first into the security moat. It was worse. In places – not everywhere – the air was thick with aggression and violence and the kind of large, florid-faced man who cannot handle his drink. Before the match even started there were scuffles in the crowd around me.

One man left bleeding from a headbutt. Someone tried to defuse another scrap. "Come on, guys, we're all on the same side," he pleaded. I looked at the buffoons hitting each other in front of their wives and children, and wondered if I was happy being on the same side as them.

Two burly Pieter van Zyls sucking brandy from plastic squeeze bottles amused themselves by standing at intervals during the game and stretching theatrically, sniggering when women asked them to sit, offering to fight the men. Still, the thrill of the game made me forget such people, and I was happy as I poured out of Ellis Park with the crowd. I was not happy for long.

Two different individuals, wretched with alcohol, entertained their friends by shoulder-charging passers-by and knocking them to the floor. I was walking beside a man about my age, wearing an Australian rugby jersey. We fell into casual conversation. He was complimentary about the Springboks and we shared a laugh. That is what rugby is about. The next minute, three men with red faces and flecks of spittle on their moustaches were in front of us, screaming something Afrikaans in the face of the Australian, and me for associating with him. Things were becoming ugly until an elderly lady remonstrated with the men in Afrikaans. She turned and apologised as they stumbled off to go beat up their wives. "We are not all like that," she said.

Thankfully, that is true. The overwhelming majority of the crowd were decent folk who love the game and who spent a happy afternoon with loved ones. But those others – that awful species of South African that is even less fun to be around in victory than in defeat – are a blight on the nation. "Fans like me are what rugby is all about," Pieter van Zyl said two weeks ago. It is not true. If it were, I would start watching hockey.

How short can 100 metres get?

BUSINESS DAY, 19 SEPTEMBER 2002

SOME PART OF the joy of being a sports fan is that sport is not a precise science. You can discuss forever whether these or those tactics should have been used, you can niggle over the nuances of selection and the imponderables of temperament and talent. It is impossible to quantify how good a given team or a given player might be, which allows for additional hours of pleasurably heated debate about whether young Ali would have whipped young Tyson, say, or how the 2001 Australian cricket team would have fared against the 1971 SA team.

Such arguments are the very stuff of being a sports fan, and the deep pleasure they afford lies in the fact that they can be endlessly recycled and rehashed, picked over and tweaked and wrangled without any real prospect of resolution. In the right hands, such arguments can be as fruitful and creative and intellectually engaging as the most ardent academic dispute over the mechanics of evolution or the wave-particle nature of light. And yet there is another sporting event whose magnetic appeal lies precisely in the fact that it is measurable and quantifiable, and there is no room for dispute or debate. It is not a sport that much arouses the passionate imagination, but it speaks to a primal sporting – which is to say, human – curiosity.

Almost the sole appeal of the 100m sprint for men is to answer the question: "Who is the fastest man in the world?" Increasingly, that question is inseparable from the question: "Who is the fastest man that has ever lived?" This week Tim Montgomery became the latest man to be the fastest man ever to have lived. His new world record of 9,78 seconds, set in Paris, was the shortest recorded time in which a man has run 100m from a stationary start. Even Ben Johnson, the thick-skulled, drug-cheating Canadian disgrace, only ran 9,79, even with chemical assistance.

At the time, before the drug scandal broke, observers were scratching their heads and wondering how it was possible for such a quantum leap forward in human physical achievement. Now the record is hailed, but it has hardly caused jaws to drop and headlines to be written. It is just taken for granted now that human beings are not only capable of continually physically improving, but are expected to do so. When we were little kids, it used to be a favourite topic of conversation to speculate whether there was a point, a kind of invisible golden line running through our communal DNA, that would prove to be the cut-off boundary of human speed. Surely, we speculated, there must be some point beyond which our bodies cannot go and will never go. For instance, no human being will ever be able to run 100m in two seconds, which means there must, somewhere on that timeline, be a time faster than which no human will ever run. Nine seconds? Eight seconds? We could not guess.

And yet as long as a new sprinter keeps coming along every few years to lower the record by a thousandth of a second, it is hard to imagine the moment when the next wave of athletes, with their training and their nutrition and their genes, is not going to be able to run a thousandth of a second faster than the previous wave. Human beings are faster now than they have ever been before – the world record is always held by a sprinter of the current generation – and there is no reason to assume that trend is going to change. The 100m is more than a sporting event. It is a small showcase of selective human evolution. Where can it all end? I look forward to watching and finding out.

Martina Navratilova

BUSINESS DAY, 30 JANUARY 2003

I AM NOT ORDINARILY someone who admires lesbians. Lesbians and I, historically, do not get along. We struggle, you see, to find common ground. We are often trying to meet the same women, we squabble over the same pool tables and I am always afraid to take off my denim jacket in case a lesbian tries it on. Have you ever tried retrieving a denim jacket from a lesbian? You could lose an arm that way.

So no – by and large, lesbians and I are like icebergs and cruise liners. We may occasionally share the same waters, but it is usually better for all concerned if we do not bump into each other. And yet there are some notable exceptions. It would be my very great honour to bump into Martina Navratilova. Of course, if I did, I know who would come off second best. She may be 46 years old, but that is one tough old broad.

Back in the 1980s I was never a Navratilova fan. Chris Evert-Lloyd was my gal. I used to sigh for her little frilly skirts and her slender wrists and I used to lie awake at night gasping with pleasure at the thought of her two-fisted backhand. She was slight and feminine and I could imagine one day when I was older taking her to the matric dance. If Chrissie was the good princess in the morality play of women's tennis, Martina was the ogre, the beast that kept cropping up to deny virtue its rewards. She stalked the courts like a panther stalking Bambi. "It is not fair!" we used to cry. "Martina's too muscular and fast! She must be cheating. Real women are just not built that way!"

Martina today is as strong and muscular as she has ever been, but when she steps on court in the presence of today's lady tennis players – Davenport, the Williams, the other Williams – she looks as Chrissie once did. She looks like a girl playing men. And who would have predicted, 20 years ago, that it would be Martina who staked the lasting claim in the affections of those who follow, however peripherally, the world of tennis? Yet it was Martina who turned out to have the personality, the charm, the intelligence. And it is Martina who is still winning tournaments.

Last weekend, at the age of 46 years and three months, Martina Navaratilova won the Australian Open mixed doubles title, playing with Leander Paes. That is 29 years – 29 years! – after her first Grand Slam mixed doubles crown, and provided her with the final title in her collection. She has now won the singles, doubles and mixed doubles titles at every single Grand Slam tournament. It is scarcely credible. And despite having returned to competitive doubles tennis "for the fun of it", and despite having found a full and active life outside the game, she is as fiery, focused and competitive as ever in her long career. It is inspiring to watch.

Martina is one of those rare, life-affirming stories that the soulless world of professional sport still manages to produce, despite itself. Like George Foreman in the 1990s, or Steve Redgrave's heroics for the English rowing team, or Roger Milla playing for Cameroon, or Courtney Walsh almost single-handedly carrying the West Indies through their lowest ebb, Martina is a parable of commitment and intensity that defies the youthist propaganda of a commercial world that all too easily forgets its real heroes. Martina reminds us of the days when the money meant less than the winning.

A World Cup protest

BUSINESS DAY, 6 FEBRUARY 2003

YOU MAY NOT have noticed, sitting so far away, as you are, but I am writing this with no clothes on. Yes, you heard me – no clothes on. Naked, in other words. This is not just because I made a number of unwise decisions at the J&B Met last Saturday, not least the decision to carry on betting even after the seventeenth complimentary glass of the sponsor's product in the sponsor's marquee. The last I remember is yelling, "I'll put everything I have on The Badger in Race 10. See! Even my shoes!"

But no, it is not just for reasons of poverty that I sit here writing all draughtily, feeling very thankful that modern technology allows me the safety of the personal computer, rather than the perilous keys of the old-fashioned typewriter. No, indeed, I am naked because I have gotten political. I am making a protest, damn it all.

I was inspired by the footage on the television news this week of a gang of flabby lady journalists who apparently whipped off their kit and lay down on a deserted patch of Cape Town to protest against Bush going to war. Now, there are too many obvious jokes to be made at this point, so I shall constrain myself to saying that once I had stopped laughing, my own political conscience was pricked. I too believe there is a pressing issue worth protesting, and so I am.

I shall remain in my pristine naked state as a statement against the commercial branding of cricket and sport and everything I hold dear. I do not mind the sportsmen themselves selling their faces and their names and spaces on their bats to large companies, but I most vehemently object to the principle of being told by the ICC what I may or may not wear to the ground during this year's Cricket World Cup. All you good businessmen reading this column can tell me all you like how the money generated by exclusive rights is necessary so that we can afford all the fireworks and the giant cardboard zebras at the opening ceremony, and so that Ali Bacher can buy a nice houseboat when he retires, but I do not care. It is a matter of personal freedom.

If, after I have paid the better part of two grand to a scalper to watch the opening game on Sunday, I choose to go to the ground dressed like that clown from McDonald's, bouncing on a giant inflatable waving a banner saying "I only drink Fanta Grape", I should be able to, dagnabbit. And then, of course, the guys on the bank behind me should have the right to smack me around a bit for obstructing their view.

But I should most certainly be able to eat and drink whatever I please. For years now it has been almost mandatory to bring your own tasty treats to Newlands, otherwise you end up having to buy your sustenance from Anil's Fine Boerie Rolls, or some such similar house of pain. No longer. Now, the only takeaway you are allowed to bring into the ground is apparently "a litre-bottle of unbranded water". Vodka, in other words. Security is certainly going to be a thing to behold. If you get caught sneaking in a pipe bomb, you will be summarily ejected. If you get caught sneaking in a box of Nando's flame-grilled chicken, you will get roughed up and *then* summarily ejected. Heaven help you if you get caught with a pipe bomb inside a box of Nando's flame-grilled chicken.

Well, I will not stand for it. In two days the World Cup begins, and I shall not be a stooge of the multinationals. When the anthem plays I shall be at home, naked, standing to attention, one hand over my heart, the other hand clutching any item of fast food it feels like clutching. I will not be branded, I tell you. I will not be herded. I will stay home and clutch my freedom. Plus, I do not have tickets to any of the games.

World Cup opening ceremony

CAPE TIMES, 10 FEBRUARY 2003

PERHAPS YOU HAD to be there. I have spoken to a number of people who were at Newlands for the opening ceremony of the Cricket World Cup, and most seemed amiably impressed. "It was colourful," said my friend Dan, "and, you know, loud." He paused. "And there was a good feeling in the stadium."

I was glad to hear that, because there was not an especially good feeling in my living room. The ceremony on television was underwhelming. It was so underwhelming it would have had to borrow platform shoes and stand on tippy-toes just to reach the whelming mark.

The problem was that it suffered by comparison – not with the Sydney Olympics, but with the 1995 Rugby World Cup. In 1995 we were less determined to produce a two-hour musical infomercial about why tourists should come to South Africa. The 1995 opening was not an extravaganza – there were speeches, PJ Powers, some people running around clutching lengths of crinkle-paper, but then there was that single, simple image that lives forever in the imagination: the airliner passing low over the stadium and stirring, shaking, *moving* everyone who experienced it.

Memorable ceremonies need a defining image: the archers lighting the flame in Barcelona; a trembling Muhammad Ali bearing the torch in Atlanta. Saturday's ceremony had no such moment, and for all the rah and razz about Africa, it had no real identity. It was a bafflement of people in leotards and plywood costumes, a fussy, jumbly, interminable medley of local music, and the longest, pushiest, most expensive travel brochure ever produced. It was as if the budget had been taken from the Cape Tourism Authority, and they were determined to get their money's worth. Look! We have a mountain! And the sea! And a fashion industry! And … and animals! And the first heart transplant! And we invented the Rooivalk helicopter! Come visit us! Bring dollars!

An important advantage of being at the stadium is that you did not have Robert Marawa's witless voice-over. "Welcome to untamed Africa!" gurgled

Robert Marawa. Untamed Africa? Since when has Newlands been untamed? Have they banned lawnmowers below Main Road since last I visited? Have the bears escaped from Tygerberg Zoo?

Still, at least Robert Marawa didn't have to be Marc Lottering. Hasn't that poor man suffered enough? For some reason, Lottering had to pretend to be a safari guide taking a gormless posse of tourists around the field. (Yes! Tourists! With foreign currency! Hint, hint!) Every so often we cut back to Lottering's gang of mugs, lined up and dancing for the camera like extras in a Boney M video. At first I was puzzled. What on earth were they doing? Ah, then it became clear – that mechanical dancing, the laughable clothing, those clenched jaws and rictal grins … they were a subliminal sales pitch. Yes, you prospective tourists, in addition to all its other attractions, Cape Town has a ready supply of recreational drugs!

It was surreal, especially after I discovered that SABC3's coverage lagged five minutes behind Supersport's. If you really liked those crêpe-paper meerkats, you could duck over to the SABC and feast your eyes a second time. If the SABC maintain this time-lag policy for the games, we can make a fortune calling friends without DStv and betting big money on what is about to happen.

There was a maritime sequence. I watched agog as a giant octopus and a whale squared up belligerently. "The octopus and the whale battle for control of the seas," explained Robert helpfully. At last! Some action! But who do we root for? Who is the good guy? In balletic slow-mo the whale poked the octopus in the belly with its nose. Then they drifted off again on their own currents, papier-mâché beasts passing in the night. Now I'll never know who has control of the seas.

The low point was the tournament anthem. It was so nondescript, so utterly without hook, that by the time it was over I could scarcely remember hearing it. It was as though I had overheard it being played at a low volume on the neighbours' television while asleep.

Like the anthem, the ceremony wound to an end without any highlights. It just did not work on television. There was no rhythm to the evening, no heart. There was no drama, no Madiba, no magic. A lot of work went into the occasion, but not much imagination. I do not say this to dull a joyous mood. I am proudly South African. I am as proud as I was before the ceremony. But the ceremony did not make me any more proud than I already was, and that is a shame.

Cricket World Cup 2003:
A toast to the minnows

BUSINESS DAY, 20 FEBRUARY 2003

I WAS SHATTERED WHEN we lost to the West Indies in the first match, but even had we won, I could not have been more genuinely delighted than I was watching Kenya beat Sri Lanka this week. What happened in that match was a triumph for sport, and for the dream of what sport used to mean.

Amid all the fluster and hullabaloo of the World Cup so far, I have been finding solace in the smaller teams. I watched in raptures as the Canadians beat the Bangladeshis in their first match, this team of part-timers, this hodge-podge gaggle of plumbers and builders and high-school teachers from a frozen land, tubby, elderly and not uniformly fleet of foot, expecting nothing of this tournament and with nothing but the joy of the game in their hearts. I was just as delighted with the Netherlands slugging it out with the Indians, the Namibians hanging tough with Pakistan.

There is something reassuringly pure in watching the small teams pitting themselves against insuperable odds merely to stand tall with giants. With the exception of Bangladesh, the most undeserving test nation under this or any conceivable heaven, they all deserve to stand tall. It is soothing to watch them. There are no cross-currents or clouds to obscure your pleasure. There are no doping scandals or salary wrangles; there are no power plays or petty politics; there are no niggling rumours that so-and-so is about to quit to play county cricket, or that such-and-such has lost his passion for the game. It is just 11 men doing their best to play well a game they still love, a game that has not become just another way of earning a living.

And how they are performing. John Davison of Canada, in an innings out of *Roy of the Rovers*, scored the fastest century in World Cup history. John-Berry Burger of Namibia cracked an even-time 80-odd against England. And then the Kenyans smacked Sri Lanka. Of course Collins Obuya's 5-24 was the highlight, but it was not Obuya who won that match. The Sri Lankans were simply blown away by the most passionate team performance of the tournament so far.

The Kenyans fielded like South Africa used to field. They threw themselves around; they sprinted after balls from which no runs were likely to accrue; they encouraged and congratulated and consoled and urged each other on. Two images will live with me from that game: the Kenyans gathering after each wicket, their arms around each others' shoulders and jumping up and down at the joy of being together and fighting together; and Collins Obuya, having dismissed Chaminda Vaas, sprinting from sheer exuberance towards the boundary ropes like an English football player.

For me, the biggest game of the World Cup will be Kenya against Bangladesh. It is a clash that represents for me the fundamental tension in world sport: commerce versus the game itself. Bangladesh should not have test status ahead of Kenya. Compared with the fire and heart and passion of the Kenyans, the Bangladeshis are like a mini-Pakistan. They were only given test status because the bean-counters at the ICC calculated they could make more money from the larger Bangladeshi market. For a few extra bucks they turned their backs on the Kenyans and left them to flail about on their own.

When Kenya beat Bangladesh and move into the Super Sixes they will have made a firm point on behalf of the so-called minnows that have given me so much pleasure these past weeks. I have, I realise now, been feeling my own passion for the game dwindle as I watch the jaded self-absorption of some of the big teams, treating each match like just another day at the office, their minds on their endorsement contracts or the golf course, all romance and wonder drained out of their games. It has taken the minnows to remind me of how it used to be.

"We play every game as though it's the World Cup final," said the Netherlands captain this week. The Canadians will not only not be paid for their time here, but they have had to take annual leave from their day jobs back home, and they did it willingly, for the simple love of cricket. Along with the bravehearts of Namibia and the heroes of Kenya, they remind me of what is glorious about the game, and how much we have lost since becoming professional. On behalf of sport lovers everywhere, I want to thank them all. The World Cup would not be the same without them.

Cricket World Cup 2003: Saluting the winners

BUSINESS DAY, 27 MARCH 2003

I WANTED INDIA TO WIN the World Cup final. I wanted them to win for a number of reasons, but mostly because of Mershen and his son. I met Mershen as we shuffled along with the crush of people trying to enter the ground on Sunday morning. He and his son were both wearing the powder-blue Indian replica kit, and they had driven down from Zimbabwe for the final. Mershen's son was 10, and he hopped from one foot to the other, tugging at his father's shirt, fair bursting with excitement. As we edged closer to the security check, a roar from the stadium told us that the game had started. Mershen's son was beside himself with dread that India might be batting first, and that he might miss Sachin Tendulkar.

"He hasn't been able to sleep properly for three days," Mershen whispered to me. "He can't believe he is going to see Sachin bat. All he can talk about is Sachin this and Sachin that and how many runs do I think Sachin will make and will Sachin hit a six?"

A man with a transistor radio turned and said that Australia were batting first. Mershen's son looked up with shining eyes. "Daddy!" he said. "We're going to see Sachin bat!" Mershen ruffled his son's hair and put one hand on his shoulder. Behind my sunglasses my eyes suddenly blurred and I felt deeply happy for this man and his son. That small boy will remember for all his life the day he came to Johannesburg and queued with his father at the Wanderers under clear blue skies to watch the World Cup final. I hoped against hope that Sachin would score a century for them.

I was not alone. As I sat in the Mondi Paper suite later that day, looking down on the impressionistic watercolour of the great green oval surrounded by swirls of clustered yellow and powder-blue shirts, I felt profoundly thankful that I was not Sachin Tendulkar, walking out to bat, bearing the dreams of a billion people. My heart leapt as he pulled the fourth ball of the innings to the boundary. The very earth shuddered, as though every Indian in the world had jumped at exactly the same time.

Then he skied the next ball and there was a low, breathless gasp from the stadium. It felt like some enormous punch to the crowd's collective gut. There are many stories of the unearthly sums of money that Sachin Tendulkar makes from endorsements, but as he walked slowly back to the pavilion, shoulders slumped, a man irredeemably alone and accompanied by the unheard howls of a continent, it occurred to me that he works hard for every cent.

And so Australia won, as they were always going to win. I have always loathed the Australians – from principled bad sportsmanship as much as anything else – but on that Sunday afternoon I finally surrendered. After a certain point, you simply cannot begrudge them victory. They win because they deserve to win. They win – over and above their talent – because they do everything right. They have the right back-up staff, the right philosophy, the right minds working behind the scenes. And they win because they have the right attitude. I have made much of how refreshing it has been to watch the enthusiasm and the passion of the Kenyans in this year's tournament, but it finally dawned on me, watching the Australians celebrating their wickets, watching them rush around Ricky Ponting at the end of the match in a spontaneous overflow of joy, that Australia is at least their match.

Where every other major team in the world seems to be stricken with in-fighting or personality clashes or the flatness of its jaded senior players, the Australians are a model of unity and mateship and enthusiasm. Cynics will say that it is easier to stay fresh and enthusiastic when you are winning. Perhaps, but after seeing the inexorable rise of the Aussies these past four years, it rather seems the other way round. I never thought I would hear myself say this, but my congratulations to Australia. We all have a lot to learn from you.

Henry Olonga and courage

BUSINESS DAY, 3 APRIL 2003

IT IS EASY to forget, sometimes, that sport stars are people. They inhabit a realm that is, for most of us, a realm of dreams, a theatre of the imagination. They are just the figures – tiny on the pitch or somewhat larger but equally distant on our televisions – that act out the roiling dramas that seem to spring whole from our own hearts. Sport, for most of us, fills a need that goes beyond support for this team or that team. It is more than just a way to pass a couple of hours on a Saturday. The attachment to sport is an attachment to a world within a world, a world of dramas and myths and archetypes that speaks to deeper parts of us than simply the parts that calculate who has won. Sport is as necessary to the soul as dreams or stories are, which is why we sometimes forget that sportsmen are not figures in dreams or characters from fiction.

That is why the public reacts with shock when their sport stars reveal themselves to be human beings – when they fix matches or refuse autographs or when you see them in a mall and they are like everyone else and do not much feel like discussing last weekend's match. It is an enormous burden that sport stars assume. When they step away from the sport arena and say or do something that has nothing to do with sport, the result is almost inevitably disappointment and disillusion, as though someone has turned on the house lights while the magician is doing his show, and suddenly you can see the hidden wires and trapdoors and false bottoms.

But every so often a sportsman does something to assert that he is a human being as well as a sportsman, and the result is relief and gratitude and admiration. That is how I felt as I watched Henry Olonga being interviewed on *Carte Blanche* this weekend. The world has been scandalously silent about the courage of Henry Olonga and Andy Flower. What they did – at the beginning of the World Cup – with their black armbands and their dignified statement about the death of Zimbabwean democracy encourages me as a human being.

Unbelievably, there are still the crabbed and inward voices of those who complain, with that desperately tired old argument, that Olonga and Flower were wrong to "bring politics into sport". What Olonga and Flower did was to remind us all that we are human beings first, before we are sportsmen or sports fans, and that human beings have a responsibility to their own conscience and their sense of what is right.

It has become clear in the past month how much courage Henry Olonga's action demanded. Unlike Andy Flower, he was not poised to jet off to play county cricket in England and then state cricket in Australia. His principled stand saw him stripped of his place in Zimbabwean cricket, and then stripped of his home. Now he hides in Johannesburg, afraid to return to the place where a madman tramples on a nation.

While the English cricket team disregarded issues of morality and made their decision not to play in Zimbabwe simply a matter of safety, Henry Olonga explicitly disregarded his safety, and made his stand as a moral imperative. Against the unedifying backdrop of administrators and the media complaining that the situation in Zimbabwe might erode World Cup profits or tarnish the lustre of the tournament, men such as Henry Olonga and Andy Flower and Errol Stewart (who refused to tour with the A-team on the grounds of moral conscience) have given me faith that human beings still can cling to beliefs and values that surpass profit and revenue and the narrow description of their jobs.

I am used to being inspired by sportsmen on the field. I am used to being transported by sport into a place of heroes and villains, of courage and determination and action such as you only find in movies or old books. Flower and Olonga and Stewart remind us that these qualities can exist inside all of us. They deserve our gratitude.

Potchefstroom Olympic bid

BUSINESS DAY, 17 APRIL 2003

TODAY IS A mighty day, my friends. Today we stand on the threshold of a bright new beginning for world sport, and the good readers of this column are the first to know about it. This very evening Cape Town sees the launch of "Potch 2012" – the official Potchefstroom Olympic Bid. No, I am not joking. I know whereof I speak, because I am one of the directors of Potch 2012, and already an army marches behind us.

The bid is to be launched tonight with the support of the mayor and people of Potchefstroom and with a glittering cast of sport and entertainment celebrities. Should we win the South African nomination and then the actual bid itself, we promise a new beginning in the sordid history of world sport.

The Potch games are being dubbed the "Back to Basics Games". The idea arose from a thoroughgoing disgruntlement with the commercialised, professionalised, degraded nature of sport today. For years we have watched in sorrow as the Olympics pay lip service to the noble ideals of sport while painting it with the harlot's colours of branding and sponsorship. The Cricket World Cup in our own country was nearly unseated by wrangles with sponsors; the cricket itself belonged not to the players or to the crowds or even the people watching at home, but to the companies that offered most money.

For decades the ideals of sportsmanship have tarnished under the pressure of money. Sport has always been a business, but increasingly it is *only* a business, and that is draining away our enthusiasm and the simple pleasure of play. If we are successful with our bid, we will use the Games as a moral renaissance. Potchefstroom will be the first sporting event in two thousand years at which absolutely no one will make, lose or misplace money.

There will be no prize money at Potch 2012, and the Games will not be sponsored. We will ask television companies to defray the basic costs of broadcasting facilities, but thereafter we shall ask not one cent for rights. Everyone is welcome to screen the Potch Olympics, from the richest to the poorest, from

NBC to e.tv. This expanded media coverage should off-set any disappointment about the availability of stadium seating. There will not be much stadium seating, as the stadium is not very big. There will be no admission fees and attendance is on a first-come, first-seated basis.

The Games will be marshalled by the same volunteers who did yeomen service at the Cricket World Cup. For this reason, purple is the official colour of Potch 2012. There will be no athletes' village at the Games. As a gesture of old-fashioned South African hospitality we are calling upon the people of Potchefstroom to open their homes to the world's athletes and make a room available for a visiting sportsperson for the duration of the Games. If you do not have a room, a sofa in the lounge will do. If you do not have a sofa, then God bless you.

Residents will obviously not be asked to house sports administrators or Australians. Sports administrators will not in fact be invited to Potch 2012. No one has ever, in the history of sport, said: "That was a nice event, but it would have been so much better if there had been more administrators." Anyway they eat too much. While the Australians will probably be allowed to attend the Games, it would not be fair to the people of Potchefstroom to expect them to welcome an Aussie in their own home, where their family sleeps.

We want no money from these Games. We do not believe that sport needs money and we do not believe that money adds to our enjoyment of sport. Potch 2012 will be an exercise in international sporting spiritual renewal, a moral rebirth for the spirit of competition. So get behind us, good people of South Africa, sign up at the official website, and chant with us the official motto: "Potch – it could be worse".

There is no place like home

BUSINESS DAY, 5 JUNE 2003

I AM PLEASED TO be back in the country. I have been away this last week and more, inspecting the sporting environs of England and Ireland, and I cannot begin to tell you what a relief it is to be back in a place where people understand the importance of sport.

While I was over in the so-called First World I could not for the life of me find information, let alone coverage, of the series between Australia and the West Indies. While the West Indians were running up three consecutive victories over Ponting and his pack, I was pacing the streets of London, flipping fruitlessly through the newspapers, wondering just what these people do for information. England is just about as parochial as America when it comes to sport. Unless it is soccer or an English team is involved, it simply has not happened.

While I was there the English newspapers were reacting with dazed incomprehension at the revelation that David Beckham is not especially well known in New York. He is over there working the talk-show circuits with the Spice Girl formerly known as Posh, but discovering that no one actually knows who he is. The English papers, even the posh ones, could hardly digest this news. To make up for it, England turned its TV news shows over to David Beckham's wrist.

I watched the match last week between Bafana Bafana and England – the match in which, as the news organs of the kingdom kept reminding us, Beckham broke a bone in his wrist – from a pub in Ireland, so I was spared the full assault of English parochialism. The Irish were politely uninterested. They could not give a flying O'Flanagan about any English sporting team, with the exception of Manchester United, and to them South Africa is just a place to go on holiday. The lads I was sitting with in Gleason's public house in Clonmel did briefly rouse themselves to ask me why, if this match was launching our World Cup bid, we were playing it on a pitch that looked like it had recently been used for the running of the Grand National, but they did not press the point.

Then we all drifted off to gentle slumber as Bafana Bafana, a goal down and the world to play for, pushed the ball around at the back, helpfully proving that their disastrous tactics in the last minutes of our last match in the last soccer World Cup were not in fact the result of miscommunication – they were just our tactics. The Irish crowd in Gleason's did briefly come to life when Beckham was injured and taken off, but we soon settled back to our Guinnesses. It was only when I arrived in England that I understood the magnitude of what had happened.

For two days and more the evening news led with interviews with Beckham's doctor, people who knew Beckham's doctor, people who hoped one day to be Beckham's doctor. There were 3-D computer-generated reconstructions of Beckham's wrist, there were painstaking slow-mo replays of the incident, complete with arrows and figures to indicate areas of pressure and force and wind speed. There were vox pops and financial forecasts, there was even a special feature explaining the medical technology involved in making David Beckham's wrist better. What was the thrillingly high-tech technology? Setting the wrist in plaster. Blair and Bush and the Middle East could not get a look-in. It was all D. Beckham's wrist.

While this blizzard of nonsense was going on, there was literally nothing with which to soothe the starving sporting soul. We do not appreciate how good we have it here when it comes to global sports. When there are developments in Australian or Scottish or New Zealand sports teams, our newspapers bring it to us. When almost any match is being played anywhere in the world, we can watch it on television or read the results the next day. As Martin Tyler declared ruefully during the Bafana match: "They are incredibly knowledgeable about their sport in South Africa. Do you know, they receive coverage of more Premiership matches than we do!"

Whatever else England has going for it – the fabulous weather, the friendly and attractive people – it cannot touch us for sport. Ah, it is good to be back.

Bring me the head of Stuart Dickinson

BUSINESS DAY, 19 JUNE 2003

THIS WEEK, I HAVE done two things that are very good for the sporting soul. This time of year is so fraught with anxiety and the acid twist of nervous anticipation that we must take advantage of this slight lull to refresh ourselves – to boost our systems and replenish our strength before the thunder of the Tri-Nations and the slow, relentless simmer of the cricket tour to England.

The first thing I did was watch last weekend's match between England and New Zealand. Obviously this did not settle any nerves as regards the looming spectre of playing both the All Blacks and the All Whites this season. The match was played with an intensity and controlled ferocity that made me gloomy just watching it. But while the game itself offered no encouragement to the South African fan, it was sheer balm to hear foreign commentators finally noticing the sustained, egocentric villainy of that officious Antipodean git, Stuart Dickinson.

Dickinson, a man whose surname is precisely five letters too long, has single-handedly ruined more afternoons of South African rugby than any man I can think of, including Sean Fitzpatrick, Stephen Larkham, Hugh Bladen and the guy who accidentally spilt his beer over the decoder down at the Chalk 'n Cue. If a mad rugby-watching scientist had to create an evil monster, using only the words "self-important twerp" as his brief, he would come up with something resembling Stuart Dickinson.

Now I am not saying that Dickinson is biased and dishonest, mind – I am merely saying that from time to time Dickinson's mutton-headed incompetence is to the naked eye almost indistinguishable from how I would imagine bias and dishonesty to look. I am continually staggered that the world of rugby does not rise together, bearing flaming torches, and drag him from the public eye to a hideous death. The reason, I can only assume, is that so far Dickinson has only seen fit to torment South Africa, so no one out there is much fussed.

But then on Saturday he made the mistake of giving England four penalties in four minutes, and suddenly Murray Mexted was roused to action.

"He should have his whistle taken away!" raged Murray. The fact that Dickinson awarded the next fourteen penalties to New Zealand did little to console him. As the match wore on and the Dickster forgot who he wanted to win, he simply contented himself with handing out a penalty every two minutes and six seconds. The man is a disgrace, and it was strangely soothing to hear, for once, commentators from another country notice it too. As Murray and Grant Nesbitt anguished about the grinning, ginger-haired Jack O'Lantern apparition of Stuart Dickinson, I could only sit back and smirk. "Welcome to our world, boys," I smirked.

But even more consoling to my ravaged sporting heart was the SAB Yesterday's Heroes function at the World of Beer in Johannesburg. Yesterday's Heroes is an annual event at which SAB gathers together some of the most beloved South African sports stars of yesteryear in order to remember them, honour them and get them drunk on free booze. I am alas not myself a sports star of yesteryear, but I managed to wriggle my way through the door. "You must be a journalist," said the doorman, running a disapproving eye over my unsporty and distinctly unheroic build.

I blushed, but it was worth it. I sat in the World of Beer, bobbing in a sea of lager, and listened to the stars tell stories. Spook Hanley expressed unrecordable opinions about the modern game; Lee Barnard told unrepeatable locker-room anecdotes about certain sportmen's, er, hidden dimensions. All around, the days were called up when sport, even professional sport, was fun to play, when characters could emerge, when camaraderie was the glue that bound teams together. The very air was golden with greatness recalled in tranquillity.

These men, I reflected from the bottom of my umpteenth pitcher of draught, are not Yesterday's Heroes at all. They remain heroes – not merely frozen in our memories like flies in amber, but as a living part of all that we still cling to and cherish as worthwhile in sport. We can only hope that our children will grow up with memories as cherishable.

Andre Agassi – the womble of Wimbledon

BUSINESS DAY, 3 JULY 2003

I HAVE NOT HAD a happy Wimbledon so far. Not only, at the time of writing, are both the Williams sisters still in contention; not only did I lose my annual bet with Porky Withers when Wayne Ferreira blamed influenza for his early defeat, rather than his more usual torn muscle or twisted ankle; not only have I not yet seen a single streaker; on top of all this, earlier this week I missed out on giving Maria Sharapova the once-over to see what all the fuss is about.

It is her name, you see. Ever since an unhappy bout in my early teens wrestling with the first names, nicknames and patronymics of the cast of indistinguishable characters in an overly muffled Dostoyevsky novel, Russian names have been like kryptonite to me. I can scarcely tell an –ova from an –eva, an Anastasia from a Svetlana. When those names come up on the screen my eyes blur and start revolving in circles. How then to tell a Sharapova from a Hentushova, a Legova from a Hangova? How to tell the Queen of Scream from the Runt of Grunt from the Ally McBeal of Squeal?

I am not ordinarily much impressed by the ladies of modern lawn tennis. At one extreme are gum-chewing, jawbone-clicking loudmouths like the Williams clan; at the other are the prettily perspiring moulded plastic dolls with their eyes on the flashbulbs. In between is a legion of interchangeable chunky-legged bit players huffing and puffing and vanishing against the backdrop of billboards and bored spectators wearing sunblock. Who can tell them apart? Still, by all accounts this new Ms Sharapova could be the next big thing on court as well as before the cameras.

Personally, I rather doubt it. People are not ordinarily blessed with a double-dose of extraordinary genes, and much of the media reporting about Sharapova – a Kournikova that can play! – sounds a lot like desperately wishful thinking. Not that I would know. Having consulted the schedule and thinking I had made time to watch Sharapova play this week, instead I found myself wading through a syllabic firestorm of Svonarevas and Dementievas and even, embarrassingly, a Sugiyama. Ah well, I will just have to catch her when she teams up with Kournikova and a rejuvenated Gabriela Sabatini in *Charlie's Angels 3 – Court in the Act.*

Even more disappointing was watching Andre Agassi being dispatched at the hands of Mark Phillipoussis. In a sport desperately seeking characters, Agassi is the closest thing to it, which is depressing when you consider that he has all the personality of a tennis ball that has been left out in the rain. For the past 15 years the best thing you could say about Agassi's charisma is that he was not Pete Sampras. All his little quirks and foibles – that ghastly ponytail, those even more ghastly denim shorts, the still more ghastly body-hair and chest-wax saga – were not much more than careful attempts to put matter in a tennis-playing vacuum. Even his principal defining characteristic – a shuffling, bobbing gait that makes him resemble a chimpanzee trained to impersonate a middle-weight Eastern European powerlifter moonlighting as a bouncer at a West Rand nightclub, or perhaps just a womble – may be interesting at first but wears thin after the first set.

But the longer Andre Agassi's career has worn on, the more compelling he has become. He may not be much of a character, but he has plenty of it. Returning from the lower 140s in the world, making a happy second marriage with Steffi Graf, fighting on past the age when his contemporaries have moved on to lives outside of tennis ... the Agassi story becomes increasingly interesting. The very fact that he is still grimly playing rather than finding some other means of fulfilment may well testify to the swirling void of his inner life, but it does not really matter any more. Agassi has become a hero to the no-longer-young everywhere. With his guile and his fiery talent and fiercely competitive heart, he tells us that it is still not too late. He brings some romance to the game. I hope he does not go just yet. Tennis still needs him.

A moment of rugby relief

BUSINESS DAY, 17 JULY 2003

THE AEROPLANE TO Cape Town last Saturday morning was a sea of green, but it was a rolling sea, a gently heaving and swelling sea, not the tempest-tossed maelstrom of foam and thunder, breakers and troughs I had been fearing. The passengers were well behaved and for the most part sober, and as much as that pleased me, it also had me worried.

I suppose the subdued mood had something to do with the fact that the cabin crew took one look at the rows of frowning hearties in Springbok jerseys and supporters' caps and announced that there would be no alcoholic refreshments served that morning. It probably also had something to do with the fact that it was at an hour of the day when last night's pre-pre-match celebrations were still causing eyelids to droop and bottom lips to quiver. But mostly it was because although this was a planeload of men and women flying across the country to support their national team, it was also a planeload of men and women who were not expecting to have much to cheer about on the flight home.

There was one desultory "Bokke!" as the breakfast trays were passed around, and one misguided fellow in row 7 tried to start a round of "Shosholoza" as we circled Cape Town, but he had misread the mood. I perched in my seat, entertaining myself with the richly creative writing of the Saturday papers, but all the while worrying that the Newlands crowd would be resigned to defeat even before the game began.

Happily, it was not worry well spent. Newlands when I arrived was a cauldron of bubbling willpower. Before the teams ran out you could feel the massed hopes of the crowd forming a kind of electric force field in the air. As we watched the waves of the early Springbok assault breaking upon the Australians, the sound and fury in the stadium felt like a wall of compressed air; when Brent Russell – may his name be venerated and his progeny ever blessed – crossed for the first try the noise became so loud, the air pressure so intense, that it felt like silence, as though we had all been submerged under water.

I was sitting with the good people of the Australian Trade Commission, a one-man oasis amid a small field of optimistic marigold-yellow, and as we settled into our seats I noticed one of the Australians looking around the banked bowl of shouting green. He breathed out slowly. "Crikey," he said.

As I sat – and frequently stood, and almost as frequently leapt up and down punching the air – watching the match, it occurred to me that the Springboks are just hooking us deeper and deeper. Forget the fabled fickleness of the French – it is South Africa that is the world's most unpredictable team. Just as we can never, ever be assured that they will put in a decent performance come the weekend, we can never, ever be confident they will not.

As my good friend Jacqui O once complained, being a Springbok supporter is a little like being an abused wife: they can be awful, terrible, they can make us sob ourselves to sleep and wonder why we stick with them. And then afterwards they come to us all ashamed and apologetic and promise that it will never happen again. And we believe them, and give them another chance, and then it happens all over again, and we resolve that this time – this time! – it will be the last chance ever. And then what do they do? They are the perfect gentlemen, and our hearts melt and we are won over once again.

No other rugby fans in the world have this sense of utter uncertainty when their team takes the pitch. I will once more be at the game at Loftus on Saturday. The All Blacks will be a much tougher proposition than Australia, but then again the opposition does not really matter. When the Springboks take the pitch, it is never the opposition we have to worry about.

Graeme, Lord Smith

BUSINESS DAY, 7 AUGUST 2003

WHAT WERE YOU doing when you were 22? Were you leading South Africa into sporting battle against England? Were you setting new South African batting records? I bet you weren't. Nor was I, come to think of it. When I was 22, I had nothing on my mind of more weight than wondering whose lecture notes I could photostat before the exam, and when I would finally break a worrying 10-month drought of celibacy.

To be fair, these are not worries that will be causing Graeme Smith's broad shoulders to stoop any time soon. For one thing, he can borrow the lecture notes that I photocopied when I was 22 – although I would suggest that if he continues in his current vein he should receive all the honorary degrees and doctorates he can carry in his kitbag. More importantly, it would be a national disgrace if Graeme Smith experiences even a single day's sexual drought for the remainder of his career. There have to be some perks for shouldering the burden of a nation's hopes and expectations at such a cruelly young age, and if you cannot come right on a regular basis when you are young, successful and the national cricket captain, then some searching questions need to be asked about South African womanhood.

I still cannot fully comprehend the enormity of Graeme Smith's first two tests against England. When he passed 50 in the first innings at Edgbaston I sat back and sighed with relief. Terrific, I thought. In the first test he has a reasonable score – no one can say he has failed – so for the time being at least he should be safe from the jackals and buzzards of public opinion, not to mention the burrowing dust mites of self-doubt. Had Smith experienced a slow start to the series, the English media would have taken off after him with a hammer, a wooden cross and a bucket of nails, and the South African media would have been trailing behind them carrying a sponge soaked in vinegar. Before you could turn around, every knucklehead with access to e-mail would have been sending misspelt messages to *Extra Cover*, demanding that Lance Klusener be made captain.

But Graeme Smith did more than avoid a slow start to the series – against a full-strength England attack, away from home, he scored more runs than any South African batsman has ever scored in a test innings, and more than any South African batsman has ever scored in a single test. In his next test, at Lord's, he not only scored another double century, not only passed Bradman's mark to the highest ever score at Lord's by an overseas player, but became one of the 10 fastest batsmen in the history of test cricket – and the fastest South African – to score 1000 runs. Given the loyalty and long memories of South African sports administrators and fans, that should secure his status in the team until, oh, at least midway through September.

But of course, in the usual fashion, when we South Africans are presented with a miracle, with a golden wonder-work, we start rapping it with our knuckles to find the weak spot, the feet of clay. I broached the subject of Graeme Smith with a friend after the first test. "Yes," he said, "but it was a very flat pitch." As though no one else in either team played on that same flat pitch without scoring a double century. As though no other South African test batsman in the history of South African cricket ever played upon a flat pitch without scoring 277. As though Michael Vaughan did not describe his century in the same match as the best of his career, citing both the South African bowling and the awkwardness of that very pitch.

If Graeme Smith were Australian, you would not be able to sleep at night for the stridency of the Antipodean trumpeting. They would know – and would be quick to let us know – that they had in their possession the brightest, most extraordinary new star in the cricketing firmament. Certainly, they have made more fuss over far less than what we have in Smith. Nor are they half so quick as we are to tear down what they have built up. We in South Africa are frequently wary of the greatness among us – we are more comfortable with mediocrity. Graeme Smith is not mediocre. He is something special.

It seems to me that this series, more than any I can remember, has all the elements of great and timeless drama. It is almost Shakespearean in its themes. Consider, a moment: In the build-up to the first clash, Nasser Hussain, the weathered warrior-king of an empire he has rebuilt by strength of will from the rubble and ruins he had inherited, lays down a personal challenge to Graeme Smith, the young king of a fractured invader tribe. In his public statements he turns the clash of nations into a clash of individuals – he invests the battle with the personal fortunes of the leaders.

It is a moment when destinies come into conflict. It is Smith's destiny to rise like a young god, sweeping all before him, storming the very citadel. Hussain, on the other hand, has pre-empted his own destiny – throwing down the gauntlet, he has thrown down the kingship. Whatever future the fates had in store for him, he has short-circuited the course of his career with an act of hubris that may yet foreshadow his fall. First the leadership, now his very place in the empire is imperilled – all is smoke and fire, and when the confusion settles it is Smith who bestrides the battleground like a laughing young colossus. There are great themes here – individual will versus destiny; embattled age versus the surging force of youth; the mantle of greatness and how it lies on those shoulders upon which it is thrust.

As Nasser begins to fade, fighting on and winning battles here and there but caught up in history's inexorable drift to stage-left, where he can only brood and look on as the empire he has built starts to crack and crumble beneath the hammer blows of the invaders, the destinies of Smith and Vaughan now range against each other. No matter what happens in the last three matches of the series, or the rest of his career, Smith has announced himself as one who is chosen by the sporting gods to perform great deeds and bear great burdens. "Those whom the gods would destroy," an English fan misquoted to me recently, "they first make great." Perhaps. We shall see.